PRAISE FOR *ALL*

"How do you choose between your family or your lover? That is the life-and-death struggle in *All for You*. Told with poignancy and woven through with excellent research, Rueb Romero explores, in so many new ways, what it means to be a refugee with loved ones left behind, waiting for you to rescue them."

—MIMI SCHWARTZ, author of *Good Neighbors, Bad Times Revisited*

"This deeply personal account of the extraordinary story of two families needed to be told. Going back to her father's Jewish roots in Germany before the rise of Fascism and his subsequent dangerous journey, fraught with privation and hardships, Dena Rueb Romero shows how personal fate is inextricably intertwined with historical circumstances."

—DR. ULRIKE RAINER, Associate Professor Emerita, Department of German Studies, Dartmouth College

"Dena Rueb Romero brings to life her parents' odyssey and boundless patience during long years of separation, uncertainty, and hardship. Supported by miraculously preserved documents, this book tracks with remarkable sensitivity the harrowing 1930s and 1940s in vile Nazi Germany, dithering Britain, and standoffish America. It is a moving, tragic story, captivatingly told."

—DR. FRANZ BAUMANN, Vice President of the Academic Council on the United Nations System, former Assistant Secretary-General of the United Nations, and former NYU visiting Professor of International Relations

All for You

All for You

A World War II Family Memoir of
Love, Separation, and Loss

DENA RUEB ROMERO

SHE WRITES PRESS

Published 2024
Printed in the United States of America
Print ISBN: 978-1-64742-654-5
E-ISBN: 978-1-64742-655-2
Library of Congress Control Number: 2023919038

For information, address:
She Writes Press
1569 Solano Ave #546
Berkeley, CA 94707

Interior Design by Tabitha Lahr

She Writes Press is a division of SparkPoint Studio, LLC.

To Juliana and Mateo with all my love,

And to all who flee persecution, repression, and war.

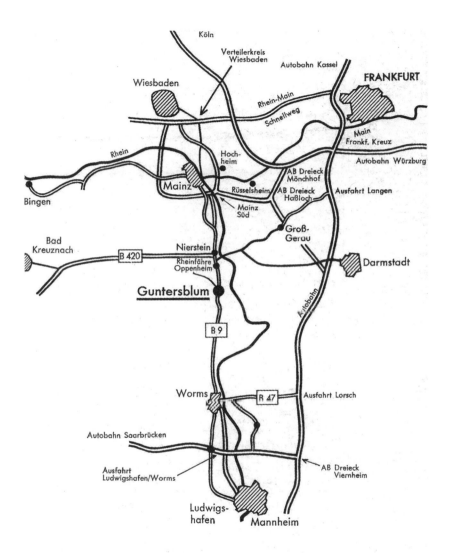

Guntersblum and surroundings; Credit: Weingut Burghof Oswald
1974 brochure, used with permission.

"*Clearly, historical events have varying degrees of intensity. Some may almost fail to impinge on true reality, that is, on the central, most personal part of a person's life. Others can wreak such havoc there that nothing is left standing. The usual way in which history is written fails to reveal this.*"
—SEBASTIAN HAFFNER,
Defying Hitler: A Memoir

"*Going into exile is 'the journey of no return.' . . . You cannot go back to the land of your childhood, where you were wholly at home; neither can you go back to a country you were forced to leave. For you want to find its former image, and that is gone forever.*"
—CARL ZUCKMAYER, *A Part of Myself*

CONTENTS

AUTHOR'S NOTE

All for You is a story about a family. It is about life and love during challenging times—dictatorship, war, censorship, and displacement—and it takes place before email or texting, before international phone calls were common, before immediate news over the Internet. It was a time when people depended on letters that could be weeks late or never arrive and on expensive telegrams that couldn't tell the whole story, a time when photographs were black and white and had to be developed and printed in a darkroom. In this account there are perpetrators, victims, those who stood by and did nothing, and those who tried to help.

Conversations and descriptions, although imagined, are based on real events and experiences, with occasional small lapses into my own invention. Whenever possible I have quoted the English written by people for whom English was not their first language and included the original German when the English translation was insufficient. I have followed the tradition of calling an older relative "uncle" even though the relationship was two or three degrees removed. Finally, if a name had an umlaut, I kept the umlaut if the person lived in Germany; for someone living in the United States, I substituted the umlaut with the letter "e." Everything changes when you leave your homeland, including the spelling of your name.

My parents spoke German to me at home. This loyalty to their language and culture let me access their words with only occasional help from a translator. The personal interludes I have inserted are to show the impact their story had on me.

❈ HANOVER, NEW HAMPSHIRE

It began in 1980 with a cardboard box, two months after my father collapsed and died.

His death at age seventy-three was unexpected, for he had been healthy, active, and still managing his business, the Camera Shop of Hanover. Now my mother and I were learning to live without him.

Shortly after his death, my mother went to her sisters in Germany; they would support her while she grieved. Before leaving, she asked me to check in on her house once a week.

The house was quiet when I went that first afternoon. The furnace made low rumbling sounds. Somewhere in the house, a clock ticked. My mission was to water the plants and to retrieve an old table in storage for my kitchen. To reach the table, I had to move a rectangular box that once held dresses—long-forgotten hand-me-downs from my godmother Susan in England. What was in the box now? It was certainly too heavy for dresses.

Had my mother been home, I would have asked permission to open the box. Knowing my mother, she would have said, "Oh, they're just some old letters. Nothing of interest to you." My mother guarded her private life. But my mother wasn't there, and I was curious. If the box had photos or documents about my parents, I wanted to see them.

My parents' German past always interested me. They had shared parts of their story: how they waited for each other, what they endured so they could marry. They glossed over the dark parts and the war because they were protective. They kept the shadows away so I could grow up in sunshine. Yet despite their efforts, pain, loss, and guilt, all unspoken, lived in our house. I needed to know about the shadows, so I decided to open the box.

Inside was a treasure trove: letters to my father from his parents, typed copies of my father's letters to them, love letters to my mother, letters to and from relatives and many people I didn't know. It was as if these items had waited for me to find them. What story did the box contain?

We were once a family of three. My mother and I were close; my father seemed distant and gave priority, or so I felt, to his business instead of to me. Once when I was playing outside, someone asked me where my parents lived. I must have been quite young because I answered, "My mommy lives upstairs, and my daddy lives at the Camera Shop." Of course, my father lived with us, but since he spent so much time at the store, my conclusion seemed logical.

As a child, I adored my father. He took me to music lessons, and sometimes the two of us, holding hands, would skip together on the way to my school. He told me stories about growing up in a small German village, stories that showed me he had once been a child like me. When I was older, we had discussions about why he opposed capital punishment. We often laughed, because my father appreciated a good joke.

As I entered adolescence and young adulthood, however, we had many disagreements. Our debates were about politics, about the Vietnam War, about calling the police "pigs." "A man is a man, not a pig," my father would repeat, refusing to hear my explanation that the police were mistreating people of color. In ninth grade, I declared I would not attend Rosh Hashanah services—I couldn't stand up for a God who allowed civil rights demonstrators to be beaten and killed. My father, who always preached tolerance, shouted, "You will attend services," reducing me to tears.

When I planned to marry, my father was seriously depressed and wasn't sure he would attend the wedding. He did come; my mother threatened she would never forgive him if he stayed away. When he cried that I would be so far away from him, I got angry. It was my mother to whom I was close, not him.

When my son was born, my husband photographed my father holding his first grandchild. It was a special moment until my father spoiled it. "You will have to watch out, little boy," my father said to the baby in his arms. "It is a miserable world."

"How could you say that to an innocent child?" I exploded, furious.

In these moments, my mother the peacemaker would try to smooth things over. She always made excuses for my father. "He loves you but can't always show it. You have to understand him. He suffered so much."

That just made me angry. "Why doesn't he try to understand me?" I would respond. It wasn't fair. I wasn't responsible for his suffering. Yet sometimes I felt guilty. How could I be angry at a person who had suffered?

There was so much about him I didn't understand. Why was he depressed? Why did he visit Germany so often? Why did he cry when he left Germany to come home?

Now my father was gone, and we would never resolve our differences. I couldn't apologize for the times I was selfish and unsympathetic. Perhaps, if I knew more about him, I would learn why he thought the world was miserable, why he so adamantly objected to calling the police "pigs," and how he came to be the man he was.

I left my mother's house with the box of letters.

What follows is my parents' story, gleaned from the letters, documents, anecdotes my parents recounted, and the testimony of others. It is my attempt to make sense of what happened before I was born. There are surely parts I didn't get right, conclusions that are incorrect. For these, I apologize.

My mother did not want me to read her private correspondence, and sadly, only some of her correspondence survived. I hope my mother, now deceased, will forgive me for violating her privacy.

My parents lived through events that upended millions of lives. May their story augment our understanding of the past.

—September 2021

PRELUDE: TWO DEPARTURES

Germany, July 3, 1937

On a sunny day in July 1937, one year before British Prime Minister Neville Chamberlain negotiates with Hitler for "peace in our time" and two years before the German Wehrmacht invades Poland, a young woman descends a stairway in the Mainz, Germany, Hauptbahnhof (Central Station). She is transferring to a train that will arrive on a different platform. Slim, with jet-black hair, she wears a suit and carries a small suitcase.

On this Saturday morning, the station is busy with groups of young people going on excursions and parents with children on their way to visit family. Intermittently a uniformed man passes by, official and self-important.

The woman finds the staircase for her connection and ascends the stairs. In ten minutes, the express train will arrive, and she will embark on a journey. Her trunk has already passed Gestapo inspection and was sent ahead. From Ostend, Belgium, she will cross the Channel to England, a country she has never seen, with a language she does not speak. A job as a nursery governess with an English family awaits her. This is her first trip outside Germany, and she is nervous but also determined. Her determination outweighs her nervousness; she knows she must leave.

The platform is crowded with people and luggage; families hug relatives in tearful leave-taking. As the woman walks down the platform, a young man approaches. He too has black hair, is of medium height, and wears a dark suit, a white handkerchief neatly tucked in his breast pocket. He looks tired, stressed. Only an observant bystander would detect a connection between the man and the dark-haired woman. Their eyes meet, but they do not acknowledge each other. As the man walks past the young woman, his hand grazes hers. In the commotion, no one notices the man slipping something into the woman's hand.

"*Achtung, Achtung,*" a voice announces over the loudspeaker. "The express train for Ostend is arriving on platform eight." The train enters the station, slows down, comes to a stop. Without a backward glance, the woman climbs aboard and takes a seat by the window. Unobserved, she opens her hand to find a small piece of paper containing three words and a photograph. The young woman smiles. She has made the right decision. She folds the paper carefully and hides it in her handbag.

Germany, September 14, 1938
(Over a Year Later)

The late morning sun shines on the vineyards along the rolling Hessian hills. In a few weeks the grape harvest will begin. The same young man, carrying a small cardboard suitcase, steps out of his parents' house in Guntersblum, the German village where he was born and where he has lived his entire life. He walks toward the train station, a short distance from his parents' house on the Wormser Strasse. His parents and brother-in-law accompany him.

The young man doesn't want to leave his parents, the vineyards he tended, his home. But if he doesn't leave now, his

American visa will expire. "Do not let that happen," colleagues and friends had urged him. "There is no future for you here."

And so, his preparations were hurried, his suitcase hastily packed. His parents accompany him as far as Mainz, where he will change trains and continue alone to Köln. From there he will fly to London.

As they wait for the train, he asks his brother-in-law to look after his parents. Before he can change his mind about leaving, the train arrives, and he and his parents climb aboard. The train takes him away—out of Guntersblum, past Oppenheim where he went to school, past the vineyards. In Mainz, he says goodbye to his parents and boards another train. He will never forget the sight of their faces as he departs for an uncertain future.

Elisabeth Bickel, the woman with the jet-black hair, and Emil Rüb, the man with the hastily packed suitcase, were my parents. They were among the fortunate, for they survived.

1. EMIL'S EARLY YEARS

*I*n the summer of 1906, the vineyards of Guntersblum, a German village on the left bank of the Rhine, promised a bountiful harvest. It was a special summer for the Rüb family. On August 23, early in the afternoon, the telephone rang at the home of Frau Dina Rüb. Widowed for fifteen years, Dina made a living selling grains, flour, and animal feed. That she had a telephone was unusual, for among the twenty-six hundred villagers, there were only eight private telephones.[1] Five of them belonged to Jewish businesspeople. Owning a telephone meant the owner was well off.

When Dina answered the phone, the voice on the line announced, "It's a boy!"

The caller was the widow's son David, twenty-eight years old, announcing the birth of his first child. The baby's mother was the former Bertha Dornberger, twenty-five years old, from Friedelsheim, a hamlet thirty miles away. After marrying in Friedelsheim on November 2, 1905, David and Bertha moved to a second-floor apartment on Guntersblum's main street. Nine months later, their son came into the world.

---

1. From the 1906 Grand Duchy of Hessen Rheinhessen address book, Volume 2, listed as "Rüb, David, Real Estate Agent, Nr. 183, Telephone Number 7." Street number 183, corner of Bleichstrasse and Ecke Promenade, was Dina Rüb's address. Source: Karin Holl.

The Rübs and Dornbergers were descended from Jews of the Rhineland-Palatinate, from farmers, vintners, merchants, and butchers who made an honest living, married, had children, and in death were buried in the local Jewish cemetery. Practicing Judaism at home and in unpretentious synagogues, they were an equal but separate minority who lived peacefully with their neighbors. "Don't stick your neck out" and "Don't cause problems" were guiding principles. Such behavior, they believed, would ensure their safety and a successful future.

Following Jewish tradition, David named his son Emil Daniel after deceased relatives. David's father, Daniel Rüb, had died when David was three years old. David's uncle Emil (whose last name was David) from neighboring Gimbsheim, acted as a surrogate father to young David and had helped launch him in the business of negotiating mortgages and loans. When his Gimbsheim uncle died, David took over the business.

The boy, Emil, had a sunny childhood. Oma (Grandmother) Dina doted on him, and, until the birth of a sister five years later, Emil was the center of his mother's attention. A maid looked after him when his mother, Bertha, was occupied with housework.

There was much in the village Emil found entertaining. From the second-floor window of the Rübs' apartment, he would watch the horses pull the brewery and wine transport wagons down the main street. Accompanying the maid shopping, he enjoyed looking into the farmers' yards to see the chickens, ducks, and geese. Occasionally, Emil and the maid had a difference of opinion; Emil wanted to continue observing the animals, while the maid, with errands to complete, needed to move on. Eventually, the maid would win those battles.

The early 1900s in Guntersblum was a time of progress. The village entered the twentieth century with the building of a waterworks facility, completed in 1907, so that, for the first time, Guntersblumers had fresh drinking water coming directly into their houses. In 1912 the Rheinhessen electric works provided the village with electric light. Far more interesting to Emil, however, was the zeppelin airship he once saw passing overhead.

When Emil was four, he went with his mother on the forty-five-minute train ride to Mainz for shopping. He loved the streetcars that transported them through the narrow streets and envied the streetcar driver ringing his bell to warn pedestrians out of the way. When he grew up, Emil decided, he too would become a streetcar driver.

A sister—Hedwig, whom everyone called Hede—joined the family on April 15, 1911, when Emil was four and a half. When she was born, Emil was evacuated to Oma Dina's house for a time, where he slept in a large feather bed. If, at bedtime, his special rag doll friend was missing, Oma Dina would call out, "Anna, where are you, you rascal?" Anna would turn up, usually under the bed, and then Emil could sleep. The times Emil spent with his grandmother were among the happiest of his childhood.

At age six, Emil attended the local elementary school. His Jewish education began later when he accompanied his father to the synagogue. At the time, eighty Jews lived in Guntersblum. Emil sat with the other boys on small benches at the front. They entertained themselves by noticing the quirks of certain congregation members so they could imitate them later. If Emil turned around and looked up, he could see Oma Dina and his mother in the women's gallery. Later, Emil attended Hebrew school on Saturday afternoons and Sunday mornings and received a solid foundation in Judaism from his teacher, Lehrer Stein.[2]

---

2. In 1940, the Rübs visited Lehrer Stein in Frankfurt, who commented that Emil was his best student.

Emil is in the second row, fifth from the left, in the sailor suit.

In 1913 David bought a large house at the southern entrance of Guntersblum, and the family moved in that summer. David hired workers to renovate the property and to install the first WC (water closet, or a flush toilet) in the village. Seven-year-old Emil was allowed to participate as a junior handyman; he learned to catch bricks tossed to him from several feet away and pass them to the next worker in line.

On the morning of August 2, 1914, a few weeks before Emil's eighth birthday, two of the young masons working on the house did not come to work. "Mobilization," the adults said. Emil soon learned what this meant: Germany was at war, and the masons had been called up for military service.

War brought new activity to the village. Military trains with slogans painted on them — "Down with France" and "Onward to Paris" — ran on the tracks at the end of the Rübs' property, and military traffic drove by in front of the house. Soldiers, about eight hundred of them, were billeted in Guntersblum homes, including at the Rübs'. Emil and his friends admired the friendly soldiers, who demonstrated their weapons and made wooden swords and guns for them.

Besides training, the soldiers participated in the community. In August the soldiers helped harvest the plums in one of David's fields, carrying the fruit in large baskets to the Rübs' house. With help from the housemaid, Bertha prepared the dough for the traditional *Zwetschgenkuchen* (plum cake). The sliced plums were arranged in rows on the dough, and the cake was then taken to the baker to be baked in his large oven. Some of the plum cakes were presented to the soldiers as a reward for their work.

Eventually, the soldiers were called to the front.[3] The morning of their departure, they assembled in the marketplace, their rifles bedecked with flowers, and practical gifts from their hosts added to their rucksacks. After their colonel thanked the villagers for their hospitality, the soldiers, accompanied by the village band, marched to the train station, singing patriotic songs. As their train departed, the soldiers waved their handkerchiefs out the window and sang a popular folk song about leaving a sweetheart behind.

David Rüb, Emil's father, was also called to serve in the military. Most likely he carried out minor administrative and office duties and did not go to the front. During his absence, Bertha and Oma Dina took care of the business and the fruit and vegetable gardens.

Four years later, in December 1918, soldiers were again billeted in Guntersblum, but this time they were not German. Germany had lost the war, and the soldiers, among them Senegalese and Moroccans, belonged to the French occupying army.

---

3. Information on the billeting of soldiers and their departure to the front from the research of Karin Holl.

Young Emil, perhaps age thirteen.

By August 1918, Emil had turned twelve and begun taking the train to school in Oppenheim, five miles north of Guntersblum. When he received the gift of a nine-by-twelve-centimeter plate camera, he became interested in photography and started photographing family and friends. He took school seriously, studied hard, and, of the students who finished school, he was one of two awarded a prize.

In the spring of 1922, fifteen-year-old Emil rode the train south to the city of Worms for high school. He studied German, French, English, Latin, math, geometry, history, chemistry, drawing, geography, natural science, and physical education. Except for physical education, he earned good to satisfactory grades in all subjects. His behavior and attentiveness were deemed *"sehr gut"* — very good.

During this time, David Rüb was becoming a respected businessman, esteemed by Jews and Christians alike for his honest, trustworthy, and cooperative manner. Already, in 1910, he was unanimously elected to the managing committee of Guntersblum's Jewish community and beginning in 1918 served as lay head of the congregation. In 1916 he began selling agricultural oils and soaps to farmers in neighboring communities. He purchased a small vineyard in 1918 and added a wine cellar and wine-shipping business to his responsibilities.

Guntersblum was not immune to the postwar hardships of hyperinflation and consumer shortages. Vegetables from the garden tended by Oma Dina helped the Rübs get by. Coal for heating and cooking was rationed and allocated only in small quantities. At night, villagers went to the Rhine, about two miles east of Guntersblum, to barter wurst, cheese, and butter for coal from coal barges anchored overnight. Because these transactions were illegal, they had to avoid the occupying French military police.

One night, Emil accompanied his father on such an expedition. "I'm cold," he complained, to which David replied, "Shut your trap!" Typical of his generation, David ruled the household and expected obedience from his son. Of course, Emil immediately became silent.

Without coal, homes were cold. At a gathering in a local guesthouse during an election campaign, Guntersblumers rose to speak, and the discussion grew heated. Finally, the Rübs' neighbor, the coal dealer Otto Clauss, took the floor. "What we need," he said gravely, "is a regime which gives us order, decency, and a good example of a how a German *Bürger* should live."

"Yes," a voice boomed from the back of the room, "and what we really need, Herr Clauss, is coal." This was typical Guntersblum humor. Who cared about order and decency when people needed to heat their homes? The comment from neighbor Clauss was indicative of those who resented Germany's defeat in the war and believed a new German order would restore the country's self-respect.

Before the war, David's main income had been from his thriving real estate business. Few properties changed hands in Guntersblum without obtaining advice from David Rüb. When a bank denied a small farmer a loan, David lent the farmer the money. David was also a bankruptcy trustee and an executor of wills. After the war, David managed to keep their house, some vineyards, and the agricultural products business. Real estate, however, was finished as an income source because nobody had money to buy property.

This ruled out a university education for Emil. On April 1, 1923, a few weeks after leaving high school, Emil began an apprenticeship in the Mainz branch of the Deutsche Effecten- & Wechsel-Bank.

By then Oma Dina, seventy years old, lived with her son, daughter-in-law, and grandchildren. Her room was upstairs, and at night she would sometimes call out, "Emil, go to the cupboard; I have such a bad taste in my mouth." Oma Dina wanted a nip of cognac to settle her stomach and to help her sleep.

The Rüb family, 1923.

Five years after the armistice, in the summer of 1923, the Rüb family assembled on the patio for a family photo. It is Saturday—*Schabbes* (the Sabbath). In the photo, the family wears their summer best, and no work will be done. *Kaffee und Kuchen*—coffee and cake—in Bertha's good porcelain dishes will soon be on the table.

This is a family at ease, confident of their place in the world. The tensions and unrest in Germany and the instability of the postwar Weimar Republic are temporarily at bay. Oma Dina sits on the chair Emil brought from the house; a regular garden chair is uncomfortable for her back. Twelve-year-old Hede smiles, happy in her white dress and shoes. Emil, a gangly adolescent of almost seventeen, stifles a grin to look serious for the photographer.

David Rüb, cigar in hand, muses on his next business venture. Guntersblumers consider him a hardworking and diligent businessman, friendly but aloof. In contrast, Bertha, his wife, is kind, warm, and nurturing. When her children were little, she read to them at night and spoiled them both, especially Emil. She kept a kosher home and skillfully managed her household. Her linen closets held monogramed sheets, and the attic stored preserves prepared with Oma Dina. Leaning back in her chair, arms crossed, Bertha looks at the photographer and smiles.

On this lazy afternoon, if anyone suggested what lay ahead, the Rübs would have stared in disbelief. They didn't feel threatened, because the Jewish community stood together. Despite postwar turmoil, life in a country village went on. Vegetables were growing in the garden; grapes would be harvested in the fall. An upstanding participant in Guntersblum affairs, David expected he would one day sell real estate again. Bertha would run her household and care for her family, and, as long as she could, Oma Dina would tend the garden. Hede dreamed of parties with boys, and Emil thought about girls and working in Mainz. The Rübs trusted that life would get better, not worse. After all, they were as German as their neighbors and fellow Guntersblumers.

2. HOW DETA GOT HER NAME

$\mathcal{T}$wenty miles south of Guntersblum, in the city of Worms, another young couple was also raising a family. They were close in age to David and Bertha Rüb, but there the similarities ended.

Katharina Seltzer and Johann Jakob Bickel already had two boys when they married on January 2, 1900, the first having been born in 1897.[4] After four more births, on March 20, 1909, a girl named Elisabeth, seventh in the pecking order, was born. Five more babies followed; the last of the Bickels' twelve children was born in 1918. Each birth, including two children who died in infancy, was inscribed in the family Bible.

Worms was an industrial city on the banks of the Rhine River with a Romanesque cathedral, the oldest Jewish cemetery in Europe, and a large monument to Martin Luther. When Katharina, a Catholic, married Johann Jakob, she converted to his Lutheran faith. Johann Jakob, known as Jakob, worked for the civil registry of Worms, a job he didn't like. His wife lived in fear he would quit his job, and they would lose the apartment they rented from the city. With twelve children to feed, clothe, and educate, money was

---

4. Sources: Interview with Elisabeth Rueb, anecdotes told by members of the Bickel family, and Bickel family documents.

Elisabeth Bickel (standing, the tallest in the back) with her sisters.

always an issue. Sometimes Jakob pawned a piece of his wife's jewelry to make ends meet.

Katharina was occupied with pregnancies, births, and babies. At first the Bickels had a maid, but later the girls helped with the household. By the time Elisabeth was born, the older boys were making their way in the world. With time and money for so many children in short supply, Jakob and Katharina did what they could for their family. At night when the children were in bed, Katharina mended or altered their clothes, and Jakob wrote articles for the newspaper to make extra money.

Katharina didn't coddle her children. Some days she stayed in bed with what was probably postpartum depression, and the children had to fend for themselves. Jakob was authoritarian but kind, with a sense of humor his children inherited. He had nicknames for each child. Elisabeth was Schwarzie (Blackie) because of her jet-black hair. Elisabeth enjoyed playing outside with her brothers and climbing trees. At night, in the bedroom upstairs, she whispered and giggled with her sisters.

Despite their limited finances, Katharina made Christmas special. There was always a Christmas tree with real candles and for each child an orange, an apple, some nuts, and home-baked cookies. For the girls, Katharina would crochet a doll dress; there might also be a practical gift such as a pair of shoes, but never the bicycle or roller skates Elisabeth coveted.

The Bickel family also suffered from the post–World War I inflation. Food was scarce, so Elisabeth, then a teenager, regularly stood in line for potatoes. Katharina would also send Elisabeth with one of her sisters to local farms to barter her linens for potatoes. On some days, Elisabeth went to school without food. She wore wooden shoes because leather was unavailable; if a shoe wore out and needed repair, she had to stay home.

When Elisabeth was fourteen, she stayed late after confirmation class to talk to a boy — something her strict parents did not allow, afraid that their daughters could replicate their premarital example. As a consequence, Jakob carted Elisabeth off to her paternal grandmother's house in Heilbronn, fifty miles from Worms. Before leaving her there, he gave Elisabeth some money. "Don't cry," he said. "Take this money to buy something to eat and stamps to write home."

After Jakob left, Elisabeth looked around and decided she did not like her grandmother's house. "I need to buy toothpaste," she told her grandmother. Elisabeth put on her coat and hat, grabbed her bag, and was out the door. She ran to the train station and, with the money from her father, bought a ticket for the next train going toward Worms. In Ludwigshafen, she had to change trains. Since Ludwigshafen was under French occupation, one needed French currency to purchase a ticket. Undaunted, Elisabeth changed her marks into francs, bought a ticket for Worms, and arrived home at two in the morning. When Katharina answered the door, she thought her daughter's ghost stood before her. Grounded for a month for running away, Elisabeth was nevertheless proud of her independence.

As the Bickel children got older, they were expected to learn a trade and earn money. After basic schooling, Elisabeth attended a yearlong finishing school for cooking, sewing, darning, and household skills. At her first job, she spent a year as a household helper, receiving only room and board.

At sixteen, she attended a childcare course at the kindergarten of the Dörr & Reinhardt leather factory in Worms and worked in a home for children of unwed mothers. She had wanted to become a social worker, but without a high school diploma, this was impossible. Instead, she chose the next best thing—to be a children's nurse. She always liked children and had looked after her younger siblings, so her choice of profession was a good fit.

In 1929, she qualified for state certification in infant care. After attending nursing school in Bremen and working in a hospital for women, she received certification as a maternity and child health nurse in 1931. Her credentials earned her the title *Schwester* (Sister) Elisabeth.

In those days, giving birth was a major medical event. After the birth, the mother usually rested in bed for one to two weeks, and those who could afford it hired a private duty nurse to care for mother and newborn. This job was ideal for Elisabeth. She was well-liked by children of all ages and by their parents. Children couldn't pronounce Schwester Elisabeth, so early on a child dubbed her "Deta" (pronounced *Deh-ta*). The name stuck, and from then on, she was Deta to children and parents alike.

Deta earned stellar references from her employers, who described her as "reliable, conscientious, and trustworthy." She found jobs by word of mouth in the homes of employers with names like Herz, Schwank, Mayer, Wolf, Schwarz, Breitenstein. That her employers were Jewish made no difference to her. Her

Elisabeth (Deta) Bickel as a young nurse in Worms.

father always said, "Whether Jew, Christian, or Hottentot, we all believe in one God."

It took time, however, to learn Jewish customs. On her first job, Deta prepared a beef broth and brought it on a tray to the new mother resting in bed. The woman took one look and shrieked so loudly that Deta almost dropped the tray. Deta had used the dairy dishes for the meat broth, which violated kosher laws. The defiled dishes had to be buried in the garden.

Despite this faux pas, Deta enjoyed her work. She liked wearing her smart-looking uniform and often joined her employers at the dinner table, where she had more and better food to eat than at home. She appreciated being in the homes of cultured people who valued art and music. That she sent most of her salary to her parents did not detract from her enjoyment.

It was a good start for a young woman in a respected profession. She looked forward to more jobs in elegant houses and even to a boyfriend or two. One day she would marry and have her own children—not as many as her parents, but at least two or three. The future looked promising.

3. A HOUSE WITH
ALL THE TRIMMINGS

To Guntersblumers, the Rübs were "*feine Leute*," decent people of fine character, kind and considerate to all.[5] "Come in for a cup of coffee and rest a bit," Bertha would say to a local delivery girl, "so you have strength to continue your rounds." When his seventeen-year-old apprentice died unexpectedly, it was David Rüb who put the burial announcement in the local paper.[6] To help elderly relatives harvest their grapes, Emil, then in his late teens, brought workers from the Rübs' vineyards. The Rübs had deep roots in Guntersblum, with their forebears in the Guntersblum Jewish cemetery going back to 1803.

The style and décor of the Rübs' house at 4 Wormser Strasse announced, "Here lives a comfortably off middle-class family."[7] The ground floor parlor had a grandfather clock, heavy oak furniture, carpets, paintings, and sideboards containing crystal, porcelain, and silver for twenty-four people. A large tile stove provided heat. The parlor was used for guests on Friday evenings after Schabbes services and on special occasions.

---

5. From interviews with Guntersblum residents who knew the Rüb family.
6. *Oppenheimer Landskrone*, April 3, 1925.
7. Description of the house at 4 Wormser Strasse comes from Emil's inventory of the contents.

The house at 4 Wormser Strasse, Guntersblum; Credit: Emil Rueb.

Toward the back of the house were a family dining room, a kitchen, and a pantry. The kitchen had everything a Jewish housewife needed for preparing and serving meals. Upstairs were four bedrooms and a bathroom; the WC was on the landing. The patio at the back of the house, site of the 1923 family photo, had a kennel for the family dog, and a swing. From the patio, one walked through a small gate and down a few steps into a garden extending all the way to the train tracks. As Oma Dina's nephew commented, it was a house with all the trimmings.

Like many German Jews, the Rübs valued *Bildung*—personal development through education and culture. Besides Hebrew prayer books, the bookcases in the family living room held a twelve-volume lexicon; collected classics by Goethe, Kleist, and Heine; works by Franz Werfel and Stefan Zweig; books and monthly magazines on art and literature; and a Latin dictionary. There was a radio and also a piano, which Bertha and Hede played.

In this house, Hede and Emil moved through adolescence into young adulthood. Almost five years apart in age, the two siblings had opposite temperaments and were not close. Emil enjoyed reading and discussing current affairs; Hede liked boys, fashion, and dancing. Emil was uncomfortable at parties; Hede enjoyed masked balls and dressing up at Karneval (Mardi Gras). Hede was fun-loving, lively, and outgoing, while Emil was quieter and more reticent. Their handwriting exemplified their differences—Emil's was sloping and small, Hede's round and full.

Their education differed as well. Hede started school in Guntersblum and then commuted to a girls' school in Worms. Next, she attended a finishing school for home economics run by Catholic nuns in Worms, and later, from December 1929 through the spring of 1930 when she was eighteen, a household training school in Hamburg. There she made friends with young women whose portraits she pasted in her photo album. "To my best friend here, remember the jolly time we spent together," one friend wrote. On returning to Guntersblum, she worked in her parents' household and business.

At eighteen, Emil completed his apprenticeship at the bank. His reference letter said he was diligent and of good character, could work independently, and had fulfilled his responsibilities to the bank's satisfaction. The bank could "recommend him to anyone." Emil, however, had no interest in banking.

David decided his son would join the Rübs' business as a traveling salesman. Emil would receive room, board, clothing, laundry, and ample pocket money instead of wages. Naturally friendly and enjoying a good joke, he got along well with his customers. On his own initiative, he added insecticides and fungicides to his wares. To better understand his products, he commuted for a semester to Fresenius Chemistry School in Wiesbaden.

As Germany slowly recovered from the postwar hyperinflation, David's real estate business revived. In 1927, David bought a car. He purchased new vines, replanted two vineyards to increase grape production, and started a mail-order business selling oils, soaps, washing powders, insecticides, and other chemical products. He hired a salesman in addition to Emil and added an office, a garage, and a stockroom to his property. In his home office, outfitted with filing cabinets, a safe, a type-writer, mimeograph machine, and a telephone, David worked at a large rolltop desk. With his son in the business, David could return to consulting in financial and property matters.

Although improvements to their house, vineyards, and business were made with borrowed money, David anticipated being out of debt by 1935. Business for father and son went well, requiring an office assistant and a stockroom worker. Because Bertha assisted with the business, a housemaid, clean-ing woman, and washerwoman helped in the household. The Rübs often had a *Haustochter*—"house daughter," a young girl who did errands and light housework in exchange for meals. Marianne, a *Haustochter* from a poor family, appreci-ated the good food Bertha offered her and Hede's help with her schoolwork.[8]

Hede at home, Guntersblum 1930;
Credit: Emil Rueb.

---

8. 2010 Interview with Marianne Flinner who recalled Hede's kindness and that she taught Marianne fractions.

Emil, volunteer fireman.

Like his father, Emil participated in Guntersblum community life. In 1928, he joined the volunteer fire department
and posed proudly in his helmet and blue uniform with gold
buttons. Arriving at his first fire call in uniform, he was
almost dismissed from the department; the uniform, the chief
informed him, was only for parades. Intelligent and sensitive,
Emil was a liberal in a community of mostly conservative
farmers. He joined the Guntersblum Chamber of Commerce, becoming its manager in 1929. He belonged to the
Young Democrats Club (Reichsbund der Jungdemokraten),
the German Physical Fitness League, and the Central Union
Club for German Jews. In 1925, David Rüb joined the
newly formed Reichsbanner, a Social Democrat organization
supporting parliamentary democracy.

The Rübs were active members of Guntersblum's close-
knit Jewish community.[9] For Emil, the Jewish holidays meant
a break from school, good food, and time to read and socialize
with other Jewish boys. He especially loved Purim, the story of
Esther and the victory of good people over bad, and he looked
forward to the reading of the story in the synagogue. Shavuot,
celebrating the giving of the Ten Commandments, was another
favorite because it fell in the spring when everything was in
bloom. And of course, Friday evenings, the weekly beginning
of the Sabbath, were festive occasions in the Rüb household.

In Guntersblum, Jews and Christians associated respect-
fully. In 1930, the local newspaper congratulated David and
Bertha on their silver (twenty-fifth) wedding anniversary[10]
and the following year noted Oma Dina's seventy-eighth
birthday.[11] One year, Hede's school chum invited her over
on Christmas Eve because Hede wanted to participate in their

---

9. "We did not have a feeling that we were lost or that we were amidst this
overpowering Christian majority—we were 2–3% of the population—we
somehow never felt lost because we always stood together." Emil Rueb, quoted
in *The Jewish Community of Guntersblum*, Dieter Michaelis, 1997.
10. *Oppenheimer Landskrone*, November 7, 1930.
11. *Oppenheimer Landskrone*, August 22, 1931.

celebration. Joining her friend's tradition, Hede dressed as an angel and recited a Nativity poem. The Rübs appreciated the festive atmosphere of the Christian holidays, especially Easter and Christmas.

Like all families, the Rübs imagined the future. Everything in the house was expected to last, with quality linen and good porcelain to be handed down to the next generation. One day Hede would marry and move away with her husband. Emil would take over the family business, marry, and live in the large house with his wife. Naturally, Hede and Emil would choose Jewish partners and raise Jewish children. In fact, Bertha hoped that Emil would marry Lotte, Uncle Emil David's granddaughter and thus a far-enough removed cousin. Perhaps Bertha pictured grandchildren at the Passover Seder, the youngest grandson reciting the traditional four questions. Later the children would hunt for the *afikomen*, the hidden piece of matzoh. And after the children were in bed, the adults, sated and content, would exchange news and gossip about relatives and Guntersblumers, over another glass of good Guntersblum wine.

A quiet evening in the Rüb household circa 1931. (From left to right) David, Bertha, Oma Dina, Hede; Credit: Emil Rueb.

❖ HANOVER, NEW HAMPSHIRE

In my possession from 4 Wormser Strasse, Guntersblum, are two pewter plates, a monogrammed silver soup ladle, Hede's albums, her costume jewelry, and some monogrammed linen.

In 2000, the then residents of 4 Wormser Strasse showed me the house. They had made many changes, but according to the owner, the wooden banister was from my father's time. When I climbed the stairs to the second floor, I imagined the imprints of hands—my grandparents', Hede's, my father's, Oma Dina's—still vibrating on the banister.

4. SUNSHINE

If money had been available and Emil could have decided for himself, he would have attended university and traveled instead of working in his father's business. On weekends he watched enviously as young adults on outings drove by his parents' house. Surely the nearby cities of Worms, Mainz, Frankfurt, and Mannheim offered more entertainment than Guntersblum on a Sunday afternoon.

Photography helped Emil relieve the tedium. In the early 1930s, when his first camera leaked light, he replaced it with an inexpensive Zeiss camera. He enjoyed finding interesting subjects, making sure the light was right, and mastering the camera.

One winter night in early 1932, when Emil was twenty-six years old, he knocked on Dr. Huhn's door. Dr. Huhn was the much-loved village doctor whose wife, Bertel, was Jewish. Their daughter had just been born, and Emil wanted to congratulate them. It would be a distraction from a quiet evening at home.

"Emil, how are you?" Dr. Huhn opened the door. "Join us for a glass of wine."

Emil hung up his jacket and followed Dr. Huhn to the living room. There, sitting next to the new mother, was a slim young woman in a white uniform with a nursing sister's cap on her head.

"Emil, come in," said Frau Doktor Huhn, beckoning him to sit down. "Come meet our *Kinderschwester.*" The Huhns had a nurse to help look after baby Erika, who had been born a few weeks before her due date.

"Schwester Elisabeth, allow me to present our friend Emil Rüb," said Dr. Huhn. "Emil, this is Fraulein Bickel from Worms, but everyone calls her Deta."

"Good evening, Schwester Elisabeth," Emil smiled as he shook her hand, noticing her black hair and trim figure.

Schwester Elisabeth with baby Erika, 1933;
Credit: Emil Rueb.

Deta smiled back, and Emil was intrigued. She seemed different from other women that Emil knew; Deta was unpretentious and friendly. He wanted to know more about her.

To the city-born Deta, Guntersblum was a hinterland. *Where have I come to?* she had wondered, depressed and homesick when she first arrived. Then she met Emil.

The friendship with Emil developed naturally, fitting into the comings and goings of village life. In good weather, Deta took her little charge for walks, and if she ran into Emil on the street, she stopped and chatted with him. "May I accompany you a little way?" Emil would ask if he had time, to which Deta always answered yes. Sometimes Deta wheeled the baby carriage on the Alsheimer Strasse in case Emil drove by en route to his customers.

Emil usually had his camera with him, which he used as a prop for social situations when he felt insecure. One day he decided to photograph the child in the baby carriage Deta pushed. The photo would be a gift to the child's parents. Of course, he also photographed Deta. Photographing Deta's charges soon became a collaborative effort. Deta would distract the child while Emil readied the camera, and then prompt the little one to look at him.

"This Saturday is my day off," Deta mentioned to Emil on one such encounter, "and I am going to a concert in Mannheim." The day of the concert, Deta took her seat in the auditorium. Moments before the concert started, someone slid into the seat next to her. It was Emil. Deta knew then that he was interested in her. Soon the two young people were leaving secret messages for each other under a milestone on the Alsheimer Strasse.

When Deta went home for the weekend, she passed the Rübs' house on her way to the train station. Her high heels clicked loudly on the cobblestone streets, and Emil listened for the sound of her footsteps to observe her from his second-floor bedroom. Besides admiring Deta's competence with children, Emil was attracted to her warmth and good looks.

Likewise, Deta was drawn to the sensitive young man. She understood his restlessness, his yearning for the world outside Guntersblum. In the village, he felt confined. Deta empathized with Emil's yearning, for she too wanted more than what she saw at home.

Deta didn't have money, but she had style, energy, and good humor, and she was falling in love. She liked Emil's fine manners, his intelligence, his integrity. He was kind and gentle, even a little shy. He was also handsome, and as a twenty-three-year-old woman, Deta felt a strong attraction to her twenty-six-year-old friend. That Emil was Jewish made no difference. She liked him, and that was that.

Slowly their relationship grew. Emil would pick Deta up in his father's car, and they would drive through the countryside. The car provided a modicum of privacy for a kiss, and, as their attraction became stronger, for Emil to unbutton Deta's blouse. Once Deta brought her latest charge with her, a five-year-old boy. "There seems to be something wrong with both of you," the lad remarked from the back seat, as Emil held Deta in his arms and kissed her.

The relationship raised eyebrows in Guntersblum, where villagers formed opinions about their neighbors. People sat at their window or stood behind the curtains to see who was passing by. At twenty-six and from a good middle-class family, Emil was an eligible bachelor. Guntersblum noticed.

Emil's parents, David and Bertha, did not approve of his friendship with Deta, and Emil never officially introduced Deta to them. If Deta saw David on the street, she would greet him with a pleasant, "Guten Tag, Herr Rüb." David wasn't rude, but he wasn't friendly and didn't initiate conversation. The same was true for Oma Dina, whom Deta occasionally passed in the Rübs' garden plot by the railroad station. One evening, Emil invited Deta to his parents' house after David and Bertha had gone to bed. The next day Dr. Huhn took Deta aside. "It would be better," he advised, "if you don't go there when the Rübs are not present. People talk."

That a young man from Guntersblum's small Jewish community was seeing a non-Jewish woman went against the norm. Jewish men married Jewish women; that was how things were done. Bertha criticized Deta, foreseeing dire consequences if the relationship continued. "She is probably a gold digger. She will take advantage of you. She won't keep kosher, and your children won't be Jewish."

Emil struck back. "If you say one more word against Fraulein Bickel," he threatened, "I will leave the house for good." Emil had no tolerance for intolerance. That day, he had planned to visit Deta in Heppenheim where her parents had moved, and his mother was not going to dissuade him. Cousins Erich and Lotte, visiting from Würzburg, accompanied him on the outing to Heppenheim on the Bergstrasse.

It was a beautiful summer day, and the three cousins and Deta spent a relaxing afternoon in a meadow outside Heppenheim. Emil was still upset at his mother. Deta did her best to calm him down, gently laying her hand on his back. Neither Cousin Erich nor his sister Lotte, who had a crush on Emil, cared that Deta wasn't Jewish. Deta's friendly nature won them over.

Emil and Deta.

Deta with Emil's cousin Lotte.

Sitting together, Lotte and Deta posed for Emil's camera. *How beautiful Deta looks,* Emil thought. Deta made him feel confident. The physical and emotional attraction between them was stronger than family obligations and religious tradition. Surely their love could overcome his parents' objections, especially after they saw Deta's fine character. Surely Deta's parents would be supportive. But Emil was getting ahead of himself. He wasn't ready to marry and support a wife. There was still time for that.

❈ HANOVER, NEW HAMPSHIRE

*M*y parents didn't show physical affection to each other. On my mother's birthday, I would insist that my father give her a kiss; I don't remember if he complied. My mother told me that when they were first married and my father returned from a business trip, he shook hands with her instead of embracing. This probably was typical of their generation.

How I wish to have been a fly on the wall that night when Deta and Emil first met. I would love to have observed my parents when they were young and attracted to each other. I like seeing in their letters that there was a spark between them, "chemistry" my mother called it, and that they desired each other sexually. This is apparent in a photo my father took of my mother asleep in the grass (see page 45); the photographer was obviously enamored with his subject. It was that heady time of being infatuatedly in love.

5. UPHEAVAL (1933)

*I*n the 1929 illustrated children's book *Die verkehrte Welt* (*The Upside-Down World*), a donkey sits in a wagon pulled by two men, instruments play on musicians, and brooms sweep the street with upside-down street sweepers.[12] In this world gone amok, the expected order of things is reversed: the child puts the tongue depressor in the doctor's mouth, washes the mother's face, feeds the father porridge, and intimidates the teacher. As in the children's book, when Adolf Hitler was appointed chancellor on January 30, 1933, Germany became a world turned upside down.

Less than a month after Hitler was appointed, the Reichstag, where the German Parliament met, was gutted by fire. The fire was attributed to Communist insurgency and resulted in the mass arrest and imprisonment of Communists. The Reichstag Fire Decree, passed the day after the fire, suspended civil liberties, including freedom of expression, of the press, of free association, and of public assembly. *Die Weltbühne*, a leftist periodical with articles against National Socialism that Emil often read, was an early victim of the suspension of civil liberties. On March 23, the Enabling Act allowed Hitler to rule by decree and gave him dictatorial powers.

---

12. Herbert Roth and Otto Schubert, *Die Verkehrte Welt* (R. Piper & Co., Verlag München).

Antisemitism in Germany was not new, but it now grew uglier. Hitler and his followers blamed Jews, Communists, and Social Democrats for Germany losing the war in 1918, insisting that Jews had betrayed Germany on the home front. This far right conspiracy theory accused Jews of stabbing Germany in the back. On April 1, 1933, Nazis organized a boycott of Jewish shops, Jewish goods, Jewish doctors, and Jewish lawyers in cities and towns. According to the *Völkischer Beobachter*, the Nazi party daily newspaper, the boycott was to "strike particularly at Jewish traders in the countryside" and "to reach into the smallest peasant villages."[13]

The small Jewish community of Guntersblum felt the impact of the new regime. Once again, David's real estate business was vulnerable, this time under pressure from local Nazi officials, making it impossible to sell properties. When Emil visited customers in neighboring villages, he was threatened and his automobile damaged. On one occasion, he was chased out of a village by a pro-Nazi mob. One after another, Emil's customers regretfully said that they could no longer buy from him. Local organizations couldn't have Jewish members; Emil had to withdraw from the volunteer fire department and the chamber of commerce. People feared repercussions if they worked for Jews, and as a result, the Rübs couldn't find workers for their vineyards and fields.

The first year of the Hitler regime brought extortion, blackmail, and weeklong absences by David because of threats to his safety. Local Nazis sometimes requisitioned the Rübs' car and then insisted David pay for the gas; they required Emil to drive Jewish and Christian Guntersblumers to the nearby concentration camp in Osthofen.[14] David spent

13. Yahil, Leni, *The Holocaust: The Fate of European Jewry, 1932–1945*, Oxford University Press, 1990, p. 60.
14. Osthofen: from March 1933 to July 1944, a concentration camp in the town of Osthofen, about 8 miles from Guntersblum. Anna Seghers's 1939 novel *The Seventh Cross* is loosely based on Osthofen.

one night in jail, his son accompanying him for fear that David might be beaten. Afterward Emil went into hiding for a few days.

Local tax officials claimed the Rübs had more taxable income than David reported. In a tax inspector's office in neighboring Oppenheim, the inspector declared, "Everyone in Guntersblum knows you have a fortune." Then, pointing to a picture of Hitler on the wall, the official shouted at David and Emil. "Stand up, the two of you. Go stand up under the picture. Do you still dare," he barked, "in his presence, to deny you are hiding a fortune from taxation?" The attacks from tax officials, often based on anonymous accusations, resulted in legal expenses that further drained the Rübs' finances.

The longtime understanding between Guntersblumers and the town's Jewish citizens was eroding. There were house searches of Jewish homes and arrests of Jewish men as well as those of Communists and Socialists.[15] If a Nazi party member thought (or pretended to think) that a Jew had cheated him, he would go at night, accompanied by other party members, to that person's house to extort him. There were incidents of mistreatment, beatings, and detention in Osthofen.[16] Doing business with Jews was forbidden.

---

15. "Stolpersteine in Guntersblum," *Guntersblumer Blätter*, Ausgabe 02-2020, p. 85.
16. Dieter Michaelis, *Die Jüdische Gemeinde Guntersblum: Von den Anfängen bis zur Vernichtung durch den Nationalsozialismus*, Wissenschaftlicher Verlag Berlin, 2014, pp. 104-111.

May 1 Parade, 1933. In April, the Guntersblum Town Council voted Adolf Hitler an honorary citizen of the town; Credit: *Guntersblum: So war's einmal Band II*, by Frank Frey and Albrecht Langenback, Geiger-Verlag, Horb am Neckar, 1993.

Emil's cousin Erich, a 1931 law school graduate who completed his doctoral thesis in September 1932, was employed as a junior attorney for the government. In April 1933, his degree became worthless: Jews were no longer allowed to practice, and Erich was suspended from his job. Unable to make a living, Erich quickly decided to emigrate. He asked an uncle in New York for an affidavit, applied for a United States visa, and arrived in New York in January 1934. (To obtain a U.S. visa, an immigrant needed an American citizen to sign an affidavit confirming that they would take responsibility for the immigrant and that the immigrant would not become a public charge.) His sister Lotte (whom Bertha wanted Emil to marry) joined him in January 1937.

The need to emigrate was clear to Erich, not only for himself, but for his family as well. Emigrating was his response to the changing circumstances around him. Choosing to leave was less clear-cut for Emil. In a letter to Erich at the end of 1934, Emil advised, "Remember, when thoughts of home stir in you, know that return to the family is always open but not to the *Heimat*. She has scorned you because you are a Jew and will only receive you as a guest." Emil wasn't ready to risk that separation for himself.

For Germans, *Heimat*—the place where you were born and raised—was more than its literal translation of "home-land." It was where you felt secure, where your roots reached back for generations, where you belonged. To leave your *Heimat* meant losing the life you were making, your identity, and yourself. It meant acknowledging that your version of *Heimat* did not match reality.

Unlike Erich, Emil didn't have an established profession. Furthermore, Emil had difficulty with change. The family business he helped manage, the vineyards he tended, his parents, and Oma Dina all tied him to Guntersblum. Who would get up at night when Oma Dina wanted a nip of cognac? Who would look after his parents, especially when the Nazis threatened his father? And where would he go? The United States did not interest him nor did starting over again at almost thirty years of age. "I would never feel comfortable over there," he commented to Erich.

There must have been considerable discussion at the Rüb dinner table. How would they keep their business going if nobody bought from them? Neither David nor Emil had anticipated the Nazis' antisemitic laws. The motto they lived by—"Don't stick your neck out and all will be well"—was not working, and life as they knew it was changing faster than they could imagine. This was not a time for indecisiveness. The initial thinking that Hitler wouldn't last was proving incorrect.

Despite his reluctance, Emil came to agree that establishing himself outside Germany and arranging for the family to join him was the only sensible course. Palestine in the Middle East was not an option; Emil was too old for the Youth Aliyah movement, which helped young people aged fifteen to seventeen to immigrate. He therefore decided to use family contacts to buy an orchard in France. On August 20, 1935, three days before his twenty-ninth birthday, he went to the county seat of Oppenheim and was issued passport number 183. After delaying six months, on February 1, 1936, Emil visited the French consulate in Mainz where he obtained a visa for a six-day trip to France, a *"visite sans intention de séjour"* (visit without intention of staying).

Later that month, Emil took an express train to the French border. Across the tracks from the German station was France, which Emil described as "the land of freedom from anxiety and never-ending Nazi oppression." After passing German and then French security controls, he met the woman expecting him, the relative of German friends and owner of a farm in France. She was in a horse-drawn carriage on the French side.

The woman greeted him warmly and then drove him up the mountains to her farm. They discussed Emil's immigrating to France and his making a living as an apple grower. The woman gave him an introduction to a Jewish merchant in Bitche, the neighboring city; the merchant in turn would introduce him to a local high court judge, also Jewish.

The next morning, Emil took the bus to Bitche and met the judge. After listening to Emil's story, the judge explained that the French Defense Authorities did not favor immigration into their area on the French-German border. The judge added, "I have no sympathy for you German Jews. You have aligned yourself so much with Germany and moved away from Judaism that you deserve what is coming to you."

Upset by the judge's comments and his mission unsuccessful, Emil returned to Germany, relieved to be home. The life he had always imagined for himself didn't include leaving his *Heimat*. Then, on April 3, his beloved Oma Dina died. The Rübs said Kaddish at her grave in the small Jewish cemetery at the edge of Guntersblum. They intended to purchase a tombstone later, when they could afford one.[17]

Writing to Cousin Erich in September 1936, Emil described his attempts to keep their business functioning. David and Emil added wood-conservation supplies, paint and varnish, and wine cellar materials. Emil still drove daily to sell soaps, oils, and fats and to collect bills. He was enjoying learning about agricultural work and took on additional responsibilities because they could not hire help. In the little free time he had, he did photography. He omitted saying that many of their customers refused to pay their bills.

But diversifying their business did not improve the Rübs' finances. Local people were still not buying from them. Emil again considered starting anew elsewhere and sending for his parents. With Oma Dina gone, his ties to home had loosened. Bertha recommended Emil visit her first cousin Sigmund Dornberger in London. Their fathers were brothers who were once in business together. Perhaps family ties would prevail.

Sigmund Dornberger came from Friedelsheim, the same hamlet as Bertha. For reasons unknown, he left Germany in 1897 for England, becoming a British citizen in 1903. In 1916, because of the enormous antipathy toward Germans during World War I, he anglicized his name to "Stewart Thornhill." He married, had four sons, and divorced when his youngest son was an adolescent. A tough, decisive businessman, he developed a thriving business importing glass, china, and earthenware from Europe. Surely Uncle Sigmund would help a struggling relative from Germany.

In January 1937, Emil travelled to London, but things did not go well when Emil rang at his uncle's door. Stewart

---

17. This was one of the last burials in the Guntersblum Jewish Cemetery. There is no tombstone for Oma Dina's grave, and the location of her grave is unmarked. In 2022 the Guntersblum Stolpersteine Gruppe (stumbling stone group) ordered a memorial stone which will be placed in the Jewish Cemetery in 2023.

Thornhill did not welcome this unknown nephew and had no interest in helping the son of a cousin with whom he had no contact. "The war [World War I] has torn all bonds between us," he said, washing his hands of Emil. Stewart Thornhill offered neither advice nor hospitality, not even a cup of coffee, and the interview ended quickly.

The rejection took Emil by surprise. At the least, Emil assumed, this "English" uncle would invite him in, ask about Emil's family and the situation in Germany; at best, he might offer a job in his company or refer him to a potential employer. In Guntersblum, Jews helped Jews. Raised with this understanding, Emil thought others would do the same.

Back on the street in the gray afternoon, Emil felt he had been kicked in the stomach. With little money and no return ticket, speaking only school English, he was without options. He also hadn't had a meal and was living off cookies his mother had packed in his suitcase and drinking tap water in his hotel. How was he going to get home? In his almost thirty-one years, he had never been so low spiritually and financially.

Seeing a post office, he entered; he would write home about his experience. A young German woman noticed him as he tried, in his limited English, to buy a postage stamp. Curious about the sad young man, she asked him, "*Sind Sie Deutsch?* (Are you German?) Where are you from? What brings you to London?"

Relieved to have a human contact in his own language, Emil explained his situation. When the woman learned he hadn't eaten properly, she took him to a Lyons Corner House restaurant and bought him a meal. Afterward, the woman gave him directions to Woburn House, where the German Jewish Aid Society was located.

Restored by food and the woman's kindness, Emil took his leave. On the way to Woburn House, he stopped outside a photography store. In the show window was a display of

large-format cameras that caught his eye. These cameras—
heavy, bulky, limited in use—were outdated in Germany.
With the Leica camera and 35 mm photography, Germany
was in the vanguard.[18]

He stood for a few moments, surveying the cameras
in the show window. And then he had an inspiration. Why
not turn the hobby he loved into a profession? As a trained
photographer, he would have a marketable skill for when he
emigrated. Right there, he decided to return home and study
35 mm photography. Despair gave way to hope. Although
he was not religious, he knew he had received a moment of
grace. Hopefully, his father would support his plan.

With his newfound clarity, he walked another half hour
to the German Jewish Aid Society in Bloomsbury. There he
was ushered into the office of a kindly gentleman named Mr.
Davidson. "How can I be of help to you?" Mr. Davidson asked.

In his stilted English, Emil explained his situation and
his plan to study photography. Mr. Davidson shared Emil's
interest in photography, and the two men spent half an hour
discussing the latest German cameras. "Do you need money?"
Mr. Davidson asked. "I can give you five pounds toward your
trip home." Accepting help was hard, but Emil had no choice.
To ease his conscience, he took only three pounds.

Emil left Woburn House with renewed energy. He
liked what he saw of London and that he could walk the
streets without fearing arrest or being threatened. Freedom
to choose was in the air he breathed during his short stay. On
the journey back to Nazi Germany, he felt like a prisoner
returning to jail, his parole revoked. But now he had a plan.

In Guntersblum it was cold and damp, and darkness
came early. Along the Rhine, the morning and evening fog

---

18. In 1924 Oskar Barnack developed the Leica, introducing *Kleinbild
Photographie*, miniature photography, known as 35 mm. Now pictures could be
taken with a smaller camera instead of with bulky, large format contraptions.

could be as thick as pea soup, but weather did not deter Emil. First, he had a promise to keep. To Mr. Davidson, the gentleman at Woburn House who gave him money to return home, Emil sent the brochure he had mentioned about the Robot, a small German camera developed in 1934.

On February 23, as the morning fog lifted, Emil boarded a train at the Guntersblum station. With money from the Hilfsverein der Deutschen Juden, a Jewish aid organization, he enrolled in Photo Schule Laszlo Rozsa (the Laszlo Rozsa Photography School). That day he would meet Rozsa, school director and teacher, at the entrance to the Frankfurt Zoo. Laszlo Rozsa, a Hungarian Jew, taught photography, developing, and printing. Rozsa was an Associated Press photographer and had worked at the *Frankfurter Zeitung* as a reporter and photojournalist since 1924. When the National Propaganda Ministry no longer recognized his credentials in 1936, he lost his job. The photo school was how he made ends meet.

Smoking his usual cigarette in a black cigarette holder, Rozsa was waiting for Emil at the zoo entrance, a Leica camera hanging from his neck. The hour and a half with Rozsa energized Emil. Under Rozsa's tutelage, Emil photographed the monkeys and then went with his teacher to develop and print the film.[19] Although Emil had much to learn, Rozsa confirmed that he wasn't a total novice, affirmation that Emil appreciated. "Take pictures," Rozsa advised, which is exactly what Emil did: photos of children, a market, the Worms Cathedral, his briefcase leaning against a fence, whatever struck him as a good subject.

David was skeptical about Emil's chosen profession and doubtful his son could earn a living as photographer. For Emil, going against his father's reservations wasn't easy. As

---

19. Before cell phones with cameras, photographers captured images on film. The film then was developed into negatives; the negatives were transferred onto light sensitive paper and then "bathed" in chemicals until the image emerged. Finally, the photographs were dried and pressed flat. This process could take up to two hours.

a young man in his father's house, Emil had struggled. He lacked confidence, was highly self-critical, and depended on others for validation. Being discriminated against as a Jew further depleted his self-esteem, and he blamed himself instead of the Nazi boycott for the family business losses.

Despite David's lack of support, Emil embraced his chosen métier. Several times a week he commuted to Frankfurt, a ninety-minute train journey with a change in Mainz. He enjoyed working in the atelier with young Jewish colleagues also preparing to emigrate. The photography course gave Emil purpose and hope. It also postponed the inevitable—departure from home and *Heimat*. Deliberate and methodical, Emil would leave only when he was ready.

There was another reason Emil resisted leaving Germany: he was still seeing Deta.

6. DETA RESPONDS TO HITLER

From June 1933 to January 1934, Deta worked in Guntersblum for the Oswald family, who owned vineyards and a winery. This time, there was no new baby; Frau Oswald was ill and recuperating in a clinic, so Deta looked after the Oswalds' daughter, Margot. Deta's room at the Oswalds' was on the ground floor facing the street. In the morning, she often found a note under the shutters, signed "E." The feelings between Emil and Deta had grown too strong to end their relationship. Their courtship, however, was not without difficulties.

One time, when Emil and Deta boarded a train together from Guntersblum to Mainz, two Nazis followed them on board. Sitting next to each other, the young couple made a plan. "When we arrive in Mainz," Emil whispered to Deta, "we'll separate. You go in a different direction from me, and we'll meet later." The two men also got off the train in Mainz, appearing to follow the couple, but Deta slipped away.

This was not the first time Emil and Deta thought they were being watched and felt unsafe. Another time, at the Guntersblum train station, some girls wearing the *Bund Deutscher Mädel* uniform (Hitler Youth for girls) noticed Deta's black hair. "Hey, Jewess," one of them called to her.

"We ought to get some scissors and cut your hair." Neither Emil nor Deta corrected the girls' mistake.

In September 1935, Hitler's Law for the Protection of German Blood and German Honor, issued during the Nazi party rally at Nürnberg and therefore called the Nürnberg Laws, made it illegal for Jews to marry non-Jews. In addition, Jews no longer had the rights of citizenship; instead of citizens, they were now *Staatsangehoerige*—state subjects. It was dangerous for Emil and Deta to be seen together.

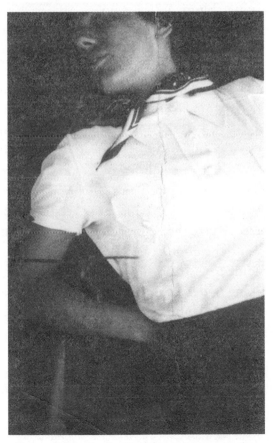

Photo of Deta taken by Emil during a secret meeting.

The couple began meeting in secret, often at the home of Jewish friends in Oppenheim. Deta was unafraid, but Emil lived in fear of arrest because an affair between a Jew and an "Aryan"[20] woman was a crime. It was a bad time for a relationship between a Jew and a Christian and too dangerous to act on their sexual desires. Had Emil been willing and able to leave Germany, Deta would gladly have joined him.

Aware that Emil and Deta were seeing each other, the Oswalds could have reported them to the authorities but did not. They were fond of Deta and knew that Emil was well-liked in Guntersblum. When a police officer accused Frau Oswald of employing a housemaid involved with a Jew, she told him to get out of her house.

Deta saw how Jews were being treated. From the kitchen window at home in Worms, she observed a Jewish neighbor being kicked and pushed by Nazi thugs. Not only did this behavior violate every value Deta had, she had to acknowledge that Emil too was vulnerable. She felt an icy shiver. If she was powerless to help her neighbor, how could she protect Emil?

Deta's resistance to the Third Reich was personal. When a Nazi demonstration took place in the street, bystanders were expected to give the Nazi salute. To avoid saluting, Deta would run into the doorway of the nearest apartment building, pretending to visit a resident in the building. The Nazis were not going to determine whom she could love.

When her assignment with the Oswalds ended, Deta had to find another job. Under the Nürnberg Laws, as an "Aryan" under forty-five years of age, she could no longer work in Jewish households. With little money in her pocket, hungry, and on foot, she spent an entire day in Frankfurt

---

20. "Aryan," an obsolete nineteenth-century term referring to language structure, was misused by the Nazis to denote a mythical race superior to "non-Aryans" — Jews, Blacks, and Roma and Sinti (Gypsies). According to Nazi beliefs, this terminology signified who belonged and who did not. In reality there is no such thing as an "Aryan master race."

knocking on the door of every obstetrician she could find
for a job referral. Her efforts were successful; a family in
Frankfurt employed her for two months at the end of 1935.

In February 1936 she was hired by a family in Darmstadt
where the wife was expecting. The family seemed nice enough
and included Deta at their dinner table. One evening, the
husband excused himself from the table, saying, "I have to
get ready for a meeting." Soon the husband returned wearing a Nazi uniform. Deta kept her personal sympathies to
herself, and the job lasted only a few weeks. By May 1936,
unable to find employment in private homes, Deta worked
in hospitals run by the Lutheran Diocese in Vilbel, Hanau,
and Nordhausen.

Emil did not tell Deta when he travelled outside Germany.
Letters could be incriminating, so they did not correspond.
Sometimes he telephoned where Deta worked since the Rübs
had a telephone at home. When time allowed, Emil scheduled
a business trip to Worms to see Deta. They met outside a
school, away from the main streets where they were less likely
to be noticed.

By now Deta's parents knew she had a Jewish boyfriend
and feared for her safety. As mentioned earlier, the Bickels
were extra vigilant of their daughters due to their own premarital episodes. Now in their sixties, they had already lost
three of their twelve children—the most recent in 1932, a son
who was found drowned in the Rhine.

"Aren't you ashamed of yourself, arriving home so late?"
Deta's mother complained when Deta returned from seeing Emil.

Deta's oldest brother, Friedrich, also scolded her, saying,
"You could be arrested if you are seen with Emil." Friedrich's
wife was a Hitler supporter, and their three children were in
the Hitlerjugend. Even Jakob Bickel, Deta's tolerant father,
wrote Emil that he would turn him over to Nazi authorities
if Emil continued seeing Deta.

Shortly after Emil's return from London, the Bickels received an anonymous letter. If Deta didn't end her relationship with a Jew, she would be charged with *Rassenschande* — despoiling the "Aryan" race — and sent to a concentration camp. Furthermore, Jakob, now retired, could lose his pension. Jakob and Katharina Bickel were neither Nazis nor Nazi sympathizers; they did not hang the obligatory picture of Hitler in their apartment.[21] The anonymous letter, however, frightened them. Deta wasn't frightened, but she had had enough. The Nazi regime was reaching too far into her private life. It was time to act.

Since marriage with her dark-eyed young man was impossible in Germany, she would leave. If Emil wouldn't emigrate on his own initiative, he might follow if she left first. This was a true leap of faith, for Emil had not mentioned marriage or even engagement. Perhaps Emil was not as far along in the relationship as Deta, unable to consider marriage when his family's economic survival was threatened. But Deta knew what she wanted. If she could not be with Emil in Germany, she would go elsewhere. Outside Germany, she could do more to help him get out.

In the hospital where she worked, Deta befriended a social worker who understood why Deta wanted to leave the country. The social worker asked her brother's girlfriend, then working in England, to help Deta. The girlfriend responded with information about an English family — Mr. and Mrs. Hill, who were seeking a nanny. The Hills were nice people who lived in Bedford and spoke no German. To work in England, Deta needed an entry permit and residence visa, which took

---

21. Jakob Bickel belonged to the Heppenheim Bekennende Gemeinde (Confessing Church) that opposed the pro-Nazi Evangelical Church. On October 14, 1938, he and a second representative of the Church Council went to the Reichskirchenministerium, the Reich Church Ministry in Berlin, to protest the removal of their Pastor.

During the Third Reich, two women brought Katharina Bickel the *Ehrenzeichen der Deutschen Mutter* (Cross of Honor of the German Mother), an award for having borne so many children. Katharina threw the award down the toilet.

fourteen days to receive. For the residence visa, all that was required was Deta's first and last name, place of birth, and her father's name and occupation. If Deta could travel to London's Victoria Station, Mrs. Hill would meet her there.

A letter to Deta from Mrs. Hill, translated by an acquaintance into German, soon followed: "You would like to know some details before you accept the position. My husband is a teacher here at the Bedford school. We have three children— one a boy nine years old, a girl of six, and a baby boy almost two years. The oldest is in a boarding school and is home on vacations. Your duty would be the baby. Meals are brought by a maid to the nursery. We have two maids. I must ask you to keep the nursery clean yourself and naturally the children's clothes. When my husband has vacation, we go to relatives in the country. We would of course take you with us.

"We can discuss vacations later. I propose that you have a half day free every week and every second Sunday afternoon. But if you wish to go away for a Saturday and Sunday, I would be willing. Now about salary. I can't pay you more than 36 pounds a year. If you accept the position, I will do everything to make you happy."

Mrs. Hill would reimburse Deta's travel expenses when she arrived. "You will of course think everything over carefully as it would be unfortunate if after a short time you wished to return." Deta had already thought things over, and she accepted the job. She took a few English lessons and applied for a passport in Nordhausen, where nobody knew about her relationship with a Jew.

The next hurdle was telling her parents. "I have an opportunity to spend a year in England," she told them. "It will be good experience and an excellent opportunity for professional development." That was true; going to England would be good experience. But Deta had no intention of returning to Nazi Germany.

Before her departure, Deta and Emil arranged to meet in Bensheim, forty minutes walking distance from Heppenheim. "Come with me," Deta told her fifteen-year-old sister, Luise. "I am going to see Emil, and I need you to come along." It was a lovely evening in mid-June, when the linden trees were in bloom and their perfume filled the air.

"We're just going out for a stroll," Deta told her parents, Luise's presence a subterfuge for her plan. Jakob and Katharina Bickel assumed Deta had broken up with Emil after the anonymous threatening letter.

"Don't stay out too late," Jakob ordered.

In the twilight, Deta and Luise walked to Bensheim where Emil waited under the railroad trestle. "I won't be long," Deta told Luise, who moved around the corner to give her sister some privacy.

There, Luise paced anxiously. Deta seemed to take forever. What if they were discovered? If they didn't return home soon, their parents would worry.

After what seemed an eternity, Deta reappeared, and the two young women walked back to Heppenheim in pitch darkness. Deta said little, wondering when she would see Emil again. Luise was terrified. To her, every knot on the linden trees lining the road, every creak of a branch, was a villain waiting to attack them. Fortunately, the villains were only in her imagination, and the two sisters arrived home safely.

A few days later, Deta's sister Käthe accompanied her to the railway station in Worms. Anyone leaving the country had to announce their departure fourteen days ahead of time so that customs could inspect their luggage for taxable items or smuggled currency.

"What's in there?" the Gestapo official challenged, pointing at Deta's trunk.

"*Mein alltägliche Schmuck* [my everyday jewelry]," Deta replied. Deta owned nothing of value, and the Gestapo officer didn't frighten her. Her trunk was accepted and sent on to England.

On July 3, 1937, then twenty-eight years old, Deta bid her parents, *"Aufwiedersehen."*

"When will you be back?" her mother asked, sad to see her daughter go.

"In a year, I promise," Deta answered, kissing her mother goodbye. Luise accompanied Deta to the Heppenheim train station, from which she would start her journey. She suspected that Deta hadn't been completely honest with their parents and that Deta's plans involved Emil. But Luise said nothing and wished Deta a safe trip.

Sad to leave Emil and nervous about not speaking English, Deta was also excited. She was traveling abroad for the first time in her life. As the train passed the familiar countryside, she wondered what England was like and how the Hills would treat her.

In Mainz, Deta changed trains at the Hauptbahnhof. Would Emil be there? Even if he were, she knew they shouldn't speak to each other. The embrace under the Bensheim railroad trestle was their goodbye. In the darkness that night, Deta had wanted to hold onto Emil forever; now all she could do was store his embrace in her memory.

A few minutes remained before her train arrived. As Deta looked among the crowd on the platform, she recognized Emil with his briefcase. She walked slowly toward him, pretending not to see him, yet noticing the circles under his eyes, the sadness in his face. As Emil brushed past her, he slipped a small piece of paper into her hand.

At that moment, her train entered the station, and it was time to go. Holding the paper tightly, Deta climbed aboard and found a seat. She looked out the window, hoping to see Emil one last time. The platform was full of people bidding farewell to relatives and friends. It looked like they too were departing from Germany. Deta couldn't find Emil in the crowd; he must have already left to catch a train to Frankfurt or to Guntersblum.

Note with self-portrait of Emil, slipped to Deta on the Mainz train platform.

Deta carefully unfolded the paper in her hand and read "All for you!" The only signature was the tiny photograph of Emil at the table with the two glasses and the bottle of wine. Deta smiled. How handsome he looked! Had one of his photography colleagues taken the picture? The note and the photo gave her courage; she was ready for whatever lay ahead.

But Emil hadn't left. He was still on the platform, watching Deta's train depart. How would she fare alone in a foreign country among people she didn't know? How would he manage without her support and encouragement? When would he see her again?

❊ HANOVER, NEW HAMPSHIRE

*I*n 1999 I recorded my interview with my mother. I wanted to know more about her childhood, how she met my father, and their courtship. She was the only one of her siblings who left Germany, and her courage was impressive.

It was fortunate that my mother let me record her. A few months later, she was struck by a car and, although she survived, her memory was affected.

I have often thought of my mother at the kitchen window in Worms seeing the man being beaten by Nazi thugs. What would I do if I saw someone being threatened or harassed because of religion, skin color, gender, or sexual orientation? Would I act on my beliefs, or would I be a passive bystander? I have no answer to these questions. Perhaps there is no answer until the moment when one is forced to choose.

7. POSTCARDS ACROSS
THE CHANNEL (1937–1938)

eta always remembered her first night at 104 Clapham Road in Bedford. The nanny she was to replace still used the room off the nursery, so Deta slept in the attic. Just as she was about to fall asleep, she heard the sound of scurrying mice. The woman who, at fourteen, had run away from her grandmother's house was not going to spend the night in an attic with mice. Deta took her blanket and pillow, tiptoed downstairs to the salon, and lay down on the satin-covered sofa. Exhausted from her travels, she fell asleep, dreaming of Emil.

The next morning, she arose early and returned to the attic. With horror, she saw mice droppings on her bed. In her minimal English, she alerted Mrs. Hill, who sprayed a chemical in the room to combat the mice. Fortunately, the official nanny's room soon became available. The mice were a minor concern. Adjusting to new surroundings, to employers and children she couldn't understand, and to being far from home — that was the real challenge.

Emil corresponded regularly. Buy a compact English–German dictionary, he advised, and be careful with the left-side traffic. He enclosed a postcard of the Oxford Regatta team arriving in Frankfurt, for Deta to show her employers.

Emil was present when an "acquaintance" took the photo, probably a veiled reference to Emil's photography teacher.

How does a Jewish man in Nazi Germany stay connected with his beloved, now over five hundred miles away? A relationship with an "Aryan" German woman, even one outside the country, was illegal, and telephone calls were beyond his means. Emil decided on weekly postcards, often written on the train between home and Frankfurt. A postcard called less attention. It announced to a censor, "What I have to say is so harmless that anyone can look at it." He created postcards with his photographs—flowers from the Rübs' garden, a fish swimming in an aquarium, a child Deta had cared for in Guntersblum, children trying on shoes in a store. In his small, even handwriting, Emil filled the postcards, which he addressed to "Fraulein Elisabeth," with news of his activities.

Anyone reading the postcard would surmise that Miss Elisabeth was just an acquaintance, since Emil used the formal *Sie* instead of the familiar *du*. Instead of a self-portrait, he sent a postcard of his shadow. He signed the cards, mailed without his return address, "your devoted E." What Emil did with Deta's letters is unknown, but it was crucial that they not be found, so he must have hidden or even destroyed them.

Despite her bravery and resolve, Deta was terribly homesick. If she had had the money, she might have returned home. But if she returned home, Emil might stay in Germany, where they could never be together. Therefore, she faced her homesickness. Knowing Deta was missing home, Emil recommended that she tell her employer, "I should like to hear a German broadcasting station, please." Hearing German might help her feel less lonely. "Ask the older girl to tell you the names of things," he continued. "Point at an object and say, 'What is the English word for this here?'"

To keep up Deta's spirits, Emil occasionally sent a newspaper or magazine and, from time to time, a novel. "How is your English progressing?" he asked. "Do the air and the food agree with you, and with the weather changing, are you dressing warmly?"

In Rozsa's studio, Emil was in his element. His days were full of new impressions and people, some of whom he captured on film. There was much to learn, and Emil delighted in learning. One day he worked in the photo lab from three in the afternoon until ten at night. Pleased with Emil's work, Rozsa praised him to the other students, whom Emil helped with their assignments. When Rozsa was absent, Emil even substituted for his teacher. Deta noticed that Emil enjoyed his time in Frankfurt, admitting only to herself that she was jealous she couldn't enjoy it with him.

While he was happy in the studio, two weeks after Deta left, he wrote to her, "At home I have [many] concerns and hardly find time to write." What were these concerns? He still had to help with the family vineyards and the insecticide and fungicide business. He had little money to buy photography equipment — a camera and lenses — which he needed to present himself as a professional photographer. Occasionally borrowing a camera from Rozsa, he was embarrassed not to have the same equipment as his colleagues. Later Deta sent money, and gradually he assembled the apparatus he needed.

In the summer of 1937, the discussions at the Rüb home were more intense. If France and England held no opportunities for Emil, should he go to the United States? Who would supply the affidavit confirming he would not be a public charge? David and Bertha were torn; they relied on Emil and didn't want him to leave. "Amerika" was so far away. But if he stayed, their financial situation would not improve.

Possibly Hede's upcoming wedding weighed on Emil's mind. In November 1936, Hede became engaged to Carl Hartogsohn, Jewish religion teacher and aspiring cantor. Carl, six years older than Hede, was an Orthodox Jew from

Emden in northern Germany. After being certified in kosher slaughtering, he worked as an itinerant cantor and religion teacher in several small Jewish communities on both sides of the Rhine. He was also a trained plumber.

From December 1933 to September 1936, based across the Rhine in Gross Gerau, Carl was spiritual advisor to thirty neighboring communities under the auspices of the rabbinical centers in Darmstadt and in Mainz. In Gross Gerau, he taught Jewish youth, founded and directed a choir that sang in the synagogue, and contributed to the cultural life of the congregation. He achieved recognition for promoting Jewish life under difficult circumstances, for his steadfast and consistent character, for his speeches rich in ideas, and for his trained baritone. By September 1, 1936, however, many Gross Gerau Jews had left, and Carl was no longer needed there. He found employment as a cantor and teacher at the synagogue in Höchst, a suburb of Frankfurt.

Guntersblum was one of the communities Carl served. He gave Hebrew lessons in the Rübs' dining room, which was how he met Hede. Six months later, their engagement was announced in *Der Israelit*, an Orthodox Jewish newspaper edited by Naphtali Hartog Hartogsohn, Carl's brother.

Carl Hartogsohn teaching Hebrew to two little Guntersblum girls.

What drew the lighthearted Hede to Carl? At twenty-five, perhaps she decided it was time to settle down and start a family. Maybe she had enough of small-town life and wanted to free herself from parental supervision and from Guntersblum. Carl had a job and was well-respected. Whatever the attraction was, she opened her warm, caring heart to him and loved him with the same loyalty she brought to her earlier friendships.

Emil, a questioner and a liberal, was not happy about this new family member with his conservative views and holier-than-thou attitude. But Bertha and David were glad their daughter chose a man for whom Jewish life and traditions were paramount and whose position in the Jewish community gave him status. Of course, Emil also should marry a Jew, but later, after he established himself outside Germany and sent for his parents.

Hede and Carl Hartogsohn 1937, newlyweds; Credit: Emil Rüb.

On August 25, 1937, Hede and Carl had a civil marriage in Höchst and on August 29, a religious ceremony and reception. The religious ceremony and reception took place in Frankfurt at Hotel Ulmann, which had a kosher kitchen. Anna, sister of a Guntersblum tailor, sewed the buttonholes on the suit her brother made for Carl for the wedding. "Be especially polite," her brother insisted, "when you deliver the suit to the rabbi," as the tailor called Carl.

Emil couldn't afford a new suit and claimed that this was the reason he wouldn't attend the festivities in Frankfurt. The issue of the suit may have been a cover for jealousy that Emil felt over Carl's joining the family. Emil was present, however, at the dinner celebration in the Rüb home, where the menu included goose, pastry filled with new peas, and a rich dessert.[22] Naturally, Emil commemorated the occasion with a photograph of the newlyweds in the garden behind the house. Fun-loving Hede was now a twenty-six-year-old married woman. On September 3, she left Guntersblum and her parents' home for her new life at Heimchenweg 47, Höchst. Hede was in love and looking forward to a future with Carl. They would face the world together.

Autumn came to Guntersblum, and the leaves of the black grape vines turned red. "In the middle of the grape harvest," Emil wrote Deta in late October, "in haste I allow myself to send you a greeting. The grapes are very sweet, especially the black ones. The work was once more enjoyable—the output could be better. You see that I obviously can't live without my grape culture." Emil helped with the harvest because local workers wouldn't work for Jews. With fewer people working, fewer grapes were picked.

In the same letter, Emil mentioned photos he developed from the Frankfurt Land Speed Record Week, a car race on

---

22. Marianne, the *Haustochter*, was included at the dinner and was impressed by the menu.

the Autobahn from Darmstadt to Frankfurt. Major "Goldie" Gardener, an Englishman, drove 148.8 miles per hour in the race. If Deta saw a newspaper photo of Major Gardener racing, he wrote, ". . . then I certainly had several of the pictures in my hand, unfortunately only in the lab."

Emil informed Deta of his plans in coded wording only she would understand. A "visit to Cousin Erich," "to Erich and Lotte," or "taking a vacation" meant travel to the United States. Joining Deta in England was impossible because he had no one there to sponsor him. Fortunately, an affidavit from the United States arrived in November.

Earlier that year, Emil had sent two portraits of Tante Elise Schlösser to her sons in New York. Tante Elise, from the neighboring town of Alsheim, was the sister of Emil's deceased grandfather. In the photo, Tante Elise reads a letter from her sons Emil and Otto, owners of a delicatessen and restaurant in Queens, New York. Impressed with Emil's photographs, Uncle Emil Schlösser agreed to sign as guarantor. But Emil still dragged his feet. Home, family, and the vineyards were part of his identity; he had no confidence in his ability to start anew.

When he didn't hear from Deta, Emil wondered if the November rain and dense fog delayed her letters. The fog was so bad that on November 16, en route to a wedding in London, the airplane carrying members of the Grand Ducal Family of Hesse (relatives of the young Prince Philip) crashed. "Don't you find the misfortune of the Grand Ducal Family awful?" he asked. "If you see pictures of the funeral in Darmstadt in the English newspaper, they were taken by acquaintances of mine."

In England, Deta had a decision to make. In early October, on her day off, she visited Gretel Marx, wife of a Harley Street gynecologist living in London. Dr. and Mrs. Marx, both Jews from Mainz, had left Germany in 1933 when the

Nazi regime prohibited Jewish doctors from practicing.[23] From Frau Doktor Huhn, in whose home Deta and Emil first met, Mrs. Marx heard that Deta was in England and invited Deta to visit.

"You look wonderful, Frau Doktor," Deta commented, when she sat down with Mrs. Marx in the living room. It was good to see someone from home and to speak German. "If I may say so, you have even gained a little weight."

"Oh," Mrs. Marx laughed, "soon I will gain even more." Deta looked puzzled. "You see," Mrs. Marx continued, "I am expecting. I know your reputation and that you have excellent references. I was hoping you would come to work for me and look after the baby. The baby is due in January."

"I would love to," Deta replied, "but I am committed to the Hills for a year. Mrs. Hill arranged for my work papers."

"Your loyalty speaks well of you," Mrs. Marx said. "Please think it over. I can hire a temporary nurse until you are able to come." Deta agreed to consider her offer.

Christmas and New Year came and went. In January 1938, Emil was still in Guntersblum. There were multiple obstacles to accepting Cousin Erich's invitation, Emil complained, none of which he told Deta. In early March he underwent surgery for a hernia, presumably caused by carrying heavy pails of water to the Rübs' new vineyards. Emil waited till after the operation to tell Deta because he didn't want her to worry. Recuperating at home, he assured Deta he was as lively as a fish. Despite some pain at night and some fatigue, he wrote, "I am a complete man. The scar can barely be seen."

Months later, in mid-June 1938, he wrote Deta, "Under no circumstances will I spend my birthday here," insisting he would celebrate "over there." But on August 23, his birthday, he was still in Germany. He predicted he would be "at Cousin

---

23. Because Dr. Marx's medical credentials weren't recognized in England, he earned a medical degree in Glasgow and Edinburgh.

Erich's" by September 20. Why was it so difficult to leave a country that every day demonstrated it didn't want him?

In his indecisiveness, Emil took three steps forward and four steps back. He documented one forward step on a postcard, his photograph of a stone road marker, saying that his trip to "this beautiful city" was successful. The unnamed city was Stuttgart, location of the American consulate. Emil's passport now contained a stamped visa dated May 20, issued by the American vice-consul at Stuttgart, Germany, quota number 16463. The 60 Reichsmarks to finance Emil's Stuttgart trip came from Deta. But even then, Emil didn't set a departure date.

Deta had an easier time making decisions; she had more experience being independent and taking care of herself. Despite her reservations about leaving the Hills, Deta accepted the position with the Marx family. In June 1938, she moved to 6 Aberdare Gardens, London, to look after six-month-old Susan. In a German-speaking household, Deta would feel less isolated.

Deta with baby Susan, 1938.

While Deta adjusted to her new job and to London, Emil substituted for Rozsa for two days in August, supervising fifteen students. He was putting together his photo equipment and had already acquired some lenses, lamps, a tripod, a Leica enlarger, and miscellaneous darkroom items. Getting the equipment out of Germany required permission from the Devisenstelle, the foreign exchange control office in Darmstadt, and paying a hefty tax. Delays and requests for more paperwork from the Devisenstelle made this a cumbersome task, and Emil attempted to extend his American visa. "I need to try," he told Deta, "since otherwise I can only bring the basic necessities, which is unfortunate because then my professional equipment baggage will be very small."

On September 1, 1938, he wrote Deta, "Such a vacation that I am about to undertake is no easy thing." This was an understatement, for "vacation" meant departing from the life he knew and starting over in a foreign land. It meant leaving his parents behind in uncertain circumstances. There would be no going back.

Delaying, however, was impossible, for the much sought-after American visa was soon to expire. On September 8, 1938, Emil sent Deta a postcard. "Esteemed Miss Elisabeth, you must be amazed to hear from me first today, but I just couldn't write sooner. . . . I still don't know exactly when I can go on vacation. My efforts to bring my equipment—they will probably not have a positive result—take up day and night. To that are added other worries so that I just don't see how I can put my plans into action. Still, I have to expect that the soonest I will see little Susan will be Wednesday morning. That causes great difficulties here but there is nothing to do about it. I still plan to wrangle twenty-four hours out of it. Will it be possible? . . . Thank you for your good wishes for my trip. . . . We are all well here in the most beautiful fall weather. Hopefully, it will stay that way for a few weeks. For today a devoted Sunday greeting—E."

What were the "great difficulties" Emil mentioned? Were Bertha and David against Emil's stopping in London, preferring he embark from Hamburg? Was it that Bertha had too little time to prepare Emil's clothes? Or was the problem getting Emil's photography equipment out of the country? Perhaps the issue was needing permission to enter the United Kingdom. Any or all of these could have been significant roadblocks. On September 13, Emil rushed to the British consulate in Frankfurt to apply for a transit visa. The atmosphere in the large house in Guntersblum, already bleak, was even darker with Emil's impending departure.

The mail brought a notice from the Devisenstelle. Once Emil paid the 1,200 RM (reichmarks) tax (about $400, almost $7,600 today), he could take his equipment with him. But Emil didn't have this amount, could not borrow from his financially strapped parents, and had no time to beg friends or family. Most likely they couldn't have helped. Had Rozsa and his colleagues from the atelier not insisted, Emil would have let his American visa expire rather than leave his equipment behind. Heeding their advice, Emil carefully packed his hard-earned equipment in boxes. For the time being, it would be safe at his parents' house.

8. ENTR'ACTE (1938)

On September 14, 1938, with a heavy heart, Emil left the house at 4 Wormser Strasse. He carried one small suitcase and 10 RM (about $60 today), the only money allowed to Jewish emigrants. He would miss David's sixtieth birthday, the Jewish High Holy Days, and the grape harvest. David and Bertha accompanied him as far as Mainz. Saying goodbye to his parents was even more wrenching than watching Deta's train disappear into the distance, especially since Bertha continued to plead with him to stay. "I shall never forget," Emil told Deta, "the sight of my desperate parents when I left them in Mainz." It was one of the worst moments of Emil's life.

The decision to leave, fraught with ambivalence, was not a free choice but a response to the worsening situation for Jews. Emil was going out into the world to save his parents and himself. At thirty-two, having lived at home his entire life, unprepared to embark, Emil was forced to emigrate by circumstances beyond his control.

Had the Rübs' situation been more stable, Emil might have left in better spirits. In September 1938, however, not only was life in Guntersblum uncertain, but the accelerating Sudeten Crisis was destabilizing Europe. Two days before Emil departed, Hitler delivered an ultimatum to Czech

President Beneš. If Beneš did not end what Hitler called "the oppression of over three million Sudeten Germans," he would annex the Sudetenland by military force. After the Anschluß (annexation) of Austria on March 12, 1938, this was one more step toward war. The Europe Emil was departing was on the edge of a precipice.

Heartsick about leaving his parents, Emil descended the train at the Köln Hauptbahnhof. In view of the majestic Gothic cathedral, he met his Uncle Josef, brother of Emil Schlösser in New York (the one who had guaranteed Emil's visa). Why uncle and nephew arranged to meet that day is unclear; perhaps David had asked Uncle Josef to accompany Emil to the airport. Neither warm nor empathetic, Uncle Josef said something disparaging to Emil that hit a nerve. Emotionally depleted from his rushed departure, in the middle of the busy station, Emil broke down and sobbed. "Please don't mention this to my parents," he begged Uncle Josef. "I don't want to upset them. They are already upset by my leaving."

By the time he boarded the plane for London, Emil had regained control. This was his first airplane trip, but as the plane sped down the runway for takeoff, he felt more depressed than elated. He watched out the window as the landscape below got smaller and disappeared. There was where he was born, where he had gone to school and fallen in love, this *Heimat* that rejected him. He tried to sleep, but his mind was filled with images: the vineyards, the photo studio, his parents, the people and places he was leaving behind. And, of course, his camera and equipment, in boxes at his parents' house.

A few hours later, he landed in London, his second trip to this city. The following day, English Prime Minister Chamberlain would fly from London to Germany to defuse the Czech crisis. Arranging to stop in London had been complicated, but Emil was determined to see Deta before crossing the Atlantic. It would be a whirlwind stay, as the stamp and handwritten note in Emil's passport confirmed: "Landed on condition of direct transit through United Kingdom to USA," and "Proceeding, ex Southampton on 16.9.38, on SS *Hansa*."

At 6 Aberdare Gardens, Deta waited eagerly for Emil to come. When he arrived, he extended his hand instead of embracing her. Emil was reticent about showing affection in public, and Deta understood that an embrace would come later in private. Overjoyed to see her young man, Deta was relieved and grateful he was out of Germany.

The Marx family welcomed Emil and invited him to stay in their large house. Emil and Deta would have had more privacy at a hotel, but Emil couldn't afford a room, and an unmarried couple had proprieties to follow. Also, Deta had to look after baby Susan. Nonetheless, Emil and Deta found a moment to embrace in Deta's room. It had been over a year since they held each other under the railroad trestle in Bensheim.

Penniless and fragile—this was not how Emil wanted Deta to see him, but Deta was happy to be with him no matter his condition. Here was someone with whom she had a history, who could reminisce with her about home. She knew instinctively that Emil needed her support, and she gave it readily. How different this reunion was from their last meeting in Germany. How remarkable it felt to be together openly, without fear. The fact that Emil and Deta could have married during those two days did not enter their minds. Without money and a secure job, Emil was in no position to propose marriage.

From London, Emil telephoned his parents. "I am not sure I will get on the ship," he told his mother, but did not mention an alternative. Staying in England was impossible, as was returning to Germany.

The two days passed quickly. Soon Emil and Deta would be over three thousand miles apart. Deta wanted to accompany Emil to the ship pier, but Mrs. Marx needed her to stay home with Susan. Dr. and Mrs. Marx were house hunting outside London, in case of war and the need to evacuate. So instead, Deta accompanied Emil to Waterloo Station, where he took the boat train to Southampton. She struggled not to cry, not wanting to make the departure harder for him. This time, Deta watched as Emil's train took him away.

Did they make any promises to each other before Emil left? They were certain they loved each other and wanted to be together. Beyond that, not knowing how Emil would manage in New York made planning a future together difficult. At best, Emil promised he would ask Deta to join him when he was settled.

From Southampton, Emil used his last English stamps to mail Deta a final greeting from English soil. "Stay healthy and patient," he urged her. And then, despite the uncertainty he expressed to his mother, Emil boarded the ship. Was it courage or desperation that carried him up the gangplank? Perhaps both.

The sight of the SS *Hansa*, the first ocean liner Emil ever saw, surely took his breath away. The ship, once the SS *Albert Ballin*, was renamed in 1935 because Ballin, shipping magnate and former director of the Hamburg Amerika Line, was Jewish. Of greater consequence to Emil was that he was about to sail to a world known for its endless possibilities, far from the village he called home.

From on board, he sent Deta his first "at-sea account" and "the last mail for the next six days." The card would be mailed from Cherbourg where the SS *Hansa* docked for more passengers. Emil shared his third-class cabin with a gentleman from Worms, Deta's home city. "Next to me—within reach— hangs a Leica. I feel like a soldier without a sidearm," he wrote Deta. The Leica belonged to his cabinmate, who didn't know how to use it. Ever the patient teacher and longing to touch this equipment, Emil explained how to operate the camera.

The seven days at sea passed quickly, and the fresh air bolstered Emil's spirits. Despite being a Jew, Emil noticed that he was treated by the crew with the same respect as his fellow passengers were. Two days before the *Hansa* docked in New York, Emil attended the ship's gala dinner. On the menu were eggs with caviar, fillet of sole in Chablis with coquille and mushrooms, Californian peaches, petits fours, cheese, and fruit, followed by mocha coffee. The evening included a program of light music. One of the pieces was a waltz entitled "*Stunden, die wir nie vergessen*" ("Hours We Will Never Forget"), a meaningful title to a young man leaving behind his beloved and the first thirty-two years of his life.

More in love than ever, Deta mourned Emil's departure. She had been so happy with him and would "live off those hours for a long, long time." But each moment took him farther away from her. She wrote, "I will be sick if I can't see you again. . . . I can't breathe without you. . . . In my thoughts I follow you to the new world and will always be with you, my good Emil!" She had hidden a photo of herself in Emil's suitcase, which she hoped he had found. "Could I have hidden myself in your suitcase, I would have done so." She promised to be patient and come to him as soon as he called for her. Alone that day with little Susan, Deta found the house unbearably quiet.

Emil's postcard from the ship was a great comfort to her. She understood his disappointment about leaving his Leica behind and encouraged him to be brave: ". . . in two to three weeks, hopefully your things will arrive."

To Mrs. Marx, Deta confided, "I would rather never see Emil again than have to go through another leave-taking." Despite her promise to be strong, Deta had her own emotional collapse. "I keep thinking over and over that your picture will become alive," she wrote Emil, "and you, my dear good Emil, will step out of the frame and comfort your Detalein."

By Saturday, September 24, the cable confirming Emil's arrival in New York "allow[ed] her to find joy in living again." She was glad he was with family. "My great belief in you and my love always give me strength. . . . And if you are sad, always think that in my thoughts I am with you, day and night."

On September 23, 1938, the day Emil reached New York, Prime Minister Chamberlain again flew to Germany, landing at the same Köln airport from where Emil had departed. "My objective is peace in Europe," he told the press before taking off from England. "I trust this trip is the way to that peace." Emil, too, hoped for peace. In America he would start over. He would find work, send for his equipment, get his parents out of Germany, and reunite with Deta. Neither he nor Deta knew that the few hours they spent together were the calm before the storm.

❋ HANOVER, NEW HAMPSHIRE

*I*n my family, saying goodbye was never easy. When I received my first college acceptance letter, my mother gave me a gift she had been saving for this moment: a large black suitcase. I took one look at the suitcase and burst into tears. The suitcase meant leaving my parents, leaving home.

I was only going as far as Boston, then a three-hour drive, not a seven-day ocean voyage like my father, but somehow the trauma of his departure had found its way into me. I too worried about my parents and how they would manage without me. Would my departure leave a hole in their lives? Years later, a wise therapist identified our family myth: we associated leaving with the possibility of never again seeing those left behind.

9. TRANSATLANTIC
CONVERSATIONS (1938)

"When angels travel," goes the German saying, "the heavens smile." The heavens were not smiling, however, as the SS *Hansa* advanced toward New York. On September 21, a hurricane hit Long Island and southern New England, causing 462 deaths and much damage. According to the September 22 *New York Times*, because of the strong winds, it took six extra tugs to bring one ocean liner to her pier in New York Harbor, and another liner, the *Queen Mary,* postponed her departure for Europe. Among the incoming passenger and mail ships listed for September 23 was the *Hansa*, scheduled to arrive at 1:00 p.m. at the West 44th Street pier.

In Guntersblum, David and Bertha Rüb awaited news of their son. They had read in the newspaper about a terrible storm near the American coast and spent a sleepless night worrying. Emil might as well have travelled to the moon, for to them "Amerika" was even more remote. Fortunately, Emil's telegram signaling his safe arrival came the next day and was, according to Bertha, the best birthday present David received, better than the surprise Emil arranged before leaving. The surprise was an announcement in the Jewish Newspaper *Der Israelit*: "The head of the Guntersblum Jewish Community David Rüb celebrates his 60th birthday on September 25. For many decades Herr Rüb fulfilled the duties of head of the congregation with steadfast devotion."

Waiting for Emil when the *Hansa* docked were letters from Cousin Erich and other relatives welcoming him to his new *Heimat*. Uncle Emil Schlosser couldn't leave his delicatessen, so he gave Cousin Erich written power of attorney to pick Emil up from the ship. In addition, wrote Erich, "Women from the National Council of Jewish Women who can be helpful to you will come on the ship."

The New York Emil first saw under cloudy skies was a city cleaning up after the storm. Most of the damage in Manhattan came from fallen trees knocked down by the storm's heavy winds.[24] In the taxi with Cousin Erich, Emil was amazed by the skyscrapers and the traffic. The taxi took the two cousins to the apartment Cousin Erich shared with his sister Lotte. Here Emil would stay, at 86 Haven Avenue in Washington Heights, a neighborhood housing many German Jewish refugees. From the back bedrooms of the apartment, one could see the nearby George Washington Bridge, its lights twinkling at night.

Arriving in New York on the eve of the Jewish New Year, Emil was now a refugee. Here he would spell his name without the umlaut—"Rueb" instead of "Rüb." Learning English, finding a job, and orienting himself in the city were priorities. Adjusting to an environment so different from Guntersblum would take time. At the National Council of Jewish Women, where he went to have his photography reference translated, the translator was a former Rozsa photography student whom Emil used to help with her assignments. Renewing this friendship made New York a friendlier place.

---

24. Source for impact of the 1938 hurricane on New York City: *New York Times*, September 22, 1938.

The first opportunity Emil found was with a German photographer, Hugo Stern, formerly of Frankfurt, who had a portrait studio a few blocks from Erich's apartment. Despite the low pay, the hours spent with Dr. Stern, a sensitive and demanding photographer, helped Emil improve his skills. "Dr. Stern," Emil wrote Deta, "with much patience is introducing me to the new arrangements [developing]. I have a great deal of work, but I am learning a lot."

One night, after finishing past midnight, Emil mailed Deta a postcard on his walk back to Haven Avenue. On the postcard he had glued a tiny picture of himself in his white photo technician's coat. He wrote, "In my thoughts I am very often with you, little Detalein. Especially when things aren't going the way I wish." Finding work, Emil discovered, was an uphill climb in a city feeling the effects of the Great Depression, and he was handicapped by his rudimentary English and the lack of openings in photography. It was also the first time Emil was truly on his own, without parental comments on his choices. Becoming his own person was a new experience; he just wished he had more to show for his efforts.

Emil's postcard to Deta, October 19, 1938.

With Erich's help, he searched the *New York Times* help wanted section and sent out applications. "I am thirty-two years old, single, and came to this country some time ago," Emil began his letters. "I am thoroughly trained in the various branches of photography and especially in contact printing on large negatives." Along with Rozsa's reference, he sent samples of his work. He offered to travel to other parts of the country but needed a railroad ticket, which could be deducted from his first paycheck. The many replies that "the position has been filled" were discouraging.

In Guntersblum, the small Jewish community was in flux as, one by one, its members departed for Mainz, Frankfurt, or abroad. Longtime friends stopped at the Rübs' house to say goodbye, some of them charging David with selling a vineyard or other property. Each departure affected Bertha deeply. In normal times, friends would drop by for a chat—social connections she valued. Now she felt alone and, except for her husband, without support in a village ever more unfriendly. With her son's departure, her daughter in Frankfurt-Höchst, and good friends leaving, Bertha's world was coming apart.

The High Holy Days, Rosh Hashanah and Yom Kippur, usually special occasions, would not be so that year. "It is terribly lonely for us, and it is very difficult for both of us," Bertha wrote her son on September 18, 1938. Rosh Hashanah services would take place in the Rübs' home instead of at the synagogue. The arrival of Emil's first letter on Yom Kippur, however, raised Bertha's spirits. David brought the letter to Bertha's bedside, where she was fasting. She wrote to Emil, "I was able to fast even better, and everyone in the synagogue was also glad." These were the last services in the Guntersblum synagogue; on September 27, 1938, David signed the official bill of sale, making the synagogue the property of a non-Jewish Guntersblumer and no longer a holy place.

While Emil sought employment in New York, the Rübs harvested the grapes in their vineyards with help from Jewish friends, among them three young children, and Hede and Carl who came from Frankfurt. To feed the harvesters, Bertha prepared the traditional potato soup and plum cake. Unfortunately, the weather was cold and rainy. Bertha got a sore throat, and Hede came down with a cold and cough and had to spend several days at home in bed. Her husband, Carl, stayed to help finish picking the grapes.

In England, while Prime Minister Chamberlain met with Hitler in Germany, Britain instituted air-raid precautions and opened fourteen gas mask stations in London.[25] "Hitler has recalled all German ships," Deta wrote Emil on September 28, "and things look quite bleak. In my room are two suitcases that I have to pack because tomorrow I will go to the country with Susan and the elderly lady [Mrs. Marx's mother]." Evacuation was a precaution in case of war.

Deta's mother, also fearing war, asked her to come home, but Deta telegraphed her refusal. To Emil she wrote, "Although my four brothers will have to go to war, I tell myself that it had to come to this. It couldn't continue the way it has been. The German people will now hopefully recognize how badly they were treated in the last five years." She encouraged Emil to be glad he could at least breathe freely and not to worry about his parents: "It can't go worse for them than it already has been."

On Friday, September 30, 1938, Prime Minister Chamberlain persuaded Hitler to sign a peace treaty with Britain. Chamberlain returned to London declaring, "The settlement of the Czechoslovakian problem, which has now been achieved, is, in my view, only the prelude to a larger settlement in which all Europe may find peace." That evening

---

25. *New York Times*, September 24, 1938.

a relieved Deta wrote Emil, "Today I unpacked the suitcases. There will be no war!"

As letters between Emil and his parents crisscrossed the Atlantic, Emil became frustrated with the delays in communication. "Don't ask me anymore about many people who don't interest me," he declared, meaning fellow Guntersblum refugees in New York. "They all know that I am not doing well. They know how to find me if they need me. Today I can't afford the luxury of seeking them out so they can tell me their problems." It was one thing to be in Guntersblum with little money and no prospects, and another to be financially dependent on his cousins, with only part-time work and no job in sight.

The biggest stumbling block to advancement, Emil believed, was not having his photographic equipment and negatives. The negatives were to prove he was a professional photographer and not a casual snap shooter. Still, he tried to be optimistic. "At some point I will succeed. . . . And if the [Rübs'] business isn't going so well," he reassured David, "it isn't such a tragedy. If I can get ahead here, everything will be all right. In the meantime, I ask you not to lose patience." (Their business, David had written, was "as good as nothing," meaning they had few customers and negligible income.)

The Rübs carried on. David had a tooth pulled. In mid-October, Bertha went to Mainz to make a condolence call, visit an acquaintance, and have her hair done. Most likely she also bought groceries because in Guntersblum, shops didn't want to sell to Jews. Although no longer working for the Rübs, Marianne, their former *Haustochter*, came at night to pick up a shopping list and money. The next day, she shopped, carefully going to different venders; since Mariana came from a poor family that bought groceries only in small quantities, asking for a full half pound of butter would have raised eyebrows. The next night, Marianne returned with her purchases. This continued until a schoolmate, a member of the *Bund Deutscher Mädel* (the Hitler youth organization for girls), saw her and threatened to report Marianne if she continued helping the Rübs. Marianne had to stop coming.

David arranged to have Emil's clothing shipped to him and worked on selling their vineyards, wine cellars, and properties as well as those of his emigrating Jewish neighbors. Bertha did laundry, a major production in a German household where household and personal linens, all white, were boiled in a huge pot in the special *Waschküche*, the laundry kitchen.[26] The two women, probably Jews, who came to help stayed the night. The Internal Revenue Office claimed David owed 200 Reichsmarks tax (over $1,000 today, an impossible sum). "And what should I do," David asked his son in his November 6 letter, "if the radio doesn't work, which happens often? Toilet and doorbell are also broken." Clearly, David depended on Emil for technical assistance.

In her letters, Bertha repeatedly asked Emil to visit the Gimbels in New Jersey with whom she was distantly related. The New Jersey Gimbels were a potential connection to the Gimbel brothers, owners of Gimbels, the New York department store that competed with Macy's. Bertha hoped the department store Gimbels might offer Emil a job, perhaps even an affidavit of support for the Rübs. Surely Emil's photos of Gimbel family gravestones would yield affidavits for Bertha and David, as Emil's photos of Tante Elise Schlösser did for him.

---

26. Before modern washers, laundry for larger homes was done in a separate building or room called the *Waschküche*, literally translating to the "laundry kitchen." Some families hired a washerwoman who came once a week to do the laundry. Deta's family had a washerwoman, and since the Bickels lived in an apartment building, the washerwoman probably did the laundry in a basement laundry room. The Rübs had an outbuilding in their yard for laundry.

Coincidentally, on November 6, Emil also wrote a letter home. "In this country," he began, "one must organize the time well so that the most important is always handled first. According to this I should now—at three o'clock in the afternoon—actually be working on an assignment at Dr. Stern's that will bring me some money. Or I should be studying English. On the other hand, there are a few things I must speak with you about. I urgently need my negatives. . . . Americans appreciate experience more than references. I can't keep stammering excuses that I still don't have my negatives."

He gave detailed instructions where his negatives were located, some still in cans with tape around them, which must not be opened. David should put them in a small box, take them to the Gestapo in Mainz for inspection, and mail them at the post office. On November 6, 1938, Emil and his parents believed they still had some control over their lives.

10. BLURRY PHOTOS:

BAD DAYS

photograph: A line of five men, the tallest in front, walk single file in the street. A sixth man, unseen because he is out of frame, is in front and carries the town bell. Bareheaded, the men wear black robes with prayer shawls garishly knotted over the neck and the waist. Three men carry large scrolls in their arms; a fourth man carries a smaller scroll. On the sidewalk, school children walk alongside the parade. Through an open window, a woman leans on the windowsill to watch. Two men in SA uniforms and armbands escort the procession, along with a man in work clothes at the front.

The six men are members of Guntersblum's Jewish community. David Rüb, second in the line, holds the largest scroll: a Torah without its protective covering. The heavy scroll is cumbersome, so he grips one handle in his right hand, the other in his left, his left shoulder bearing most of the weight. If the scrolls unroll, it will be harder to carry them, and they must not touch the ground. It looks as if the scrolls are already coming undone.[27]

---

27. One of seven photos taken on November 10, 1938, and mentioned in Ludwig Liebmann's testimony (see footnote 28). The photos were in the Landesarchiv in Speyer and because of German privacy laws, released only in 2008.

Guntersblum, November 10, 1938. The second man in line
carrying a Torah is David Rüb. Source: Landesarchiv Speyer,
Bestand X 3, Nr. 111, used with permission.

On the morning of November 10, 1938, the Guntersblum constable went to the Rübs' house. "Rüb," he said, without the usual *Herr*, "you are to come with me."

When the constable knocked on their door, David and Bertha were having breakfast. "Why?" David asked. "What is wrong?"

"You have to come to the town hall," the constable answered.

Puzzled, David put on a jacket and accompanied the constable the short walk to the town hall. Inside, David was escorted downstairs.

"In there," the constable ordered.

"There" was the basement jail cell, where two members of the Jewish congregation already waited. One by one, the remaining men from Guntersblum's Jewish community were brought to the town hall and locked in the cell. Outside the building, a mob assembled, shouting threats: "You decrepit Jews." "Your last hour has come." "Cut their throats; hang them."[28]

Around one o'clock in the afternoon, the men were brought upstairs. Their tormenters had removed Torahs, prayer shawls, and black robes from the synagogue. The six Jewish men were told to put on the black robes. Next, the prayer shawls were draped and knotted around them in a mocking fashion, the Torahs thrust in their arms. Some of the perpetrators were Guntersblum Nazis the Jewish men knew.

Now the real torment began. The Jewish men had to march through the village streets while school children watched and onlookers insulted, threw stones and dirt from the street, and spit at them. The last man in the line was short; when his prayer shawl slipped and dragged on the ground, someone stepped on it so he couldn't move forward. Later, in the smaller streets, the men were beaten with fists, sticks, and clubs.

---

28. September 9, 1946, written testimony of Ludwig Liebmann, former Guntersblum resident and one of the six men paraded in the street.

"Aren't you ashamed of yourselves?" a woman bystander shouted at the perpetrators.

"Be quiet," voices from the crowd warned her. "Shut your mouth, or you too will be taken away."

The procession was photographed, the photos to appear the next day in a local store window.

Fourteen-year-old Marianne, who had brought the Rübs groceries, was at school when the men were brought to the town hall. The children were told school was over for the day. Marianne ran with her friends to the main street where she saw the Jewish men being led through the streets to the sound of the ringing bell. She recognized David, who looked at her briefly. As he raised his hand in her direction, she saw the gold signet ring with the rust-brown stone he always wore. Did he want to say something to her? Or was he thinking, "And you too are standing there, watching—you who were in my home and ate at my table?" Where, she wondered, did he find the strength to endure this torment? But there was no hatred in his eyes, only humility and goodness. Of this she was certain. She carried this memory with her for her entire life.[29]

Around four o'clock, the parade returned to the town hall. In the yard, a bonfire was prepared and gasoline poured on it and lit. Standing in a circle around the fire, the men were forced to throw the Torah scrolls into the fire along with their robes and prayer shawls; then they had to stand and watch until only ashes remained. As they watched, they heard rumors that their homes were being "cleaned up." That evening, the men were transported to Oppenheim and held there for the night. Except for some bread and wurst given to them in the Guntersblum basement cell, they had no food or water the entire day.[30]

---

29. Marianne Flinner interview. Emil Rueb's inventory confirms David had a signet ring.
30. Sven Felix Kellerhoff, *Ein Ganz Normales Pogrom: November 1938 in einem deutschen Dorf* (Klett-Cotta Verlag, Stuttgart, 2018).

While her husband was marched through the street, Bertha waited at home. In the afternoon, a Guntersblumer wearing an SA uniform and carrying an axe on his back entered the house; he was joined by others, including SS men from nearby Osthofen. By 4:30 p.m., a witness saw that all the windows were smashed and the curtains pulled down. Glass from the broken windows lay on the street. Because of the tremendous racket coming from the house, a mother passing by with her young child stopped and looked inside. There she saw the same man with the axe, swinging it wildly and destroying the furniture. Bertha stood at the door in great distress. "Frau S.," she addressed the woman, "is there no Lord God in Heaven who can help?" The woman could watch no longer and continued toward the railway station.[31]

The vandals locked Bertha in one of the buildings on the property, perhaps in the laundry kitchen or in the storage area where David kept oil for his agricultural business. More vandals, some from Guntersblum, others from neighboring towns, entered the house, along with schoolboys who were encouraged to participate in the destruction. From next door, the coal seller Clauss, who once advocated for a regime bringing order and decency, watched as linens, bowls, porcelain, and marble platters were ruined, tables and chairs smashed to bits. In the living room, the bookcases were tipped over, the books spilling onto the floor, the *Knaurs Lexikon* landing open; someone wearing heavy boots walked on it, leaving dirt and a boot print. This was one of a few books David later sent to Emil in New York.

In the kitchen, the large cupboard was turned over, making a huge racket.[32] Former customers ransacked David's office and destroyed evidence that they owed the Rübs money.

---

31. Testimony from a former Guntersblum resident, August 14, 1945, Landesarchiv (State Archives) for Rheinhessen-Pfalz at Speyer, Germany.
32. Details of the destruction in the Rübs' house come from testimonies, some dated November 1938, others post-war, in the Speyer Landesarchiv (State Archive).

Emil's Knaurs Lexikon with the dirty boot print.

Valuables were stolen and a typewriter "requisitioned" for the Bürgermeister. The men found their way to the cellar and drank the wine stored there. Toward the end of the evening, the cellar and the yard were strewn with empty wine bottles. Items in the warehouse—oils, fats, soaps, packing material, pumps, and measuring devices—were also damaged.

Somehow Bertha managed to escape and walk to the train station. She had no coat, no handbag, no money. Frau Simon, whose son had once worked for the Rübs, was walking home from the train station and found Bertha standing near the train crossing. "*Ach*, Frau Simon," Bertha said, terribly upset. "Could you lend me some money so I can buy a train ticket? I want to go to my daughter in Frankfurt." Frightened she could be sent to the Osthofen concentration camp if she were seen helping a Jew, Frau Simon was going to send her son behind a building to give Bertha the money. Just then Hede appeared, looking for her parents.[33] Hede and her mother boarded a train for Frankfurt and took a streetcar to Hede and

33. February 14, 1993, interview with Frau Simon.

Carl's apartment in Höchst. The next day, David was released and joined them in Höchst.

That evening, the mob continued vandalizing Jewish homes. They would have burned the former synagogue, but a neighbor came out to protest. "If you burn the synagogue, you will burn my property next door," he admonished.

How did Bertha keep herself together that day as the home she had tended, the possessions she prized, were smashed and destroyed? She must have been terrified, for her husband and for herself, and in shock as her orderly world was attacked. And from where did David muster the dignity Marianne saw as he was paraded through the village?

The Rübs knew many of the people who marched David through the street, who terrorized Bertha in her home. Some were David's customers. One can only imagine the Rübs' fear and humiliation. That their son was safe in New York was small consolation. "Is there no Lord God in heaven who can help?" Bertha had asked a passerby. That day in Guntersblum, the answer was no.

❈ HANOVER, NEW HAMPSHIRE

What happened in Guntersblum on November 10, 1938, is heart-wrenching. How could people mistreat and abuse their neighbors as they did that November day? Why did they?

Ludwig Liebmann's testimony was among the papers in the box I took from my mother's house. A friend of my father's, he was one of the Jewish men forced to march through the Guntersblum streets. His testimony was how I learned the details of this terrible event. Later my research took me to the State Archives in Speyer, Germany, where I received copies of the seven photographs taken that day, released by German law in 2008 to the public. Thankfully, my father never saw the photograph of my grandfather carrying the Torah. It would have devastated him.

For the perpetrators—unfortunate, misguided men—there is no space in my heart.

What I feel is anger, disgust, and the need to wash my hands. Reading the archived records of that day is touching dirt. But washing my hands does not make the pain go away. How do I live with the knowledge of that day? All I can do is tell my grandparents' story.

11. AFTERMATH:
THE HOUSE IS COLD

*"In the meantime, a tremendous
amount has changed."*
—Carl to Emil, December 4, 1938

Throughout Germany on November 9 and 10, 1938, there were attacks against Jews and Jewish property. The Nazis coined the term "Kristallnacht" (Crystal Night) for this period because the glass from destroyed windows and objects from Jewish homes, synagogues, and shops littered the streets. Kristallnacht was nothing less than a pogrom, carried out with malicious intent to inflict as much damage as possible.[34]

On November 7, a young Jewish man, distraught over his parents' deportation from Germany to Poland, had shot German diplomat Ernst vom Rath in Paris. Vom Rath's death on November 9 became the pretext for the nationwide reprisals against Jews. These reprisals, promoted by the Nazis, included burning synagogues, looting and vandalizing Jewish businesses

---

34. The preferred term in Germany today is *Reichspogromnacht*.

and homes, and arresting Jewish men. The men were sent to concentration camps.

The *New York Times* November 11, 1938, headline read, "Nazis Smash, Loot, and Burn Jewish Shops and Temples until Goebbels Calls Halt." At the Jewish-owned Frankfurt hotel where Hede and Carl had celebrated their wedding, windows were smashed and furniture thrown into the street. When Emil read about this, he panicked. Had his parents been arrested? Were they still alive? How would he find out about his family? The uncertainty and worry were unbearable.

On November 15, a cable arrived from Germany. It had been delayed because the Haven Avenue apartment number was missing from the address. The cable read: "Affidavit Expected Papa and Carl."

This, Emil explained in a November 17 letter to Deta, was "Adolf Hitler German and means, 'Papa and Carl detained; send affidavit for entry permit to the United States so that they will be released.'" Reading between the lines, Emil understood he must immediately obtain affidavits for his father and brother-in-law so they could apply for American visas and exit Germany. "Adolf Hitler German," a term Deta understood, was how one communicated safely in the Third Reich and still got the message out.

But Emil needed more information. Where were David and Carl being held? Each day without news was torture. Perhaps Deta could help. Emil cabled her on November 17: "Call Evening Guntersblum 7 Carefully ask if Papa and Carl still detained and well STOP Will try to get sponsorships STOP Cable brief answer." Guntersblum 7 was the Rübs' telephone number.

On receipt of Emil's cable, Deta telephoned Guntersblum that evening, but the call did not get through. When she tried the next morning, she learned that Guntersblum 7 had been forwarded to another number—Guntersblum 53. At this number, Frau Johanna Wolf, once Deta's employer, answered the phone. The Wolfs were also victimized on November 10. In their house, vandals destroyed porcelain and lamps, smashed furniture, and slit open feather comforters, emptying the down feathers out the window.[35] Eugen Wolf, Frau Wolf's husband, was detained. From Frau Wolf, Deta learned that David and Bertha were safe with Hede, but Emil's brother-in-law was "away."

With this update, Deta cabled Emil on November 19: "Papa returned parents Hede well in Frankfurt Brother-in-law in custody Information received from Wolf." But which "brother-in-law" was detained: Hede's husband, Carl (Emil's brother-in-law)? Or Hartog (Carl's brother and Hede's brother-in-law)?

Clarification came later.[36] Carl avoided internment, because he developed heart palpitations and, thanks to a non-Jewish doctor, was hospitalized. Detained in Buchenwald for seventeen days was Carl's brother Hartog Hartogsohn. Only through the intervention of the British consul in Frankfurt were Hartog and others released, with the proviso they leave the country.[37] The consul issued visas for England; Hartog would leave Germany at the end of December.

Information trickled out slowly, carefully camouflaged. From Frankfurt Höchst, Bertha wrote on November 15, 1938, "Hede and Carl brought me from home at the end of last week. Papa was not at home at the time and came a day later."

Hede added, "Parents want to stay here as it is too cold at home."

---

35. *Stolpersteine in Guntersblum*, Guntersblumer Blätter, April 3, 2020, p. 53.
36. February 3, 1939, Hartog Hartogsohn's (Carl's brother) letter to Emil sent from London, England.
37. The Frankfurt British consul general Robert T. Smallbones reached an agreement with the Gestapo. The British Consulate would issue a transit visa to the detained men if they were released. The men returned to Frankfurt and reported weekly to the local police station until they left Germany for England. It is estimated that Smallbones saved 48,000 Jews, among them Carl's brother Naphtali Hartog Hartogsohn (en.wikipedia.org/wiki/Robert_Smallbones).

Three weeks later Hede reported, "On Wednesday I was in my hometown. The furniture has been modified, lower. We are leaving the glass panes out. As there was no light and no heat, I was glad to get back here." Hede's true message was also in between the lines: the furniture had been smashed and the windows broken. The house was uninhabitable; 4 Wormser Strasse, the house once carefully managed by Bertha, where David ran a thriving business, from where Emil and Hede set out into the world, was no longer home.

Höchst had not escaped the horrors of November 10. The synagogue where Carl was employed was burned and, on November 11, the interior ravaged, chandeliers and furniture destroyed.[38] Jewish stores and homes were vandalized, and Jewish men arrested and sent to Buchenwald. David explained, "Carl can no longer fulfill his functions as his office no longer exists."

The message was clear: Jews needed to leave Germany. David and Carl wanted to go to Holland or England until they could travel to the United States; the women would follow later. To emigrate, however, one did not simply walk into another country. Each country had entry requirements, quota restrictions, and attitudes toward Jews; the Third Reich had exit regulations. To enter the United States, one needed a visa and an affidavit of support from a relative or permanent resident, and relatives weren't always willing to accept responsibility for another person, even if they were related.[39]

Emil turned to Uncle Emil Schloesser for help with affidavits. In return, Emil had to promise that he would support his family once they reached the United States and that he

38. Beck, Fenzl, and Krohn, *Juden in Höchst*, from the series *Die Vergessenen Nachbarn (Forgotten Neighbors)*, the Frankfurt Jewish Museum, Drückerei Henrich GmbH, 1990, pp. 61–63.
39. After November 9–10, Emil received letters asking for help to exit Germany. Carl's brother wrote on behalf of his five sisters; an acquaintance of Bertel Huhn sought affidavits for himself and his wife; a school friend asked if Deta could help her obtain a temporary position in England until her American visa came through. As a recent immigrant with few resources, Emil was unable to help.

would take the first best job offer. Only then did Uncle Emil Schloesser sign four affidavits, which Emil promptly mailed to Frankfurt. Convincing Uncle Emil hadn't been easy.

Emil always planned to maintain his parents once they arrived; at their age (David sixty and Bertha fifty-seven), Emil thought they had worked enough. Hede and Carl could come as a household helper couple but must compromise their Orthodox tradition and work on the Sabbath. Later, a job might materialize where they could have Schabbes off, but first they must take whatever was offered. If there were no other way, Hede answered, they would work on Schabbes. "Of course, we don't want to be a burden to anyone. We are not afraid of any work." Neither was her mother. "I can also still work. I can sew, darn socks, etc. . . . . I suppose," wrote Bertha, "somewhere there is still a place for the four of us." For now, the Rübs planned to rent a room near Hede and Carl.

As late as November 23, Emil hadn't grasped the impact of November 10 on his family and that their home was uninhabitable. "Hopefully, you, dear Papa and Mama, are in Guntersblum again and from there can prepare for your leaving. I would prefer that because of my things. . . . If, for example I had my enlarger, I could present myself better and have a better chance at finding a job. . . . If you are not burdened by other worries, please think of my things. . . . Do not let the permission [to take his equipment out of the country] expire. As I see it, it is luck that I have the permission. At least try again to help me." Emil ended his letter, "Don't lose your heads, trust me . . . and [in English] 'last not least' especially stay healthy."

Before Emil could post his letter, he heard from his parents. "I am shocked at what you omitted from your letter," Emil replied. "You simply present the fact that you no longer live in Guntersblum." That David and Bertha had left Guntersblum so abruptly, that their house was now boarded up and uninhabitable, was difficult to absorb. It was especially troublesome because Emil assumed his parents would stay put when he left. His parents remaining in Guntersblum was the anchor he needed as he found his way in New York. Now that anchor, that bit of imagined stability, was gone.

Go to the Frankfurt Jewish Aid Society, Emil advised, to ask about awaiting their American visa in London. Perhaps Uncle Thornhill in London, who refused to help Emil in 1937, could take in "*liebe Mama und Papa*" until they could enter the United States, "this generous country [where] of course there is space for them." And in a handwritten note on the bottom of his letter, he added: "Were my apparatus and books in the living room affected by the cold weather? Or can they no longer be used?"

Emil couldn't stop obsessing about his photography equipment. How could he present himself as a photographer without camera and lenses? As with any professional, the tools of his trade, he was convinced, were essential. Hede finally wrote Emil the truth: "The apparatus is in small pieces. Not nice. The weather is thoroughly bad for it." Emil had to accept that his enlarger, dryer, lens, and almost all his books were destroyed. This loss, conflated with the expulsion of his parents from Guntersblum, was difficult to bear.

Other than money, Emil didn't know how else to help his parents, and to send money, he needed more income. His wages from Dr. Stern—$10 a week and meals ($190 today)—were insufficient. Every day, Emil walked from one photographic studio to another, searching for better-paying work. From England, Deta sent the Rübs what money she could.

The bad news from Germany had one positive result. In late November, the Jewish owners of the Mayfair Portrait Studio in Times Square saw Emil's advertisement in the *New York Times* and contacted him. Two days later, Emil was employed. As he wrote a former photography colleague, the studio owners gave him a job "so they could help me and my people. Three weeks ago, I don't think they would have hired me." Now he was "among the enviable class of people who earn their living."

Emil worked as a darkroom technician from nine in the morning until six at night and earned $20 a week, doubling his income. But deciphering orders was difficult because of his limited English, and his new supervisor spoke no German. Fortunately, he was familiar with the work, thanks to his time at Dr. Stern's. The money Emil sent his parents was now for their support instead of to redeem his photographic apparatus. "You see," he wrote them, "that this time *malheur* [misfortune] lies close to the good," meaning that his employment resulted from their misfortune.

In Höchst, the Rübs and the Hartogsohns coped as best they could. Carl's angina had improved; he would be released from the hospital on November 27. Hartog returned from his "trip" (Buchenwald Concentration Camp) and would leave soon for England.

Recovering from his Guntersblum trauma, David stayed mostly in Hede's apartment. Bertha took day trips to Guntersblum to retrieve their mail from the post office and to clean up the house. "I am always so glad when I am back here [in Höchst], tired and worn out," Bertha wrote, her nerves frayed. Adding insult to already terrible injuries, the Rübs had to give up their telephone and radio, both damaged on November 10, and pay the repair costs for the telephone.

The Hartogsohns' small Heimchenweg apartment was filling up with items Bertha rescued from the Guntersblum house. Hede, who visited Carl daily in the hospital, wrote that outside of Emil's metal bedframe, nothing else from the Guntersblum house was worth bringing. There was more upsetting news: the Hartogsohns were being evicted and, with David and Bertha, would have to find housing elsewhere.

Hoping it would arrive in time for Hanukkah, Emil sent money and tried to buoy his parents' spirits. "You must absolutely eat well and turn your attention here rather than on the disintegration over there. For here is being built up what there is being lost and you mustn't be impatient waiting to experience it." Under no circumstances should the family spend money on an expensive cargo container to ship their things. A cousin in New York was paying $5 a month for storage; the possessions of another refugee family from Guntersblum sustained water damage in transport. Bring only boxes with bedding and clothes and, he advised in an effort at humor, his iron bedframe. For himself, he urgently needed to purchase some new pants and see a dentist. Could his parents manage if he sent only 50 RM (about $20, or $375 today) a month?

Given recent events, remaining positive in Höchst was a tall order. The inhabitants of the Heimchenweg apartment wanted to be "over there," as soon as possible. But, as Carl noted, everything took a long time, and their efforts to leave were unsuccessful. The Hilfsverein informed Hede and David that an American visa depended on where they were in line; there was no way to expedite the process. The Hartogsohns' number was 15,238 and the Rübs' 44,183. This meant a long wait. The quota for Germans to enter the United States that year was 27,370, and the United States State Department saw no urgency to help persecuted German Jews. "Everything is so terribly difficult," Hede wrote. Safe in New York, Emil had no idea how difficult things were and how much more difficult they would become.

❈ HANOVER, NEW HAMPSHIRE

The letters I found from David and Bertha were the closest
I came to "hearing" their voices. My grandmother's
plaintive statement—"somewhere there is still a place for the
four of us"—runs through my head, unvoiced, soundless, and
as real as if she had spoken these words aloud.

12. STATE OF AFFAIRS

(DECEMBER 1938)

For the Rübs, the Hartogsohns, and for Jews in Germany, 1938 had gone from bad to worse. In Frankfurt Höchst, it was bitterly cold—so cold, wrote Hede, that the milk froze in the Heimchenweg kitchen. And now, in this cold, they had to find housing. On December 21, the two families moved to Seilerstrasse 9 parterre, a ground floor apartment in the traditionally Jewish area of Frankfurt's East End. The apartment had two bedrooms, a kitchen, a bath with WC, and central heating. The move, on what Bertha called "the coldest day," happened four days after David and Carl found and rented the apartment. For their room, David and Bertha would have their beds and linens brought from Guntersblum. "Dear Papa and I still have to look for everything," wrote Bertha, "because we have no closet. This is temporary." At least their housing was warm. Hartog, Carl's brother, came for lunch before departing for England, and Bertha and David visited and were visited by acquaintances.

Across the Atlantic, in early December, Emil wrote his school friend Madeline Heyman in Germany: "I am sitting in a comfortable warm room and from time to time look out at the Hudson, which has similarities to the Rhine." Clearly Haven Avenue was living up to its name, for it had become a haven for Emil. "I am ashamed," he continued, "that I was so ambivalent about the beauty of this country. A Haydn symphony accompanies my writing; so much beautiful music that we hear in the course of a day would not be offered to you there in an entire week. The level of the films is much better than I imagined. The Americans are much nicer than I pictured. They place humanity above all else." His job at the Mayfair Portrait Studio exemplified this.

The Christmas season was flourishing in New York, and in mid-December, Emil wrote Deta that the "American Christkindchen" (the Christkindchen was the bearer of Christmas gifts in Germany) would travel to England on the *Queen Mary* with a gift for her. For this purpose, Emil visited Macy's, where Christmas music played and the atmosphere reminded him of a German department store. But Emil no longer believed in a German Christmas: "Boarded homes, destroyed books, furniture, photographs, and equipment, accepted by [the non-Jewish] people of over 25 million,[40] speak against everything beautiful, good, and holy. Not a single one of the 2,600 Guntersblumers has written me that he was sorry that my father was beaten. But where you [Deta] are, it is Christmas and peace, and I lay my head on your lap and let you stroke me. . . . I hope to have you here in the course of the new year."

On Christmas Eve, he wrote Deta that the previous week he had "bathed" between five and seven hundred nice Americans—their photos, that is, many of their faces showing the anticipation he loved on Deta's face, especially when she had a secret. Even in his all-Jewish workplace, the Christmas spirit was present. "I work in the heart of New

---

40. This number was a guess. The 1939 German census (not counting Austria and Sudetenland) showed 69,316,525 inhabitants, of which 277,266–318,340 were Jews. The 1933 census showed 65,362,115 inhabitants of which 503,288 were Jews.

York, and you must picture the crowds on the sidewalk as if in Piccadilly Circus or on Oxford Street. . . . In front of the building stands a Christmas tree and countless people hurry by laden with packages whose green-white wrapping suggests the contents are gifts." That day, having finished his work, he wished everyone "a Merry Christmas" and returned to Haven Avenue.

Emil was not forgotten on Christmas Eve, for several small gifts had been left for him. Deta's gifts—a new datebook, a colored pen he had admired, and a special letter—added to his pleasure. Also from Deta, via the steamship *Normandie*, were one and a half English pounds (about $7.00), which he would send to his parents. "Much joy you have given me, so much that I am already speaking with you for an hour while Erich and Lotte listen to music. How can I thank you, you good Detalein? I will have to put that aside for a later time."

On December 27, Emil wrote to Otto Schätzel of Guntersblum, in whose house Emil was born, to wish him a Prosit Neujahr (Happy New Year). This greeting was a tradition Emil needed to maintain, for Otto Schätzel was someone Emil counted "among the people who make the old homeland still something valued." After the events of November 10, however, Emil confessed he didn't miss his hometown anymore.

Finding work had been hard, he told Otto, and made him feel like a beggar. But now, "Imagine, shy Emil works in the beloved part of the largest city in the world. The work is interesting, sometimes hard. I have often had open sores on my hands, and evenings I am dead tired." Ending his letter, Emil gave in to nostalgia: "Sometimes I miss Gaensweid [one of the Rübs' vineyards], and I am very sad that I worked for nothing. A young vineyard that I helped raise became part of my heart."

Slowly, Emil was adjusting to his new life. He attended English classes three times a week, made new acquaintances, and reconnected with former Rozsa colleagues. "Sometimes I meet more acquaintances in the city than in Mainz or Worms," he told his parents. He said nothing about having to exchange his image of Guntersblum as *Heimat* for a place of violent antisemitism and what this meant to him.

On New Year's Eve 1938, looking out at the Hudson and the George Washington Bridge, Emil reflected on the year about to end—a year of dislocation, anxiety, and distress. He had been uprooted to a large city, to a different language and culture. From the distance, he had to take in the ill-treatment of his parents on November 10 and the destruction of their home, which he would probably never see again, and of his valuable photographic equipment.

What helped were Erich's support, Lotte's friendship and care, and Deta's belief in him. "Your letter," Madeline Heyman wrote to him, "speaks such courage and confidence. One could almost say that a person changes according to his assignments." Living openly and without fear of reprisals from Nazi authorities also made a difference. Much rested on his shoulders—especially the livelihood and safety of his family. Emil did his best to rise to the occasion.

13. A NEW YEAR (1939)

*"My dear good Emil, those were not
people who did that [to your father].
Only animals could behave that way."*
—DETA TO EMIL, REGARDING NOVEMBER 10, 1938
(JAN. 21, 1939)

The New Year—1939—was not a time for celebration.
The Rübs spent a few hours at 4 Wormser Strasse in
Guntersblum. It was painful to see the trappings of their
former life lying about in pieces, many items missing, the
house in disarray. But David and Bertha needed to furnish
their new refuge and could not spend time grieving. They
salvaged what they could and retrieved the few intact pieces
of Emil's photo equipment. A hired delivery van transported
their bedroom furniture to Frankfurt.

At Seilerstrasse 9 parterre, their new abode, an acquaintance installed an armoire, repairing the damage from
November 10 so Bertha could store their clothes and keep their
small room in order. "Here we have our bedroom set, of course
no more of its former quality," explained David, obliquely
referring to the damage done on November 10, "along with

the couch and the round table from Grandmother's room." It helped to have familiar things around them.

"Are you familiar with Seilerstrasse?" Bertha asked Emil on January 7, 1939. "One can ride directly to the Friedberger Anlage [a park]. I am glad I no longer have to go to Guntersblum so often as the house is very cold." Surely Bertha knew that the Orthodox synagogue at the Friedberger Anlage, once one of the largest synagogues in Frankfurt and perhaps the most impressive, was destroyed on November 9 and 10. "There are so many relatives here," she continued. "I could spend the week making visits, but I have no desire. Dear Emil, you write that we will see each other in 1939. That is my wish, hopefully very soon. Be greeted and kissed from your Mama." After a second move within two months, Bertha had no energy to visit the relatives, friends, and neighbors who, like the Rübs, had moved to Frankfurt because their former homes were also "too cold."

David promised to send Emil's remaining books and any usable camera equipment after consulting with Rozsa about whether the equipment still functioned. By mid-January, David reported that the vineyards were sold. Without the *Preisstoppverordnung*, a 1936 law imposed on all Germans that froze real estate sales to 1935 prices, he could have gotten 1,800 RM more from the sale, a loss of about $8,500 today. Selling his properties was essential to finance their emigration. A methodical businessman, David couldn't imagine emigrating without first putting his affairs in order.

Carl viewed their situation differently, seeing no point in putting nails on the wall of their new lodging when all he wanted was to leave the country. The burning of the Höchst synagogue and his brother Hartog's experience in Buchenwald reinforced his sense of urgency and his frustration they weren't making headway. If an American Jewish congregation invited him to come as a preacher, he and Hede might leave sooner, and, since he had an affidavit of support, the congregation would not be financially obligated. Whether the congregation actually employed him was unimportant; the objective was getting to the United States. Carl asked Emil to forward the references he enclosed to the New York Immigration Department of Agudas Yisroel, an Orthodox Jewish religious organization, hoping they could offer him a position.

In the apartment at Seilerstrasse 9, daily life continued. Monday was laundry day, Bertha wrote, and they would use the laundry kitchen of the apartment building. "Even that has to be taken care of," Hede added. "Not fun." Hede wasn't getting out of the house as she used to in Guntersblum and Höchst. Imagining that English and American people would laugh at her pronunciation, she nonetheless tutored seven students in English three times a week at the apartment.

On Tuesday the Rübs planned to go to "G"—Guntersblum again. It was, David stated, "impossible in the village." People with whom he had done business no longer recognized him, former clients didn't pay what they owed, and their neighbor, the coal seller Clauss, wanted their house for the lowest possible price. To negotiate the sale of one of their vineyards, David went to the buyer's house late at night; it wasn't safe to enter an "Aryan" home in broad daylight. Where the Rübs were once well-known and greeted by the villagers, they were now avoided. Anonymity in Frankfurt felt like protective armor, but in Guntersblum, it was a slap in the face.

Five months had passed since Bertha last saw her son. When would they see each other again? Had the winter clothing the Rübs sent arrived at Haven Avenue? Especially worrisome for Bertha was that David and Carl might leave Germany first. "Dear Emil, isn't it possible that Papa and I can get away? Couldn't we come to England together? . . . I am often sad and in a bad mood."

To Deta, Emil confessed his negligence in not having applied for his parents' visa earlier. "I would give up a piece of my comfort," he stated, "if I could bring them out faster from that cruel country. The consequences could be disastrous if it is too late."

As of January 1, 1939, the Nazi regime required all Jewish women to add "Sara" and the men "Israel" to their name and to carry an identity card. A large orange "J" for *Jude* marked each card.[41] Had Emil seen the photos of his parents, he would have been shocked; these are not the relaxed smiling faces in the portraits he took for his photography class.

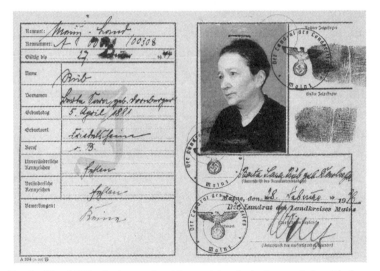

Bertha "Sara" Rüb: she has aged and lost weight; she looks worried and forlorn.

---

41. The YIVO Institute for Jewish Research in New York, which has a collection of original *Kennkarte* (id cards), provided copies of the cards for David and Bertha Rüb and for Hede. They did not have the card for Carl Hartogsohn, and I have not been able to obtain one from other sources.

David "Israel" Rüb: still the respectable businessman in a starched white collar, jacket, and tie. He too has aged and lost weight, but he carries himself with dignity.

Hedwig (Hede) "Sara" Hartogsohn: A fashionable young woman with plucked eyebrows, composed and brave. Gone is the smiling face of the young newlywed; she is now a married woman with sorrows. She too has lost weight.

Emil's year began with the loss of his photo technician job. The Christmas season over, the Mayfair Portrait Studio in Times Square no longer needed his services. Once again, he turned to the Greater New York Coordinating Committee for German Refugees and to anyone else he thought might help. Emphasizing his practical experience in entomology, he wrote to the Boyce Thompson Institute for Plant Research in Yonkers. The director's response was kind—"I am of course in full sympathy with the Jewish refugees from Germany and other European countries"—but he had no job to offer.

Emil withheld being unemployed from his parents, instead asking for their news, such as who had bought the vineyards and under what circumstances, requesting to be kept informed about the sale of the house, and reminding his parents to have the stonecutter place a gravestone for Oma Dina. He hinted he might have a better chance finding work in a smaller city. Recently, he told them, he began a vegetarian diet, which he believed was the reason he stayed healthy. He described this diet to Deta: an apple or orange before each meal, whole wheat bread, more apples, fresh vegetables, baked potatoes with their skin (Europeans didn't eat the skin) with cheese and butter, also salads, nuts, milk, and honey.

Presenting a brave front did not mean Emil was unaffected by the loss of his job. He hated not having an income and had little patience for refugees better off financially who complained. In Guntersblum, he had never experienced such dismal financial straits.

Across the Atlantic, if prizes were given for persistence, Deta would have won first place. On January 6, she went to see Emil's uncle Stewart Thornhill in Hatton Gardens, London, hoping he would sign a guarantee for David and Carl.

Mr. Thornhill was out when Deta arrived, so she spoke with his son. Emil had written the elder Mr. Thornhill, she explained, asking him to invite David and Carl to England.

"There would be no cost to Mr. Thornhill," she insisted. "Emil will support the two gentlemen, and I will regularly contribute four pounds."

"My father has already taken on the responsibility for several relatives," the son stated.

"I do understand," Deta replied, "but he must also understand that the two men want nothing more from him than a piece of paper, an invitation. For everything else, I will take responsibility."

"I will tell all this to my father," the son answered, "who will respond. Please leave your name, address, and telephone number."

That evening, Uncle Thornhill telephoned Deta. "Miss Bickel," he said, in English, "if I issue an invitation to Mr. Rüb and Mr. Hartogsohn, I will be obligated to support them, which I am unwilling and unable to do."

"Are you not obligated anyway?" Deta replied. There was silence on the line. Mr. Thornhill had hung up.

"You have no idea what expectations are put on a guarantor; otherwise, you wouldn't write me so childishly," Uncle Thornhill wrote to Emil. Uncle Thornhill was already fulfilling his family obligations by supporting his own sister, his brother-in-law, and a niece with husband and child. "For other family members . . . I am not available."[42]

But Deta didn't give up. "Believe me, Emil," Deta wrote, "day and night thoughts swirl in my head about what I can do so that your father and brother-in-law get out of Germany soon." Out of love for Emil, she would do anything, no matter how difficult. "Love," she told him, "gives strength."

She began writing and calling the few contacts she had in England, and she visited the Jewish Relief Committee at

---

42. A British sponsor had to consider how long the emigrant would wait in England for their American visa. Room and board for two people cost a minimum of 12 pounds per month. Despite Deta's promise that the guarantor would not have to pay for the emigrants, a sponsor would naturally consider this.

Woburn House where Emil had gone for help in 1937. The people there, Deta reported, were very nice, but the only help they offered was an address of an organization assisting rabbis. Was Carl a rabbi?

Next, Deta wrote Mrs. Hill, her previous employer. "Please will you forgive me," Deta began, "for asking a very great favor of you. I don't find it very easy to ask for your help since I never had an opportunity to earn it in any way, but still I trust you will understand knowing the terrible conditions under which Jews in Germany have to live." Praying for a positive response, Deta posted her letter.

To Deta's surprise, Mrs. Hill answered that she would sponsor Emil's father. "It makes us all feel positively sick to think of the dreadful things that are happening to the Jews in Germany," Mrs. Hill wrote, "and we would like to be able to do something to help if we could." She noticed that Deta's English had improved "and you now write a very good letter."

Deta immediately contacted Woburn House for the requisite form and then wrote to David Rüb. This was the start of a brief correspondence between Seilerstrasse 9 and 6 Aberdare Gardens. "Esteemed Fraulein Bickel," David wrote in February, "upon my return from Guntersblum, I found your letter of the 14th of this month, which pleased me very much and for which I am more grateful to you. The requested photocopies and waiting list number 44,183 I will have prepared as quickly as possible, and they will follow. I would be especially glad if you could also find a guarantor for my son-in-law, or I will give up mine because he is younger."

A flurry of activity to obtain forms and photocopies followed. Deta sent paperwork to Mrs. Hill, but since David didn't have an American visa, Deta couldn't verify that David would only stay in England until he received permission to enter the United States. Regretting delaying the process, Mrs.

Hill promised to forward the form directly to the committee once Deta sent the missing documents.

Emil wasn't optimistic that his father could be placed in England and recommended David leave Germany illegally. If Mrs. Hill's efforts didn't succeed, Emil still appreciated her generosity and kindness. As he told Deta: "You have no idea how much good it does me and also my people. We have long been used to being shown the door."

In New York, Emil again found luck in misfortune—an opportunity for a week's training at Leitz and then at Pavelle Laboratories, where he went daily from nine until six. He shared this news with Deta on a postcard featuring a self-portrait. Although his face is half-obscured by the camera, the photo is an improvement over the self-portrait from Germany of just his shadow.

Self-portrait of Emil sent on a postcard to Deta,
February 8, 1939; Credit: Emil Rueb.

The training course would prepare him for a potential job as a photo finisher in a Cleveland, Ohio, drugstore and the assignment to build up their photo department. If nothing interfered with this plan, he would travel to Cleveland.

"Don't be amazed," he wrote his parents, "if I tell you that in mid-February, I may establish myself 1,000 miles from here. In the interior, it is much easier to advance professionally than here. Don't worry; I have good advice, and also the Committee [of Jewish Women] is very nice to me." Describing how helpful and kind the people at Pavelle were to him, he noted, "I am only telling you this to say that in this world there are still people, strangers, who are nice to us [Jews]."

He cautioned Deta that the Cleveland plan might fail at the last minute. "This is typical here and seen as quite normal." Emil's sixth sense about the Cleveland job was correct; the employer requested Emil bring darkroom equipment he did not own and which the Resettlement Division of the National Coordinating Committee could not purchase for him.

Despite this, Emil did not give up hope. It had been a long journey from Guntersblum to New York, and there were still "thorn hedges"—barriers—to succeeding. But just as Deta was optimistic for him, he too sensed something would give and he would find a foothold.

�֎ HANOVER, NEW HAMPSHIRE

The identification cards for my grandparents and Hede with "Sara" and "Israel" added to their names reminded me of a visit to my parents around 1978.

On the table between us, addressed to my father, was an envelope with German stamps that I had discovered in a drawer. On the back of the envelope was the sender's name: "David Israel Rüb."

"I thought your father's name was David," I said to my father. "But here it says 'David Israel.' Why?"

My "why" sounded accusatory. The subtext was: "Are you hiding something from me again? I am thirty years old, married, a mother, and you still treat me like a child." My well-meaning parents, believing they were protecting me, often withheld information.

My father smiled, a smile that was kind, sad, and embarrassed. "His name was David," he answered. "But the Nazis required Jewish men to add 'Israel' to their name and the women 'Sara.'"

"I am sorry," I apologized, regretting my confrontational tone. "I didn't know." There was so much I didn't know about what my father and my grandparents experienced in Nazi Germany. "May I keep this?" I picked the envelope up from the table.

"Yes," my father responded. And then he added, "My parents would have liked you."

This was my father's way of saying that he liked me. I think he appreciated my wish to keep his father's envelope. His comment to me that day was a gift.

14. ANOTHER DEPARTURE

(MARCH 12, 1939)

On a blustery March Sunday, Emil boarded a train at Grand Central Station. Cousin Lotte waited on the platform, her handkerchief ready to wave when the train departed. From his window seat, Emil saw Lotte smiling at him. In his bag were fruit and the sandwiches Lotte prepared for his journey. In his pocket was a $10 bill (a loan from Cousin Erich), along with a slip of paper with travel instructions from the Greater New York Coordinating Committee for German Refugees. "If anything prevents you from going," the note ended, "telephone to Mrs. Mann at 0-7974." There was also a small German–English dictionary, a goodbye gift in which Lotte inscribed, "I hope your English will soon be so perfect that you don't need it often." Emil tried to smile back at Lotte. Leaving New York was hard. He had come to love this city where he had found refuge.

At twelve thirty in the afternoon, on schedule, the train began to move, and Lotte waved her handkerchief. "*Aufwiedersehen*," she mouthed to Emil. Waving back to her, Emil swallowed tears. He would miss his cousins, especially Lotte, who had looked after him. Although the circumstances were different, this departure brought back the painful image of his parents when he left them in 1938.

Once again, he was traveling to an unfamiliar place where he knew no one. This time, however, a job in a photography store awaited him. As the train gathered speed, Emil wondered what lay ahead. Would he and his new boss like each other? Were there any Jews where he was going? Would he be accepted?

The job offer was a small miracle. Months earlier, a popular photographic magazine had run an article about German photographers expelled by the Nazis. While these refugees sought work in New York, there was demand for 35 mm specialists in other parts of the United States. To help refugee photographers, the editors offered to connect potential employers with photographers seeking work.

In early January, the owner of a small camera store saw the article and wrote to Nell Mann, Head of the Employment Department of the Greater New York Coordinating Committee for German Refugees. Someone well-trained in photo finishing, with a working knowledge of printing and developing, preferably a young person with a basic knowledge of English, was what he needed. Although the starting salary of $14 a week was low compared to New York standards, it would increase if the person showed promise. Also, living expenses in his area were less than in a metropolitan area. There was an additional enticement: should the person like the situation, he could acquire an interest in the business, perhaps even a partnership.

Given the pay, the writer acknowledged that his request was a tall order. Because he wished to finalize an arrangement through a personal interview, he would call on Miss Mann when he next came to New York. Soon thereafter, Mr. Philip Carter, owner of the Camera Shop in Hanover, New Hampshire, came to the city, interviewed three applicants, and chose Emil.

As the train made its way north, the words of the Council of Jewish women rang in Emil's ears: "You are the first immigrant we are sending out. Don't let us down!" They had made it clear: if you don't take this job, we can't help you anymore.

Eating one of Lotte's sandwiches, Emil recalled what Mr. Carter said about the Camera Shop. The store was started by Philip Carter's brother Paul, a photojournalist. After training in Germany and Holland, Paul Carter worked under Roy E. Stryker in the Photographic Unit of the Farm Security Administration.[43] In ill health, Paul Carter left the Farm Security Administration in 1936, and with his older brother Philip, a businessman and engineer, opened the Camera Shop in Hanover in 1937. Sadly, in 1938 Paul Carter, thirty-five years old, died of tuberculosis.

After Paul's death, Philip Carter, four years older than Paul, wanted to keep the business going, but he needed the specialized help Emil offered. The store was in a small space above Eastman's, a Main Street drugstore, but Mr. Carter planned to move to larger quarters. There was one employee, a part-time student who did the developing. Emil wondered if he would fit in at this establishment. Did they do things differently from what he learned from Rozsa and Dr. Stern? Anxious to make a good impression, he was keenly aware that his future and the possibility of partnership in the business were at stake.

As the train traveled north, a young college student asked to sit next to Emil. The two began a conversation about Leicas that lasted almost all the way to White River Junction, Vermont, Emil's destination. The conversation about a subject Emil loved made the six-hour train journey less tedious. It also kept him from noticing the blinding snowstorm outside the train window.

43. Roy E. Stryker started the documentary photography unit of the Farm Security Administration, which employed, among others, well-known photographers Walker Evans, Dorothea Lange, and Gordon Parks. The photographers documented the Great Depression, including the "dust bowl" ecological disaster.

The train arrived in White River Junction at seven, fifteen minutes later than scheduled. Mr. Carter was waiting for Emil and welcomed him warmly. "How was your trip?" he asked Emil. "What do you think of this weather?"

"It is amazing," Emil replied. He had never seen such a storm in Guntersblum.

The drive through the snowstorm to the Carter's house in Hanover took twenty minutes. Mrs. Carter and their three children, curious about this German Jewish refugee, were waiting at the door. Supper was ready, and they sat down at the large dining room table for the vegetarian meal Mrs. Carter had taken pains to prepare. "Tell us about where you are from," she asked Emil. "What was it like there before you left?" Mrs. Carter had traveled in Germany and wanted to know how things had changed.

After dinner, Mr. Carter drove him to the nearby house where Emil was to rent a room. Before going to bed, Emil wrote "Hanover Arrival" in his pocket calendar for March 12. Then, tired from his journey, from the emotions stirred up leaving New York, and from many new impressions, he fell asleep.

When he awoke the next morning and looked out the window of his second-floor room, the newly fallen snow sparkled in the sunlight. It was a snow paradise, the first he had ever seen, and he was enchanted.

After breakfasting, he walked the short distance in the snow to Main Street. At the Camera Shop, Mr. Carter handed him a broom and said, "Every morning I would like you to clean the front office." Mr. Carter gave him the keys to the store and to the darkroom and showed him the open cash drawer and the Leica lenses, in case Emil needed to use one.

Taking to heart the admonition from the Council of Jewish Women, Emil asked Mr. Carter, "How do you think I should identify myself here?" The Council had prepared Emil by saying that the mostly white Anglo-Saxon Protestant college town of Hanover was a different world from New York's Washington Heights with its German Jewish immigrants.

"That is your decision," replied Mr. Carter.

"Is it acceptable if I say, 'I am a Jewish refugee from Germany'?"

"Certainly," Mr. Carter answered. "I have nothing against it."

Emil's first impressions of the Camera Shop were positive. The darkroom, though small, was well-equipped. Jack, the student employee, despite having no formal training in photography and developing, had managed the darkroom alone and in Emil's estimation did it "not badly." The photographic equipment for sale, however, needed improvement. It was not of the caliber Emil knew from Germany.

In the afternoon, Mr. Carter gave Emil some film and said, "Go out, take a walk, and see Hanover as a photographer." The openness and trust that Mr. Carter extended to him moved Emil deeply.

Two days later, Emil wrote Deta: "I am living my new American life six train hours from New York among students and upright citizens. Hanover—emphasis on the first syllable [to distinguish it for Deta from Hannover, Germany, which is accented on the second syllable] and don't forget to add New Hampshire because there are ten more Hanovers in the United States—has 2,000 inhabitants and is home to the 2,500 students at Dartmouth College. They are the clientele of the Camera Shop, a baby for whose care I have been brought here from New York. I am among cultured people, and I believe they like me."

To keep friends and family informed, he wrote a two-page summary about his "new American life," organizing his descriptions by categories—Hanover, The Camera Shop, Personnel, Customers, Work. In landscape and climate,

Hanover reminded him of small towns in the Taunus area of Germany, but here the townspeople were neither fascists nor pro-Hitler.

From the moment he stepped off the train, Emil was occupied with familiarizing himself with the Camera Shop, learning about the town, and settling in. Although he missed Deta, he had no time to miss New York. His workday began at eight in the morning. After sweeping, he developed films and made enlargements and copies. Closing time was six-thirty, but Emil often stayed later to finish some developing or to write letters. Each day, he grew more certain he was cut out for the Camera Shop and for his assignment to increase sales and photofinishing. Emil added his own goals: improve the photofinishing and help customers produce better photographs by increasing their technical knowledge. Achieving these goals would, he hoped, lead to a stake in the business, the enticement Mr. Carter had offered with the job.

Jack, the student employee, took Emil under his wing and pulled him along to lectures at the college, to the library, and to meet his friends. Every evening there was something to fill the time. One night Emil and Jack listened to classical music records. Another night Emil attended a class taught by Professor Rosenstock-Huessy, a German exile.[44] Sometimes they worked in the darkroom and discussed photography. Emil, who would turn thirty-three in August, often socialized with the students and enjoyed the college atmosphere.

He ate one meal a day with students who cooked for themselves and another at night in a restaurant. For budgetary and health reasons, breakfast was two oranges and an apple. The Carters often invited Emil to dinner and did their best to make him feel at home. Philip and Muriel Carter, both products

---

44. Eugen Rosenstock-Huessy (1888–1973), historian and social philosopher, was born in Berlin, the son of secular Jews, and became a Protestant at age seventeen. He left Germany in 1933 and began teaching at Dartmouth in 1935.

"Taken by a colleague at a college fraternity house while we listened to records and I retouched photos." Letter from Emil to Deta, April 6, 1939.

of private schools, came from solid backgrounds. Philip, a minister's son, graduated from Yale in 1923, and Muriel, a member of Scarsdale society, had spent a year in Paris. Emil described Mr. Carter, with whom he had a comradely relationship, as a "very cultured and decent boss," who understood slow and solid work and wanted to raise the quality of the Camera Shop's output to German standards.

Within two weeks of coming to Hanover, Emil concluded that he was the person Mr. Carter sought, and the Camera Shop, an enterprise waiting for new ideas, was the right place for him. Mr. Carter introduced Emil to the public as an "outstanding German photographer" and approved many of his suggestions. As one of the first German Jewish refugees to land in Hanover, Emil discovered that anything cultural and scientific from Germany—Thomas Mann, Beethoven, Brahms, ski teachers, and the Leica—was appreciated. Mr. Carter was proud of his German photographer. When Emil received his portrait lens, smuggled out of Germany by an uncle, Mr. Carter showed it off to the Dartmouth students; the lens, unavailable in the United States, was a novelty.

One day a traveling salesman from a well-known photography company entered the store. Since Mr. Carter was out, Emil tried to converse with the salesman but couldn't understand his English. Likewise, the salesman couldn't understand Emil's English. After twenty minutes, the two men realized they were *Schicksalsgenossen*—fellow refugees. "Nice people, the Carters," the salesman said in German. "But they still take their time to pay." Emil recounted this as an amusing story to his parents, but it was the first time he heard the store had financial issues.

Another early experience had more significant consequences. While developing a film for a medical student, Emil made a small error that he corrected, thanks to his darkroom skills. When the student came to pick up his work, Emil acknowledged his mistake. "Oh, it's okay," the student told him. "Don't worry about it." Fifteen minutes later, a gentleman in a white doctor's coat rushed into the store. He was Dr. Rolf Syvertsen, dean of the Medical School. He wanted to meet and congratulate the person who had resolved the mistake so well. Dr. Syvertsen took an interest in the German refugee photographer and became Emil's mentor, advisor, and primary supporter.

Emil committed himself to helping the Camera Shop grow, certain that obtaining partnership and partial ownership depended on this. He turned down an offer to interview as a darkroom technician with well-known German photojournalist Alfred Eisenstaedt, a job which could have been a feather in Emil's cap. The days weren't long enough for Emil's projects: improve his English, retouch photographs, learn more about the store, search for new ideas—in short, everything that might increase business and thereby secure his livelihood.

But writing a birthday greeting to Deta was sufficient reason to pause from these tasks. "Dear, good Detalein," he began, "six years [since they fell in love] you have been waiting for me, six years with little joy, many sacrifices, and unheard-of patience. Let me thank you for this today and wish that you can hold out another half year." For Emil, Hanover was a new beginning. In another six months, his income should be more than he needed, and he could send for Deta. Reassuring her of his love, he wrote, "Detalein, you are my hope, I wait only for you. In a lovely but somewhat lonely . . . little town I am working and waiting. I kiss you and hold you close."

Emil was not the same person who left Guntersblum six months before. He had survived the departure from home, acclimated himself to a large city, and now, besides supporting himself, was saving money to help his parents. Partial ownership in the Camera Shop promised a foothold and some security. The kindness and respect shown to him by the Carters, Jack, Dr. Syvertsen, the students, and Camera Shop customers were an additional bonus. Although he did not realize it, he had started on the road toward independence and autonomy.

Emil's Hanover arrival, however, did not shelter him from world events. On March 15, 1939, Hitler invaded and occupied Czechoslovakia in violation of the Munich agreement with Chamberlain. Would there be war? To Deta, Emil wrote, "England and France will only fight if there is no other option. But I wish they would wait with their *Klamauk* [fuss and racket] until I have you here." Deta should investigate the cost and set money aside for an Atlantic crossing because he might ask her to come on short notice. "Would you enjoy having my hand stroking and caressing you?" he closed.

15. A PASSOVER–OF SORTS (1939)

*T*hree weeks later, Emil spent the evening alone at the Camera Shop. It was Erev Pesach, the night before Passover, a holiday he always loved because in Guntersblum it heralded the coming of spring. Early April in Hanover was not as in Guntersblum. There was still snow on the ground, and although the days were getting longer, it was cold.

This was the first time Emil would not celebrate Passover in his parents' house. The prior year in Guntersblum, David, Carl, and Emil had read from the Haggadah, dipped the herbs in salt water, eaten the matzah with charoset, and drunk the sweet red wine. With Hede's help, Bertha had brought a delicious meal to the table. Remembering what had been made Emil homesick. To overcome these feelings, he cleaned the darkroom, an activity fitting the Passover tradition of cleaning the house top to bottom to dispose of any leavened food.

This year, Passover fell on April 5, Bertha's birthday. Although Emil needed to have dental work and to replace some clothes, for Passover, Bertha's birthday, and Hede's April 15 birthday, he arranged through a New York relative to mail some "books," code for "money." Once the shipment arrived, Emil promised to send more "books."

As he worked, Emil thought about the Jews' exodus from Egyptian bondage. The Exodus was one of God's greatest deeds, a sign that the Holy One had chosen the people of Israel to exist and, through them, to share the experience of freedom and responsibility in the promised land. But more relevant now was Emil's own exodus from Nazi repression and from poverty. Hanover, if not the promised land, was a good place to start over.

In Frankfurt, Bertha also prepared for Passover, but there was no comparison with previous Seders in Guntersblum. This year, she would make do without her special Passover porcelain; hopefully, she would find enough matzah in Frankfurt to last a week. "You would be amazed," she wrote Emil, "how I run around the city doing errands." The Rübs attended an engagement party and received visits from relatives and from Guntersblum acquaintances. Envious of those leaving Germany, Bertha mourned her shrinking social network. David's cousin Rabbi Moritz David and his cousin's wife were leaving their house in Bochum and going to a Jewish retirement home in Manchester, England. "Tante Lotte and Uncle Moritz are lucky. I wish we had such good fortune."

With Jack's help, Emil wrote to Mrs. Hill, thanking her for guaranteeing his father and reassuring her that he would support David financially in England. Would she also consider, he asked her, vouching for his mother, who dreaded being left behind? The guarantee, Emil clarified, was only "a formality as far as you are concerned; for us it will be indeed a lifesaver."

Travel without delay, Emil urged his parents, once their documents were ready. If departing on short notice, they should take only hand luggage and leave everything else behind, including his remaining photographic equipment. Emil would send them money in England. Forget about the

Wormser Strasse house, he encouraged, because in America there were much nicer and less expensive houses. Knowing it was difficult to leave treasured possessions behind, Emil wanted his parents to prioritize their lives over material goods.

When an invitation for England came, who should leave Germany first? While David was insisting that Carl, the younger man, should go first, Emil disagreed: Carl and Hede could fend for themselves. David had endured more and for much longer than Carl, and therefore had priority.

Ideally, both the Rübs and the Hartogsohns would leave soon. Agudas Yisroel in New York, to whom Emil had sent Carl's documents, couldn't help. But Hartog, Carl's brother who was safe in England, found a guarantor for Carl, freeing Emil from this obligation. The £150 promised by an uncle in Palestine and intended for Carl could now go to Bertha and Hede. Since Hede could enter England as a domestic servant,[45] the focus moved to the Rübs.

When she learned that Emil planned to leave New York for New Hampshire, Bertha had worried. Where was he going, and how far? What would he earn, where would he eat, who would do his laundry and darn his socks? How would he celebrate Passover, and where would he get matzah? How would he manage without a Jewish community and without Cousin Lotte to look after him? Still wishing Emil would marry Lotte, Bertha doubted Emil's ability to take care of himself.

On days she felt down, the self-portraits Emil sent lifted her spirits. According to Hede, Bertha "presents him in photographs" to all their acquaintances and keeps the photos in an envelope on her bedside table. From his photograph, Bertha noted that Emil had lost weight. "Do you not get proper meals?" she fretted.

---

45. Britain had strict immigration policies, but women were allowed in on a domestic service permit. This is how Deta got her job in Bedford. Without a permit, a refugee wasn't allowed to work.

By mid-April, David's emigration documents were in England, but leaving Germany without selling his properties was not in David's makeup. Trained in German *Gründlich-keit*—thoroughness—and needing the funds, David wanted to sell their Guntersblum house before the Nazis auctioned it on May 23 and retained the proceeds. Next-door neighbor Otto Clauss wanted to buy the house at auction because it would sell for less than its value.

Auctioning the house would devastate his parents, Emil wrote to Herr Clauss. David owed Clauss money, and Emil regretted that, because of his family's misfortune under the Nazis, Clauss hadn't been repaid. Couldn't Clauss wait until David sold the house? In Guntersblum, no house was ever left unsold, and surely someone would want theirs. "Therefore I beg you," he concluded, "to think humanely and to wait until a sale has taken place." Clauss mentioned to David that Emil had written, but Clauss never replied.

At Seilerstrasse 9, Passover and birthday celebrations were subdued. For Pessach, Carl's brother Hartog had food sent from Belgium. "On Erev Pessach, it will be three years since we buried dear Grandmother," David noted. "How much has happened since then. With God's help, everything will be all right again." There was still no stone for Oma Dina's grave, probably because there was no money to pay for it and the stonecutter would not work for Jews. Starting the following week, their emigration would be David's top priority. "We hope soon to be in the USA." Hede celebrated her twenty-eighth birthday and wished the next one would be in the United States. Like her mother, she lamented the departure of their acquaintances and was "often sad because I hardly hear any news."

Bertha need not have worried about her son, for Emil wrote that he was doing well and the Camera Shop was the right place for him. His ideas for advertising the business were starting to bring more clientele, and Mr. Carter was satisfied with him. He was often invited out, and he accepted all invitations. Two Jewish Dartmouth professors were especially kind to him.[46] One of them, Professor Louis Silverman, invited him home for matzah ball soup. Some evenings, seeing light in the Camera Shop, students dropped by.

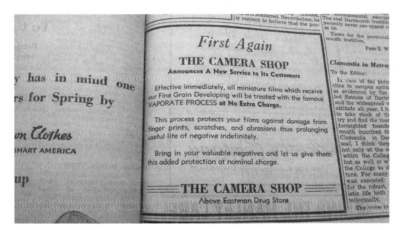

Advertisement in the *Daily Dartmouth*, the Dartmouth College newspaper, April 12, 1939.

Relieved that her son was well, Bertha sent him a package of homemade macaroons, his favorite, and a tablet of chocolate for Mrs. Carter.

To Deta, Emil gave the same glowing report, admitting he would feel even better once his teeth were cared for. He earned $17.50 a week (about $330 today) and easily covered his expenses ($4.00 for rent, $1.00 for laundry, and $6.00 for food), allowing him to save $5.00 a week. A product of his culture, Emil had one trouble: his torn socks were starting

---

46. The two professors were Louis Lazarus Silverman and Albert William Levi. Professor Silverman (1884-1967) taught mathematics at Dartmouth from 1918-1953. Professor Levi, Dartmouth class of 1932, was assistant professor at Dartmouth from 1935-1941. Professor Silverman's wife was Sonia Paeff Silverman (1888–1963), a pianist. Their son Raphael Hillyer (1914-2010) a violist, was one of the original members of the Julliard Quartet.

to accumulate. He managed to call the laundry to pick up his clothes. "But more? I find that is the job of a woman. Don't you agree?" he teased.

At the end of the Seder, the participants say, "Next year in Jerusalem," a symbolic wish for freedom after long suffering. The two couples in Frankfurt were hopeful; Mrs. Hill agreed to sponsor both David and Bertha, and the guarantee from the Palestinian uncle could now go to Hede. For the Rübs and the Hartogsohns, "Next year in Jerusalem" could only mean "Next year in Hanover." For Emil, the final words held his deepest longings: reunion with Deta and next year's Passover celebration with his parents. Surrounded by the people he loved, he could then put down roots in his new environment and even start his own family.

16. TENSIONS AND HOPES

(SUMMER 1939)

> *"Detalein, it must be possible to have*
> *you soon in my arms. Detalein, it must be*
> *made possible because I can't be and don't*
> *want to be without you any longer."*
> —EMIL TO DETA, AUGUST 3, 1939

*O*n a Sunday in late June 1939, Emil sat on a lawn chair outside his rooming house. The afternoon was sunny, not too hot, without a cloud in the sky. "I wish you a good afternoon," he called out to Mr. and Mrs. Williams, his landlords, as they drove out of their driveway and waved to him. The Williamses were kind to him. Two weeks before, Mr. Williams had invited Emil for a Sunday drive, a walk, and supper. Besides the human contact, the supper invitation meant a savings of 40 cents, which Emil could use for another expense. In July, the Williams would take a month's vacation; in their absence, Emil would watch the house instead of paying rent.

After spending hours in the darkroom, Emil appreciated the fresh air and sunshine. There were tasks waiting for him

at the store, but today he needed to attend to his correspondence, especially to his parents and to Deta. Letters were the
only way he stayed in touch. A reply usually arrived within
one to two weeks, transported by one of the large ocean liners
crossing the Atlantic. The Hanover post office was across the
street from the Camera Shop, and Emil checked the store's
postbox several times a day. In the last two weeks, he hadn't
heard from Deta, which was unusual and concerning. When
a letter came, he learned that Deta's silence was because she
had been nursing little Susan, who had been sick.

With the warm sunshine on his face, Emil closed his eyes
and thought of Deta. If only she were sitting next to him.
Through the neighbor's open windows, radio reports from
Berlin and from London interrupted his reverie. Hitler had
designs on the Free City of Danzig and the Polish Corridor,
Europe was in crisis, and the situation was "very serious."
Emil returned to his letter, reminding his parents to bring
only what they could use in a furnished room.

On this summer Sunday, the Rübs, Danzig, and the
Polish Corridor seemed light years away. Emil had settled
in at the Camera Shop, working twelve-hour days as if the
store were his. Word spread that the German 35 mm specialist
"Emil of the Camera Shop" was the person to see about a
problem with a camera. The students, professors, and locals
liked him and valued his knowledge. He wished that someone from home would say, "Good job. You amounted to
someone after all," to contradict earlier predictions from
extended family that he was a *Schlemiel* (loser). If he were
totally honest with himself, he also wished he could focus
solely on the Camera Shop.

A minor setback was having two teeth extracted. This
made him feel like an old man next to the Dartmouth students
who patronized the Camera Shop. The students gave him a lot
of work but also companionship. When they returned from

vacation, Emil developed their films, mostly of "pretty girl-friends who looked so alike that he had to be careful not to mix up the pictures," as he told Cousin Lotte over the telephone.

Earlier that month, Emil took the train to Boston, his first excursion from Hanover, paid for with his earnings. Staying in a hotel room was lonely, but he liked looking at the ocean toward England and, as he wrote Deta, toward "a Germany that is now beautiful only in my imagination." He walked in the park and visited the Museum of Fine Arts, where he admired paintings by the Impressionists, Van Gogh, El Greco, and Rembrandt. But these sights paled when Emil imagined seeing Boston with Deta. In the next month, he hoped to have a clearer picture of his future so that he could bring her over. On the train back to White River Junction, he finished a letter to Deta with, "So let me end my trip with a loving greeting to you, a long kiss, and in my thoughts let my head lie on your sweet breast."

The Boston trip gave him perspective. He would discuss his prospects at the store with Mr. Carter, and, if the answer were positive, he would ask Mr. Carter to send Deta an official invitation to come in mid-September. Deta would need such an invitation from an American citizen to obtain a tourist visa. Assuming Deta liked Hanover and wished to stay, they would marry. If only her parents would approve his plan; however, in Nazi Germany her father could not consent to what was there an illegal marriage between a Christian and a Jew.

Once together, Emil wrote, Deta would work with him at the Camera Shop. She would earn her own money and be financially independent. But she should consider carefully whether she wanted to come. Marrying would take her away from her parents with no guarantee when she would see them again. It was not that Emil didn't want her but that he didn't want to cause her unhappiness.

"Detalein, I long for you so often, for your velvet eyes, your gentle touch, your breasts, your knees . . . Would you give me a great pleasure? Sometimes I am ashamed of myself for asking. Wouldn't you send me the picture of you in a bathing suit? Or would you take a few pictures of yourself in your room and send me the undeveloped film?" Emil advised her what film and exposure to use. A day later, however, he regretted his request and asked only for a photo in which she is looking at him "so at least I have your eyes." He enclosed $15 in his letter. She should send most of the money to Frankfurt but keep a few dollars for herself.

"Do I please you?" Deta asked in her return letter. She had complied with Emil's request to photograph herself, perhaps in a bathing suit, maybe in the nude. "Oh, Detalein," Emil answered, "the photos were sharp enough for me to see you in all your beauty, which reflects the tenderness of your soul. I kiss you on the mouth and stroke these breasts that I like so much."

In June, the Rübs' vineyards were auctioned off at less than their value. With permission from a town official, neighbor Clauss wired the Rübs' garden gate shut, barring them from entering. Clauss harvested the Rübs' asparagus, rhubarb, strawberries, currants, and gooseberries, and "if it continues like this," David complained in a letter, "he will harvest everything else." It would be helpful if Emil sent "something," meaning money. Clauss had interfered with the sum David should have received from the sale of clover from the Rübs' field near the train station.

Bertha recounted that Carl's sister Clara Hartogsohn received her permit and had a job in England[47], friends visited them at Seilerstrasse 9, the youngest son of an acquaintance just had his bar mitzvah, and in two weeks an acquaintance

---

47. Carl's sister Clara (1898–1975) left Germany for England in July 1939 and moved to Canada in 1951.

was leaving for Chile. "One after another of our circle of acquaintances is leaving and I am always very sad," she wrote.

Now that Hede gave private English lessons, Bertha did more housework. Never idle, Bertha crocheted gloves, practicing on a pair for Hede. She would send a pair to Emil's landlady because the results were very nice and everyone liked them. Find out, please, she asked her son, what she and David could do there; she would very much like to learn a new skill. The Rübs sent another small package containing toothpaste, English Lavender, and chocolate for Emil and some for the Carters.

At that time, Hede thought their parents looked and felt well and didn't miss the large Guntersblum house. But her assessment was incorrect; over the summer, family strife was brewing. The tension, initiated by Carl, was about money and, according to David, caused "a few weeks of unbearable state of affairs." Having lost his Höchst job teaching religion, Carl had no income. David owed Carl 1,200 RM; David had repaid 100 RM, and his payments for the household laundry, light, and gas counted against the debt. The entire mess, David believed, was because Carl wanted to purchase clothing he deemed necessary for emigrating.

At issue was a vineyard promised to Hede on her wedding and that Carl assumed was now his property. Under the Nazis, David couldn't transfer the vineyard to Hede, and since he couldn't sell the property, there was no money for the Hartogsohns. Regarding a second property that Carl purchased from David, if Carl received less than its value when it sold, David had promised to make up the difference. This, however, could not be put in writing since Jews no longer had the right to acquire property.

"Can't you pull off getting the fellow to England or somewhere else?" David asked his son. The atmosphere in the household, according to Bertha, was "not very rosy." The Rübs stayed mostly in their small bedroom and ate alone.

Old jealousies resurfaced. "I regret," Emil wrote Carl, "that you haven't received something that really should belong to me. For I planted the new vines, for years in the greatest heat, carried water there every week and sprayed and then developed a hernia. You were often in Guntersblum sleeping sweetly while I was working . . ."

Even worse, Carl broke his promise to look after his in-laws when Emil departed. "Have you no compassion?" Emil asked his brother-in-law, for David had "suffered like Job." "I beg you sincerely and urgently to be good to my parents as your common plight now requires. Otherwise, I have no peace, which I very much need to move forward."

If Carl did not respond by return post, Emil would no longer consider him his brother-in-law; furthermore, Emil would ask Uncle Emil Schloesser to withdraw the affidavits for the Hartogsohns' American visas. He would work harder and eat less to send his parents money to pay Carl. "Please," he ended, "do me the favor and be a good person! Be kind to the old people who have lost everything; don't let them also lose their daughter."

Carl replied in two angry typewritten pages. David's unfulfilled promises—to pay a furniture bill for the newlyweds, to give Carl and Hede wine and the vineyard—made David a liar. Carl had taken in his in-laws and helped David collect debts owed him; as thanks, Carl claimed, he received only lies. If Emil wished to have Carl and Hede's affidavits withdrawn, so be it. The only one Emil hurt was his sister. Carl would emigrate on his own and then Emil would discover the countermeasures Carl would take against him. "I will never allow my rights to be taken from me," Carl pronounced. "I require that your father apologizes to me." If Emil sent monthly payments, however, Carl would consider the matter closed.

David pronounced Carl an uncultured person and said they would never live again under the same roof. Although Carl behaved badly, calling David a blackguard and raving like a maniac, David requested Emil not impose sanctions that might cause problems for Hede. "Don't be mad at Hede," Bertha begged, "for she sits, so to say, on two chairs." The Seilerstrasse situation deteriorated further. Bertha and David stayed out of Carl's way and ate alone in the kitchen. David refused to congratulate Carl on his July 27 birthday.

Emil didn't answer Carl's letter, deciding that his brother-in-law was mentally and physically unwell. He would repay Carl, but once the debt was paid, Hede and Carl would cease to exist for him. When Emil felt threatened or insulted, he withheld from anyone who offended him and made threats he didn't necessarily intend to fulfill. "Look how you have made me suffer," was his message. His anger became poison, hurting primarily himself. Underneath the anger, however, was pain, in this instance over how Carl was treating his parents and the fact that Emil could do so little to help them.

Was the uproar in the Seilerstrasse apartment really about money, or was it a sign of nerves on edge? With so much hostility outside, why didn't the two families hold together? How could Emil even consider withdrawing the lifeline of an affidavit so desperately needed? Carl's behavior to his in-laws was incomprehensible, but Emil's threat to have the Hartogsohns' affidavits withdrawn was inflammatory and added to the tension.

David continued corresponding with "Fraulein Bickel" regarding the immigration papers, birth certificates, medical certificates, and photos for England. Documents had to be retrieved; there was an error in David's birth certificate; the Rübs needed a doctor's certificate confirming they had no mental or physical handicap. David wanted Dr. Huhn from Guntersblum to provide their medical information, unaware that Dr. Huhn himself had had surgery, thereby creating another delay. "We have the greatest interest in expediting the matter," David assured Deta.

Hede also wrote to Deta. Could Deta find a guarantor for her since Carl already had an English sponsor? Otherwise Hede would wait in Germany for her American visa number to come up. In June, Hede wrote again: the guarantee for Carl, supposedly arranged through his brother Hartog in England, did not exist. Could Deta do something? "I heard today that with a guarantee of 100 pounds one could get a trainee post in a store selling electric appliances."

This amount, almost $2,000 today, seemed far out of reach, but, willing to do anything for Emil's family, Deta contacted a London acquaintance. Finding trainee positions for immigrants was becoming more difficult, the acquaintance answered, but he would help "the gentleman in question" to get into a small or midsize furniture factory. He included a form to be completed and returned. In mid-July, a grateful Carl sent the completed forms to Deta, along with a thank-you note from Hede.

In May, the German Jewish Aid Committee informed the Hills it might take years before the Rübs could leave England for the United States. This information was new to them, Mrs. Hill said, but "our signatures on the form still hold good in spite of that." She alerted Deta to a change in regulations requiring additional documents and regretted it was taking so long. "Pretty soon all babies must have documents," Emil joked, "and five years' detention before they may live in their own homes here in America."

In July, Mrs. Hill had another concern. What if Deta's permit to stay in England was not renewed and she returned home, leaving the Rübs behind without support? As guarantors, the Hills would be obligated to pay for the Rübs' upkeep, which they could not do.

She would never return to Germany, Deta replied; in fact, in September, she planned to go to America. Although neither Deta nor Emil could give a bank guarantee, they promised to pay for the Rübs' travel and living expenses. Deta would always earn more than she needed, and her fiancé, Mr. Rüb, had a good position in America. "You know that I am honest and would never let anyone down, least of all you to whom I owe so much," Deta wrote the Hills. She would be grateful to them her entire life for "helping to get this poor old couple out of Germany." With Deta's clarification in hand, Mrs. Hill signed and mailed the guarantee the same day, July 25.

By the end of July, it appeared that the Rübs could go to England, and Deta to America. After visiting the 1939 World's Fair in New York over the July 4 holiday, Emil cabled Deta to come September 1 for the fair. She should request a visitor's visa at the American consulate to spend her vacation in the New Hampshire White Mountains and emphasize that she had no intention of seeking employment in the United States, was not a refugee, and had an English permit to return to London. Next, she should find a small ship that would dock in Boston; the Red Star Line with only one travel class might be an option. Despite worrying that Deta "might find me so changed that you wish to return," Emil counted on Deta to stay.

The $20 Emil saved by not having to pay his July rent went to Deta, and in two weeks he would send another $20 to help finance her trip. Given the growing risk of war, Deta should not wait for the Rübs to leave Germany; surely an English refugee committee would help them when they reached Great Britain. Emil urgently needed Deta's help and support; he was doing double duty managing the store and supervising the move to a larger locale across the street while Mr. Carter was on vacation. When the students returned in September, his workload would increase even more.

Emil in the Camera Shop darkroom, July 23, 1939.

In August, the residents of the Seilerstrasse apartment made an uneasy truce. Carl still needed £100 to get to England, and, at Hede's request, David asked an uncle in Palestine for the money. Carl now worked as a cantor and religion teacher in Wiesbaden, a thirty-five-minute train ride from Frankfurt, where he commuted daily, sometimes accompanied by Hede.[48] On August 2, 1939, the Immigration Department of the German Jewish Aid Committee in London mailed visas to David and Bertha Rüb, which arrived three days later. Expressing his gratitude to Deta, David wrote, "As soon as we have liquidated everything and have our passports in hand, which should take two to three months, we will come there." He should hear from the British consulate soon. Bertha added: "We will now have an abundance of work till we can get away. Thanking you again, you are warmly greeted from your Bertha Rüb."

---

48. Other than confirmation of Carl's monthly wage from the Wiesbaden Jewish Community, I have been unable to find information about his work there. In May 1939, 1,225 Jews lived in Wiesbaden, compared to 2,600 in 1933. Since 1939, services were held in the partially ruined orthodox synagogue on Friedrichstrasse; the Great Synagogue on Michelsbergstrasse was destroyed on November 10, 1938.

GERMAN JEWISH AID COMMITTEE.
(Immigration Department)

IM/27241

Woburn House,
Upper Woburn Place,
LONDON, W.C.1.

Mrs Elizabeth Bickel,
6 Aberdare Gardens,
London, N.W.6.

2 AUG 1939

Dear Sir/Madam,

     We have pleasure in informing you that we have today posted a Visa Card to:-

       Mr & Mrs David Israel RUEB,
       Frankfurt/Main,
       Seilerstr. 9 pt.,
       GERMANY.

       Yours faithfully,
    GERMAN JEWISH AID COMMITTEE.

IMMIGRATION DEPARTMENT.

ED/S

Confirmation that permits to enter England
were sent to David and Bertha Rüb.

The Rübs still needed a $500 guarantee to enter Great Britain, money neither they nor Emil had. For Jews, obtaining a passport was no small matter; David would have to obtain a tax-clearance certificate proving he did not owe any taxes and that he had paid the Reich Flight Tax. Once in England, where would the Rübs go? Emil hoped housing could be found for them in a London suburb.

On August 23, Emil would turn thirty-three, his first birthday away from home. Bertha was sad she would not bake the usual birthday cake nor congratulate her son in person. "I wish you good fortune in your new homeland," she wrote, "all the very best a mother can wish for her child." In September, Emil would have been away one year; Bertha expected that with the Rübs' high immigration number, it would take another four years before they could join him.

Along with his birthday wishes, David advised his son to eat some meat, "even if it is only two or three times a week, because I can tell you from experience what it is like to be completely without meat as for almost three quarters of a year we haven't eaten any. We are overjoyed with the permit, and I will now go to the consulate."

On August 27, 1939, a blue sky summer day, Emil and Lotte spread out a blanket at a nearby Hanover lake. Cousin Lotte had come from New York for Emil's birthday. Mrs. Williams, Emil's landlady, drove them to the lake and would return later to pick them up. Emil was in good spirits because, as he told Lotte over a picnic lunch, Deta would come soon. After lunch, Lotte stretched out on the blanket to read, and Emil started a letter to Deta: "Now I wait for the end of the European crisis and then your cable informing me of your arrival or at least the fact that you have received an American or Canadian visa." He had already cabled her: "Carter's letter of invitation will leave tomorrow STOP Think there will be no war."

"I think that the situation in Europe will resolve itself," Mr. Carter wrote Deta the next day, and therefore she wouldn't have to postpone her trip. This, however, was not the case. Hitler insisted that Danzig and the Polish Corridor be returned to Germany, and Europe, the *New York Times* reported on August 28, was "on the knife edge between war and peace." On September 1, 1939, the *New York Times* headline read: "German Army Attacks Poland; Cities Bombed, Port Blockaded; Danzig Is Accepted into Reich." Two days later, on September 3, Britain and France, having promised to aid Poland if Germany invaded, declared war on Germany. Emil and Mr. Carter had miscalculated; Europe was again at war.

❋ HANOVER, NEW HAMPSHIRE

With the invasion of Poland, the winds unleashed when Hitler came to power were now ferocious storms. These storms destroyed millions of lives and scattered survivors to the ends of the earth. The trauma of these events continues, transmitted to next generations. How different my life might have been without those storms.

17. IN ENGLAND (FALL 1939)

*O*n Sunday morning, September 3, Deta walked on the beach in Folkestone, a seaside town in southeastern England. It was a clear day, and she could see across the Dover Strait almost all the way to France. Until then, Folkestone had been full of visitors enjoying their summer holiday and the good weather. Today there were fewer people.

Deta ignored the view, her thoughts crisscrossing with concerns. How was little Susan? The child had cried bitterly when Deta left. Would Deta's four brothers be called up to fight? With Britain declaring war on Germany, Deta felt anxious and unsteady. Would the war prevent her from joining Emil?

Suddenly air-raid sirens sounded. Deta started running back toward Sunshine House, the guest house where she had been staying since the end of August.

"No need to run, luv," an older gentleman waved at her. "Probably a false alarm." Indeed, Radar Defense had picked up an unidentified aircraft over the channel.

Deta nodded her thanks, not wanting to reveal her German accent. Still, she felt safer returning to Sunshine House.

Deta was in Folkestone for a much-needed vacation, courtesy of the Marx family. She had spent several sleepless nights nursing Susan through a childhood illness and was exhausted. A grateful Mrs. Marx insisted Deta take time off.

From her small but comfortable room, Deta had written Emil, "The peace and quiet is therapeutic, but also sometimes unbearable. I feel well when I am by the sea and it is high tide; the more restless the sea, the more beautiful it is." If only Emil were with her.

Deta knew firsthand that war meant loss, hunger, and disruption. Should she have heeded her mother's request to return? No, she thought, she had made the right decision; Germany was no longer home. She would inquire about her parents and siblings through the International Red Cross. In the twenty-five words the Red Cross allowed on their inquiry form, she wrote, "I am well, please let me hear from you, am worried." That afternoon she cabled Emil: "Keep calm I am alright."

From Hanover, Emil reminded Deta that they were fortunate not to be "sitting in that hell." Those who had tormented them would have to pay the consequences. "But that the few good people over there and all on the English-French side have to risk their lives for such lunacy causes me much grief." Hopefully his parents could still get to England and Deta could cross the Atlantic. He was glad Deta was out of London and asked her to stay away from a city unless absolutely necessary. Half of a Deta, he joked, was of no use to him.

Joking aside, had Emil asked Mr. Carter to issue Deta's invitation four weeks earlier, Deta might have been with him by then. That she was still in England was because of his indecisiveness, and Emil blamed himself. In normal times, blaming oneself might have been reasonable. But circumstances were not normal, and the outbreak of war caused the change in Deta's plans.

That Deta wasn't coming in September made Emil long for her even more. At thirty-three years old, he wanted marriage, sexual intimacy, and a life companion. The negatives Deta had sent, for his eyes only, were a poor substitute. When he was alone in the darkroom, he enlarged one or two of the negatives, but when he reached out to touch her, she was not there. Certain that each passing day shortened their wait, he promised he would do everything possible to bring her to him.

Safe from Nazi oppression and doing better financially, Emil saw challenges ahead. To support his parents once they arrived, he would need more income. More income depended on improving the Camera Shop's profitability, which required working longer days and staying healthy. If the Camera Shop showed a loss or went under, there would be no pay increase and even worse, no job. In fact, Mr. Carter later admitted he had considered closing the store.

Emil saw himself as the linchpin for the store's viability. It was his expertise and ideas that brought customers in the door. To increase profitability, he needed to spend less time in the basement darkroom and more time with customers. He also needed the calm and stability Deta offered him and her help in the store's daily operations. Besides his own survival, he juggled multiple obligations—to his parents, to Deta, and to the store. Which should come first? Which ball deserved priority?

After six months at the Camera Shop, Emil began to question whether he really had a future in the business. He speculated that for Mr. Carter, who had other resources, the store was just a hobby. Mr. Carter, a decent but stubborn person, liked to play the boss but was not a good businessman and occasionally forgot to pay Emil's weekly salary. Would Emil be better off starting his own business as an independent photographer and photofinisher? He certainly did not want to compete with Mr. Carter and wouldn't resign without talking with him first.

By early November Emil's work situation improved. Mr. Carter increased his pay to $20 a week and agreed to let

Emil participate in the success and profit of the business. As long as Emil stayed in Hanover, Mr. Carter wanted him to consider the Camera Shop his headquarters. The pressure on Emil to secure his job was, for the moment, alleviated.

Now, new worries arose. With Britain at war with Germany, how would the British treat Deta? And if it took too long to bring Deta to Hanover, would she give up on him?

The day after Britain declared war on Germany, Home Office Secretary John Anderson announced a review of all Germans and Austrians to determine their loyalty. By September 28, under Home Office guidance, tribunals were set up throughout England. A tribunal was an administrative body, not a court of law, to identify who might be a security risk. The tribunal issued three classifications: "A" for a high security risk resulting in immediate internment, "B" for someone suspicious who would be subject to extra restrictions, and "C" for a person considered safe and therefore exempt from restrictions and internment. The proceedings were closed to the public, and the applicant was not allowed a lawyer. In the fall of 1939 only those sympathetic to their home country's war goals or considered dangerous or disreputable were interned, not refugees from Nazi persecution.

Deta was summoned by a tribunal in Midhurst, Sussex where she and little Susan were staying at the time. Of this experience, Deta reported, "I was asked many questions, all of which I could answer well and with certainty." A cable from Emil and a letter from her previous employer Mr. Hill, now working for the War Office, verified her statements. In her tailored suit, dark hair neatly coifed, Deta confidently answered the tribunal's questions in her accented English. "No," she said clearly, "I don't support Hitler. I have never supported Hitler. My fiancé is a Jew."

The tribunal concurred that Deta was not a danger to the security of Great Britain and on October 30 classified her as "C: Exempted internment until further notice." They did, however, withhold Deta's registration book[49] for two weeks and restricted her to within five miles of London. Beyond five miles, she needed to apply for a travel permit. Since she rarely left London, this limitation did not bother her. The only travel Deta wanted was to Emil in the United States.

By early November, Deta and Susan returned to London. "London is as if dead," she told Emil. "One sees almost no children as they have almost all been evacuated. One doesn't go out at night because [with the blackout] it is almost impossible to find one's way home and it is very dangerous. Cars and busses have very little light so that one can hardly see which bus to take to get home. London is just black. I don't think that planes will come to London in this darkness. Perhaps we are safer here than in the country."

"I long for you so," Emil wrote Deta as the days got shorter and darker, "for your wonderful soul and your beautiful body." At night, he covered himself with the dressing gown Deta had given him, the only way he could hold Deta close. "Oh, Detalein, may you be here very soon."

---

49. Immigration in Britain was tightly controlled. The immigrant had to report to the police within three months of arriving to receive a registration book. A change of residence had to be reported within forty-eight hours.

18. IN GERMANY (FALL 1939)

On September 3, 1939, Bertha had news for her son: "Yesterday morning we were eating in our room. Carl entered, apologized, and extended his hand. We accepted it out of love for Hede." Had the atmosphere at Seilerstrasse 9 improved? With Germany at war, was Carl seeking peace inside the apartment? David doubted his son-in-law had changed and begged Emil to find Carl a job. The £100 an uncle had promised, the guarantee Carl needed for England, had not materialized.

With the war, Jews suffered more restrictions. Correspondence to the United States had to be mailed from the post office; letters were censored, and criticism of the regime was prohibited. What Emil's parents could and did say was that they needed money. Although Carl now had an income—he earned 189 RM a month ($1,200 today) from the Wiesbaden Jewish Community, he did not contribute to their joint household, perhaps because David owed him money. Since August, no "books" had come, neither from Deta nor from the uncle in New York through whom Emil sent money. On October 10 Bertha's only reference to the war was that they could no longer "receive anything from E," meaning that neither mail nor money from Deta were forthcoming.

Starting September 1, Jews could not be out after eight in the evening in the winter, nine in the summer. Jews were forbidden to attend theaters, concerts, or movies, to use hotels or sleeper cars, or to visit parks. Food rationing, imposed August 28 on all Germans, was particularly harsh for Jews. Ration cards would soon be stamped with a "J" to further segregate Jews from "pure-blooded" Germans. *"Es kann den deutschen Volksgenossen nicht zugemutet werden, zusammen mit Juden auf Abfertigung zu warten oder anzustehen"*: "German citizens," decreed the authorities, "should not be expected to wait or stand in line with Jews."[50]

Former Guntersblumer Ludwig Liebmann, in Frankfurt to obtain an Italian transit visa, spent two days with the Rübs and visited all "G'blumer Frankfurter." He found the Rübs in good health but circumstances "very bad for the Frankfurt Jews":

> *Available food on ration cards is less rather than more and other than their rationed share of food, Jews obtain hardly anything else, although one can obtain a few items through clandestine trade with Jews who sell at sinful prices. There are Jews who peddle wares at unaffordable prices. Whomever is caught doing so—whether the seller or the buyer—will never get out of jail.*
>
> *In Frankfurt there is especially bad antisemitism . . . with all authorities and official offices. There Jews are harassed for the slightest matter. . . . Above all, Jews must buy food in the assigned store, which must have an extra small room only for Jews, and they can only buy there at specific times. Still living in Frankfurt are about 15,000 Jews, and for them*

---

50. Wolfgang Wippermann, *Das Leben in Frankfurt zur NS-Zeit*, Frankfurt am Main (1986, p. 131).

perhaps 10 or 12 food stores are assigned. One must stand for hours to get something. The baker and the butcher in particular are assigned. One must often stand for four to five hours to obtain the ration cards, which are also distributed separately for Jews. It is all a hassle. Clothing, shoes, stockings, and so forth are completely barred for Jews. Besides the 8:00 p.m. curfew, everyone has his own burden, some greater than others, be it with the Devisenstelle [Foreign Exchange Office], the finance ministry, or with some other authority.

These details reached Emil only after Ludwig Liebmann arrived in New York in February 1940. Such a letter could not have been mailed from Germany. Yet all the while, Bertha wrote, "We are glad to hear that you are well and say the same for ourselves." Was this true? Were they really all right, or were Bertha and David afraid to say otherwise?

With the Rübs consistently writing, "We are still waiting for news from you," Emil suspected that some of his letters were not getting through. At least Emil's telegram, sent September 25 for David's sixty-first birthday, arrived despite the caveat from the Western Union telegraph office: "Accepted subject to war conditions [in] country of destination." Emil also wrote to Deta's parents, offering to forward mail from them to her, but received no reply.

In October, David and Bertha were alone in their apartment; Hede and Carl were in Wiesbaden for four weeks, presumably for the Jewish holidays. Bertha would be glad when the Hartogsohns returned to Seilerstrasse. She needed Hede's help obtaining ration cards and standing in line for food.

From the Jewish aid organization, David learned that Chile might be the only option to emigrate. The cost, however, was prohibitive: $1,000 for two people. In the meantime, the curfew curtailed their going out and their social life: "With the exception of the known firms [code for people they knew], our correspondence is now very small. . . . Guntersblumers meet seldom. For today, warmest greetings, Papa. If we could only leave now, no matter where." The Rübs were becoming more isolated and more desperate.

Hede and Carl expected to be called to the American consulate in Stuttgart in February or March 1940. "Dear Emil, how wonderful it would be if we could see each other soon," wrote Bertha, reminding him to ask their Gimbel relative in Chicago for help. This Emil did, without success.

With his increased wages, in November Emil wired money to his parents and every three to four weeks sent $6 or $7. He still worried that if the Camera Shop failed, he would be out of a job. It wasn't that he didn't trust Mr. Carter. After living in Nazi Germany, Emil knew that circumstances could change from one moment to the next. For this reason, he used his money to purchase photographic equipment in case he needed to start on his own.

Money order from Emil to his parents, which they received in December.

In New York, newly arriving Jewish refugees—a former Seilerstrasse neighbor and a distant cousin—brought messages from the Rübs. Jews had an especially hard time obtaining food, they reported. With England closed to them, couldn't David and Bertha go somewhere else? Could Emil find a job for Carl as a plumber or a cantor? The Seilerstrasse household would appreciate butter, coffee, cocoa, chocolate, and smoked meat (the last strictly kosher), which could be sent by Kurt Werner & Company via Rotterdam. The Rübs were in good health but had received no news from Emil since November 20, 1939, and, outside of the sum from the Dresdner Bank in December, no money from Emil since early November.

The Rübs needed to emigrate by spring, for, as David stated: "[W]e receive no financial support here at all, and without any, it is truly an art to muddle through because since mid-September, I pay all household expenses alone. It has come down to asking for help, which was summarily refused without any grounds." He does not state to whom he applied for assistance.

Emil had thought his "Hanover arrival" would be a turning point; by the end of 1939 Deta would be in his arms and his parents safely in England. The outbreak of war cancelled these hopes. He did, however, have a new strategy for reuniting with Deta: she would apply to a three-year nursing course at the Mary Hitchcock Memorial Hospital in Hanover. If the nursing school accepted her, Deta might join him in February 1940. Dr. Syvertsen, Medical School dean, Camera Shop customer, mentor, and person of influence, would shepherd Deta's application through the process. Emil sent Deta the Hitchcock Hospital application. With an updated invitation from Mr. Carter, Emil would appeal to Washington to issue Deta a visitor's visa through September 1, 1940. In the meantime, Deta should explore obtaining a visa from the Canadian consulate.

The war, with its blackouts and noise restrictions, put a damper on New Year's Eve celebrations in Europe. In Hanover, Emil joined the Silvermans in raising a glass to Emil's family and to "the young lady in England." At Seilerstrasse 9 parterre, other than being alive, there was little to celebrate. Frankfurt was cold, foretelling an arctic winter, and the future looked grim. At the time of year when families lit candles together, the candlelight did little to dispel the growing darkness, and the distance separating Emil, Deta, and Emil's family couldn't have been greater.

❈ HANOVER, NEW HAMPSHIRE

In December 1970, I joined my fiancé at his parents' house in Lima, Peru, where I planned to stay. To telephone my parents in the United States on Christmas (we celebrated both Jewish and Christian holidays in our home), I had to place a request with the phone company. When the call finally got through and my mother answered, I suddenly felt terribly homesick. This was my first Christmas away from home. But unlike my father in 1939, I could speak to my parents and hear their voices, and for those few moments on the telephone, I felt close and connected to them again. That was a comfort my father didn't have.

19. EVERYONE IS WAITING
(JANUARY–JUNE 1940)

"Ich will warten, warten, und warten auf Dich
[I will wait, wait, and wait for you] even
if it lasts very long until I'll have you."
—EMIL TO DETA, MARCH 25, 1940

*E*arly on Monday morning, March 11, 1940, Mr. Carter called down to the darkroom over the intercom, "Emil, please pick up the phone. You have a call."

Emil exited the darkroom, drying his hands. Who could be calling him so early? It was Mrs. Carter, with an invitation for drinks that afternoon. "Please come at six o'clock," Mrs. Carter asked Emil. "The Silvermans will be here too."

"What is the occasion?" Emil asked politely.

"We want to celebrate the one-year anniversary of your arrival in Hanover."

"But I arrived on March 12, and today is the eleventh," he said, a bit confused.

"Emil, it's leap year," Mrs. Carter replied, "which is why we chose today to celebrate."

Surprised, Emil thanked Mrs. Carter and returned to work. It was good of the Carters to remember a date so meaningful to him. Despite their differences, Emil liked and got along with his boss. Mrs. Carter, who often invited him for a meal, reminded him of his mother, and the Carters' three children were attached to him. Alice, the oldest, would sometimes sit next to him in the darkroom when he developed pictures. Thanks to the Carters and the Camera Shop job, Emil felt he belonged in Hanover.

That evening at the Carters' house, Emil was the center of attention. Mr. Carter poured everyone a glass of wine and raised his glass for a toast. "Emil," he began when he got the guests' attention, "it was a good wind that blew you to Hanover. You have a done a lot for the Camera Shop, and we are lucky to have you. Here's to future years with you."

"Hear, hear," said Professor and Mrs. Silverman and raised their glasses.

"And to recognize your many contributions to the store, we have something for you," Mrs. Carter said, and she presented Emil with a new tripod.

It was a lovely evening, with Emil staying on for dinner at the Carters. Emil appreciated their recognition, something he had not often received from his father. As he walked home, however, he couldn't help thinking that the nicest tripod did not compensate for Deta's absence. Without her, he felt incomplete and alone.

With the war in Europe, letters now took several weeks to cross the Atlantic. Emil's New Year's Day letter to his parents arrived January 27, almost a month late. The Rübs wrote every ten to fourteen days, and David began numbering their letters so Emil could gauge whether mail from Seilerstrasse was getting through. Two letters from Deta, mailed December 8 and 12 respectively, reached him January 6, 1940. "If only the papers would arrive!" Emil exclaimed, frustrated by the delay in Deta's Hitchcock Hospital application. "The European situation becomes ever more serious, and I want to have you here beforehand and stroke your breast."

Deta's application and recommendations reached Hanover on January 23, but Emil still needed evidence of Deta's schooling and hospital work. Deta quickly posted her two state diplomas, three references, and a copy of her birth certificate. Dr. Syvertsen would personally present Deta's situation to the New Hampshire State Commission of Education and to his friend at the Hitchcock Hospital. "I implored him," Emil wrote Deta, "to expedite the matter."

Now the application had to run its course, and Emil and Deta had to wait. And waiting, Emil noted, was hard. Waiting meant being dependent on people who didn't know them and on systems regulated by rules; it made the person waiting feel they had no agency or control. "Oh, these bureaucrats, Detalein," Emil complained, "they make my life terribly difficult. . . . It also takes time, nerves, and grey hair."

Despite his complaints, Emil was hopeful. "As difficult as everything is," he encouraged Deta, "somehow it will work out." And then, smiling, he wrote, "I kiss your eyes and caress your _____. Guess what it is and write me!" There was also news to make Deta smile; they had received their first wedding present—a watercolor from Mr. Ellis, an American painter who gave the painting to Emil as a goodbye gift when he moved out of Emil's rooming house.

In another matter, Emil was successful. He had written Deta's parents in the fall of 1939, offering to forward mail from them to her, hoping to surprise Deta at Christmas with news of her family. The Bickels could not contact her directly because England and Germany were at war. But Deta's parents had not replied. Their silence, he assumed, was because corresponding with an expatriated German Jew could be dangerous for them. Nonetheless, three weeks after Christmas, a carefully worded letter arrived from Deta's father, Jakob Bickel. To protect his identity, he signed as Jakob Heppenheimer [Jakob of Heppenheim]; Heppenheim was where the Bickels now lived. Perhaps one of Deta's siblings wrote for her father, because the handwriting is not Jakob's. The letter, which Emil forwarded to Deta, read:

> *"Frankfurt, 8 January 1940. Esteemed Sir, both your letters received. Please convey belatedly [to Deta] our most sincere Christmas and New Year's wishes, and best wishes for the future. So far we are all still healthy and, given the current circumstances, are doing well. Hopefully this is also the case there [Deta in England]. Many thanks for your effort."*

Deta also heard from her parents through the Red Cross, in response to her September 1939 inquiry. On January 29, 1940, Jakob Bickel wrote: "Dear Elisabeth! Parents, sisters, and Friedrich are still well. Oscar, Alfred, and Ernst [are well] considering actual circumstances. Rike [Deta's sister Friederike] wrote from Frankfurt. Trust in God. Warm greetings! Parents." Deta was reassured. Friedrich, Deta's eldest brother and a World War I veteran, had not been called up, presumably because of his age and injuries from the previous war. Whether her three remaining brothers, Oscar, Alfred, and Ernst, were drafted was unclear, but at least they were alive.

In London, Deta moved resolutely through her days, looking after little Susan and helping in the Marx household. She hid her disappointment about not joining Emil the previous September and trusted he would do everything he could for their reunion. Some days were harder than others, and then her emotions would rush to the surface.

Deta and baby Susan in London.

This happened when she accompanied Dr. and Mrs. Schwartz from Worms to the train station in London. In 1935 Deta had cared for their only child, Walter. During her time with the Schwartz family, Emil occasionally took Deta and five-year-old Walter for a drive. It was Walter who had said, "There seems to be something wrong with you," from the back seat of the car when Deta and Emil embraced and kissed.

A year after Deta left the Schwartz family, Walter came down with appendicitis. The appendicitis was not diagnosed in time, and the little boy died on June 30, 1936. Had she been caring for him, Deta was certain Walter would have survived.

Seeing Walter's parents brought back memories of the boy and outings in Emil's car, Emil's London visit in 1938, and

Photos mailed to Deta
February 20, 1940.

his departure from the same train station. Dr. Schwartz, a Jewish dentist, could no longer practice in Germany and was emigrating to America with his wife. If only Deta could have travelled with them! Their willingness to carry a small package for Emil did not alleviate her sadness, and she wept as she watched their train depart.

Emil begged Deta not to lose patience. He regretted she would not celebrate her birthday in his arms: ". . . and the birthday kiss I want to give you sounds like paper." Once reunited, he would show her "the thousand beautiful things I love in New York and in New England which will be our new *Heimat*." "Everything I do," he insisted, "how I live, how I try to progress, is under the motto to have you here soon, very soon."

Deta's letters were also replete with dreams of reuniting with Emil: "I come to you in spirit and am completely your Detalein."

Perhaps Deta could travel to Bermuda and wait there until Emil brought her to the United States as his wife. "Unless Miss Bickel's proposed journey to Bermuda is one of urgent necessity," the British Foreign Office informed Emil, "it is unlikely the authorities in Bermuda would permit her to enter." And even if Deta entered Bermuda, Emil could not marry her there because as an alien United States resident, he would not have permission to re-enter the United States.

Emil would have to wait three and a half years, till 1943, to apply for American citizenship, which would be a definite improvement over his status as a stateless refugee. On May 10, the name "Rüb, Emil Daniel Israel" would appear in the German state press organ, *Deutscher Reichsanzeiger und Preussischer Staatsanzeiger*, announcing that, along with 114 other emigrants, his German citizenship had been revoked.[51]

In Frankfurt it was cold and damp, with snow on the ground. Jews no longer received ration cards for clothes and couldn't obtain shoes or other leather goods. But Bertha worried it was colder in New Hampshire and wondered whether Emil had warm underclothes.

Like Emil and Deta, the residents of Seilerstrasse parterre were also waiting—for news from Emil and for a way to exit the country. The Rübs were discouraged that their emigration plans had come to nothing. David, who had contacted the Jewish community organization for employment, hadn't found work and received no welfare support; since December 1939, no money arrived from abroad. The house in Guntersblum still hadn't sold. Emil's parents urged him to ask friends and relatives in New York to lend the money for Hede's ship passage. "So concern yourself a little about Hede, do it for her and us," wrote Bertha, who wanted to see her daughter safe.

Maintaining they were healthy despite an occasional cold, David mentioned that if a farmer requested him, the United States might accept him as a farmer and winegrower. He already had written confirmation from the Guntersblum *Bürgermeister* that he had worked in agriculture and as a vintner. "Couldn't you arrange for one of your acquaintances with a farm to ask Papa to come?" Bertha asked.

Since the Rübs and the Hartogsohns had been a joint household for over a year, David queried the American

51. Information and copy of original page from the *Deutsche Reichsanzeiger und Preussischer Staatsanzeiger* No. 108, May 10, 1940, provided by the late Fritz Neubauer, Bielefeld, Germany.

consulate in Stuttgart about traveling on the Hartogsohns' visa. With their lower quota number, Hede and Carl expected to be called any day to the consulate to receive their American visa. Unfortunately, the consulate answered, neither age nor living in a joint household made a difference; they would not issue an appointment before an applicant's visa number came up. The Rübs would have to wait.

The residents of Seilerstrasse 9 parterre depended heavily on the food packages Emil sent. In late April, a package arrived from Holland with half a pound of tea, half a pound of coffee, half a pound of cocoa, one can of milk, one jar of *Marinaden* (probably marinated herring), and two pounds of butter, all much appreciated luxuries. The tea, Bertha noted, tasted excellent.

That year, 1940, the Rübs were alone for the Passover Seder; Hede and Carl were in Wiesbaden. "Imagine," Bertha wrote her son, "as I opened the Haggadah, your picture fell out and so you were also here." How depressing this usually joyous holiday must have been for David and Bertha, alone in their apartment. Emil's photo falling out of the Haggadah was a glimmer of light in their sadness.

Try as he might, Emil could do little for his parents. The Rübs were trapped in Nazi Germany by the war, by their lack of passports and money, by their high American quota number, and by the United States' restrictive immigration policy.[52] Deta's parents, Emil assured her, were "definitely better off than my parents, whom despite my best efforts I cannot help."

On April 9 the German Wehrmacht invaded Norway and Denmark and, on May 10 entered Belgium, Luxembourg,

---

52. Jews escaping Nazi persecution did not receive priority. At the time the United States had an immigration policy but no refugee policy. For more information on antisemitism in the U.S. State Department and on the Stuttgart American Consulate, see Michael Dobbs, *The Unwanted: America, Auschwitz, and a Village Caught In Between* (Alfred A. Knopf, New York, 2019).

and the Netherlands. Miraculously another package arrived at Seilerstrasse 9, presumably also from Holland, with a can of small sausages, one cheese, a half–pound of coffee, half a pound of tea, and two pounds of butter. With the invasion of Holland, it was doubtful that any more packages would arrive. To supplement their diet, David planted vegetables in the small garden behind their apartment building. Calling it a garden was exaggerated; the space was no bigger than a small border in their Guntersblum backyard.

On May 21, Hede and Carl travelled to Stuttgart for their visa appointment at the American consulate. Their trip was successful: their American visas, valid until September 21, 1940, were approved, and the Hartogsohns could be in the United States by August or September. Now they needed money for their ship passages and to decide whether to travel via Russia, Italy, or Portugal. "Emil, see what you can do, who could help with this," Bertha pleaded, "and if there is no other way, then only for one person." Carl sent greetings, and Hede wrote, "To a healthy and speedy reunion." When the Hartogsohns left, the Seilerstrasse apartment would be larger than what David and Bertha needed or could afford. They would either rent the two empty rooms or move to a smaller place.

With the Wehrmacht overrunning the continent, Emil appreciated that he and Deta were safe and had each other. He imagined Deta arriving by ship, meeting her at the pier, and then driving her through the city and bringing her into a little room where they would be completely alone together. "How happy I will be with your sounds of pleasure . . . and how I will always stay with you." This fantasy he wrote on a little piece of blue paper with instructions for Deta to read when she was alone.

Hede and Carl anticipated their departure, but Emil and Deta's plans were stymied. On June 5, 1940, the Mary

Hitchcock Memorial Hospital School of Nursing denied Deta's application. Worse news was en route from England. On May 28 Deta's employer, Mrs. Grete Marx, wrote. "Dear Mr. Rüb, I am very sorry to tell you that Elisabeth has been interned yesterday. We will do what we can for her. I hope it is only temporary. I let you know immediately if I get some news. These times are too awful. I am so sorry to write such bad news."

20. ISLAND INTERNMENT,

PART 1 (1940)

"Alien Arrests Net Women in Britain;
3,500 Germans and Austrians Seized
for Internment on Isle of Man."
—NEW YORK TIMES, MAY 28, 1940

On Friday, May 30, 1940, shortly before 11:30 in the morning, the crew of a large steamer prepared to dock at Douglas, capital of the Isle of Man. The ship had left Liverpool at 6:30 a.m., in view of the Liver Tower visible to mariners returning to the harbor. At this time of year, the Steam Packet ferries usually carried happy vacationers anticipating their seashore holiday. Today the passengers were 1,308 women and 155 children; the previous evening, the same boat transported 1,281 women and 104 children. None of them chose this journey, and they were nervous about what awaited them. One of the women was Deta.

Three days earlier, in the early morning, two police officers knocked at 6 Aberdare Gardens in London. "We have an order to detain Miss Elisabeth Bickel," one officer said, "and she must come with us." The knock on the door was repeated throughout Britain. Although over three thousand German and Austrian men had been arrested on May 12 (and in June, Carl Hartogsohn's brother[53] and Emil's uncle Rabbi Moritz David[54]), there had been no warning that women and children would also be detained.

Britain's so-called phony war against Germany was now a real war, with England on the defensive. On May 13, having invaded the Netherlands, Belgium, and Luxembourg, the German Wehrmacht crossed into France. On May 19 the head of the British expeditionary force in France requested permission of newly installed Prime Minister Winston Churchill to withdraw to Dunkirk in northern France. German troops were in Calais, twenty miles across the Channel from Dover, positioned, it was feared, for an imminent invasion of Great Britain.

If Germany invaded, how would the seventy thousand foreign nationals living in England respond? It was assumed that a person's first allegiance was to their country of birth; a citizen of an enemy country was, therefore, a threat to national security. Even worse, a "fifth column" within the United Kingdom might deploy spies and commit acts of sabotage. "Fifth column," a term originating in the recent Spanish Civil War, referred to clandestine foreign agents intent on undermining a country's security. That fifty-five thousand of these foreign nationals had themselves fled the Nazis was irrelevant. With the German army so close, the British government had neither the time nor the inclination to distinguish between Nazis and Jewish refugees, or between Hitler supporters and anti-fascists. "If parachute landings

---

53. Naphtali Hartog Hartogsohn, detained in England June 11, 1940, transported to Canada on July 7 and interned at the Refugee Camp at Ile aux Noix in Quebec, Canada. Released in the fall of 1943, he spent the rest of his life in Canada.
54. Rabbi Moritz David, interned on June 26, 1940, transported on July 10 to Australia, returned to England October 6, 1942.

were attempted and fierce fighting attendant upon them followed," Churchill explained to the House of Commons, "these unfortunate people would be far better out of the way, for their own sakes as well as ours."

On May 27, as English boats of all sizes evacuated British soldiers from Dunkirk, the Home Secretary declared German and Austrian women enemy aliens and ordered their arrest and detention. With a stroke of a pen, Deta was reclassified from "C"—exempted from internment—to "B"—subject to arrest and internment. This order brought the police officers to the Marx's front door and was the reason Deta had to pack quickly under the watchful eyes of a policewoman.

"Bring warm clothes and only what you can carry in your suitcase," the policewoman advised.

"Where am I going? How long must I stay there?" asked Deta.

"I'm sorry, but I don't know," the policewoman answered.

Twenty minutes later, the officers escorted Deta to their car. "Please tell Emil," Deta called over her shoulder to Mrs. Marx as she went out the door.

Deta's internment upset Emil more than her rejection from the Mary Hitchcock Nursing School. Convinced her detention was his fault, he pictured her in a concentration camp with bad conditions and poor food. He cabled Mrs. Marx to do whatever she could for Deta.

In shock, Deta didn't at first appreciate the irony of her predicament. Germany considered her a criminal because she loved a Jew. In Great Britain, now at war with Germany, Deta's German passport made her an enemy.

The police officers took Deta to a holding center, one of several throughout London, where she joined other women detainees, many with young children. Some women were stunned. A few cried. Others laughed and made conversation. From the holding center, the women were brought to

Euston Station, where they boarded a train for Liverpool. A policewoman sat in each compartment and the doors were locked, the sound of the train doors slamming shut echoing through the station.

Women detainees boarding a train in London on their way to be interned on the Isle of Man; source: used with permission from the Imperial War Museum.

Arriving in Liverpool three hours later, the detainees were taken to the Liverpool sports arena, where women volunteers offered them a hot drink and a meal. Deta spent two nights in the arena, an uncomfortable accommodation. From there, she was bussed with the women and children to the docks to board the ferry. Fortunately, the Irish Sea was calm that day, and Deta, prone to seasickness, managed the four-hour crossing without incident.

As the ferry approached the shore, the Isle of Man cliffs and hills visible, Deta wondered what lay ahead. Would she be locked up in a prison or in a concentration camp? Disembarking with the other women, Deta saw that first came formalities. She stood in line for the local police to check her registration book. Then she joined a second line to be photographed while her information was entered onto an Isle of Man National Registration Identity Card. "Look straight at the camera," the photographer instructed. The photo shows a dazed thirty-one-year-old woman with circles under her eyes.

Deta's Registration Card; Source: Manx National Heritage Archives, Isle of Man.

Next, Deta and the internees, carrying their luggage, went on foot to the redbrick Victorian train station, a five-minute walk from the docks. There they boarded what one internee dubbed "this charming little toy railway,"[55] a narrow-gauge train pulled by a steam engine. They were again locked in their compartments.

The train traveled past rolling green meadows separated by stone walls where sheep, lambs, cows, and horses grazed in the fields. Gorse, a shrub with yellow flowers, was everywhere. After a fifty-minute ride, the train arrived at Port Erin, a seaside village of a thousand inhabitants in the southwest

---

55. Maxine Schwarz Seller, *We Built up our Lives: Education and Community among Jewish Refugees Interned by Britain in World War II* (Westport, CT: Greenwood Press, 2001) p.88.

corner of the island. Port Erin claimed it was "the gem of the Golden West" and "the prettiest little seaside resort in the British Isles." Along with nearby Port St. Mary, Port Erin was now Camp Rushen, internment camp for women.

Deta was directed to the Belle Vue Hotel, a short walk from the station. As she turned the corner from the station, did she notice the view of the sea, dazzling in the early evening light? Or was she simply too overwhelmed to care? Port Erin was three hundred miles closer to the United States than London, but as a detainee, disoriented and helpless, Deta felt even further away from Emil.

The Belle Vue Hotel, Deta's new home, was up a hill, near the top of the Promenade in a row of similar Edwardian hotels. Facing west, the hotels offered a view of the sun setting in the center of a horseshoe-shaped bay below. On a clear day, one could see the Mourne Mountains in Ireland.

1937 Advertisement for the Belle Vue Hotel;
Source: Manx National Heritage, Isle of Man.

The Belle Vue, "the Rendezvous of all that is fashionable and one of the best-appointed Hotels on the Island" (1937 advertisement), had 135 bedrooms with hot and cold water,

14 bathrooms, and shower baths at the back of the building. Until the outbreak of the war, its raison d'être was to provide comfort for summer guests.

Because the women arrived on short notice, the camp staff had little time to prepare. The women had to share rooms, and, just as the government overlooked the distinction between persecuted and persecutors, so Nazis and fascists were billeted with socialists, communists, and Jews, in some cases not only in the same hotel but sometimes in the same bed. It took time to rectify these mistakes. Fortunately, Deta's roommate was not a Nazi.

Camp Rushen was demarcated by barbed wire, but within the barbed wire, until the eight o'clock curfew, Deta was free to move. The locals resented so many German-speaking women in their midst. The shopkeepers, however, anticipated new customers, and hotel and boarding house owners appreciated the Home Office payments for the internees' food and lodging, which partially offset the lost income from summer guests.

At the Belle Vue, the detainees cared for their rooms and kept the hotel clean according to a roster of housekeeping assignments. Deta was assigned to the dishwashing brigade, which she didn't mind; work would take her mind off her situation. The hotel offered three meals: breakfast (8:30 a.m.), lunch (1:00 p.m.), and tea, the term used for supper, (6:00 p.m.). The menu included stew, porridge, sausage, scrambled eggs, and tapioca—the lack of variety the internees' only complaint.

The summer of 1940 was hot, allowing for days of swimming and sunbathing. Deta joined the other internees for walks in the fields and along the seashore. Until the locals complained, the detainees could go to the Bradda Head with its small tower, a Port Erin landmark. From there, one had a panoramic view of the town, the bay, and the sea.

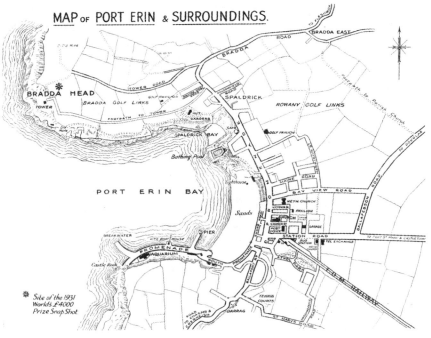

Map of Port Erin.

The camaraderie among the women helped Deta adjust to her new surroundings. She missed Susan, whom she loved as her own, and wistfully asked Mrs. Marx to send the little girl to her. This, of course, Mrs. Marx couldn't do. Reminding Deta that Emil was doing all he could for her, Mrs. Marx encouraged her to "think you are now on holiday and make the best of it."

Deta's greatest support was Emil's letters, typed mostly in English so the censor wouldn't retain them. "I shall write you every week in the future," Emil wrote, "until I am able to whisper everything into your little ear. (I hope the censor likes to read this.)" Sometimes Emil enclosed a handwritten love note in German: "O Detalein, I see your little face before me now, I kiss your black eyes, and you say, 'Stay here!'"

Emil threw himself into campaigning for Deta's release. His weapon was a typewriter; his aides-de-camp were Dartmouth professors who provided references, his adjutants sympathetic college students who helped him with his English. Believing that writers had influence, on June 9 he wrote to Carl Zuckmayer, the playwright and screenwriter who was born about ten miles north of Guntersblum. Zuckmayer and his family had fled the Nazis and, helped by journalist Dorothy Thompson[56], came to the United States in 1939. "Please see these lines as nothing more than a desperate attempt to bring my fiancée here," Emil begged Zuckmayer. "Don't think that a time of mass murder rules out helping an individual."

Zuckmayer responded quickly. "Be assured that I would gladly do everything within my power to be helpful." But, he explained, Dorothy Thompson, who had aided the Zuckmayer family when they arrived in New York, was overburdened with urgent, life-and-death requests, and she requested he stop bringing individual situations to her; she already had dozens of applications for which she needed to use all her influence. Zuckmayer promised to present Emil's case personally to Miss Ingrid Warburg, director of the Emergency Rescue Committee (ERC). This committee focused on getting Jewish intellectuals and artists out of occupied France. (If Zuckmayer had followed through, the ERC surely would have replied that Deta's case was not urgent and not part of the ERC mission.)

On June 17, Emil wrote to the playwright George Bernard Shaw, explaining Deta's situation and their relationship: "She is non-Jewish (*arisch*) and this means that the Jews, except those who know her, will not trust her, the English cannot trust her, the Germans would punish her, and the Americans are overscrupulous about receiving her." Should Deta fall into

---

56. Dorothy Thompson (1893–1961), American journalist and broadcaster, head of the *New York Post* Berlin Bureau until expelled by Hitler, in 1939 recognized by *TIME* magazine as being as influential as Eleanor Roosevelt.

German hands, she would be imprisoned for her relationship with him, for working in a Jewish household, and for not registering with the German consulate in London.

Postcard to Emil Rueb from George Bernard Shaw, postmarked July 3, 1940.

George Bernard Shaw regretted he could not be helpful: "I am afraid I can do nothing; for though I am doubtless persona grata in some official quarters I am very much the reverse in others; and my interference might do more harm than good."

On July 21, Emil wrote to Erika Mann, actress, writer, activist, and eldest daughter of Thomas Mann, but Miss Mann's priority was helping those in danger still in France. Emil tried again in August, pleading that though Deta was not a writer, painter, or an orchestra conductor, she was a special person worth saving. This time Miss Mann's representative replied: Miss Mann would be abroad until November.

On July 10, 1940, the German Luftwaffe made its first air raid over the Channel off the southern coast of England. The English Under-Secretary for War accurately predicted this might be the beginning of an even greater attack. Fortunately, the Isle of Man, known primarily for an international motorcycle road race, was not a strategic target, and Deta was safer there than she would have been in London.

Deta and Emil wrote each other weekly, but censorship of Camp Rushen incoming and outgoing correspondence delayed mail even longer. When Deta didn't hear from Emil, she worried that he had changed and was tired of waiting for her. "I have not changed a bit," Emil reassured her. "Sometimes I think I've just left you and now I'll meet you again and take you for a ride in the good old Brennabor [the Rübs' car in Guntersblum]." If Deta couldn't cross the Atlantic, Emil would "take one of the first ships going over after the war is over and marry you in England."

Emil sent this photo, dated Aug. 5, 1940, to Deta. On the back
he wrote, "I hope the censor is kind enough not to keep it."

Once the novelty of their surroundings wore off, the
Camp Rushen internees faced the lack of meaningful activity.
They needed to keep busy, especially since their stay might
be lengthy. The women accepted this challenge and by
September began offering classes and lectures to each other.
Those with a talent or a skill shared their knowledge with
others. In the mornings, Deta worked at the Hydro, the
hotel next to the Belle Vue that housed a hospital for the
internees. She took English and elocution classes, learned to
play bridge, and knit an intricate navy-blue sweater. For her
elocution classes, she kept a notebook in which she copied
sentences such as, "All works well in the waterworks"; "It
is very windy at this window"; "Work goes on when the
bombers swarm overhead."

Inside cover of Deta's Camp Rushen notebook 1940.
The Isle of Man is located in the Irish Sea, northwest of Liverpool.

Emil was certain that an influential person could prevail against the restrictions keeping him and Deta apart. He
believed their cause was just, and that rules and regulations,
although slow-moving, were "still subject if only a little to
human encouragement." All it took was finding the right
person, perhaps "a fine American lady" with friends in high
places, who would cut through red tape, and then the mail
would bring a letter announcing Deta was on her way.[57]

A fine American lady of influence did materialize. She
was Madeline Shaw[58], Dorothy Thompson's personal secretary, who often travelled with her employer and spent time at
Miss Thompson's summer home in Barnard, Vermont. How
Emil met Miss Shaw is unknown; perhaps she came to the
Camera Shop on an errand for her employer. What matters is
that Miss Shaw became Emil's conduit to Dorothy Thompson,
who sent two cables to the Home Office about Deta. Surely
Miss Thompson's intervention would have a positive outcome
because she was, Emil explained to Deta, "such a famous lady
that the English officials cannot say no again."

Seeing newspaper reports that English children were being
evacuated to Canada, in June Emil asked the London Home
Office if Deta might accompany them as a children's nurse.
The Home Office replied that only British subjects escorted
the children.[59] Emil wrote the Home Office again, enclosing a

57. Emil's belief in the power of influence was not naïve. American relief worker
Varian Fry, who helped artists and intellectuals escape Vichy France, wrote a
friend ". . . about the only way to get a visa for anybody now, is to get some very
important influential person to bring pressure on the State Department." Michael
Dobbs, *The Unwanted: America, Auschwitz, and a Village Caught in Between*
(New York, Albert Knopf, 2019, p. 219).

58. Madeline Shaw (1917–2002) worked for Dorothy Thompson in the late 1930s and
the 1940s. She must have been extremely busy; by 1937, Ms. Thompson had 10 million
readers a day and received up to 700 requests a week for speaking engagements. Miss
Shaw's prompt replies to Emil were consistently supportive and kind.

59. On September 18, 1940, the *SS City of Benares* transporting 406 passengers,
among them ninety child evacuees, was torpedoed and sunk by a German
submarine. Seventy-seven children died. The disaster ended the evacuation plans
of the British Children's Overseas Reception Board.

reference from Professor Harold Tobin, head of the Dartmouth College political science department, that Emil was "a useful and valuable resident" of Hanover. Should Deta have "permission to proceed to the United States and all arrangements have been made for her to do so," the Home Office answered, "the question of her release will be at once considered."

"I start all kinds of attempts," Emil explained to Deta in August, "receive denials, start anew." Would his Highness the Duke of Windsor, Governor of the Bahamas, "be willing to exert his influence in my favor?" Emil asked in September. Government House replied on September 12 that his Highness, although sympathetic to Emil's case, was unable to help "in the manner in which you suggest."

Emil campaigned relentlessly for Deta; networking, advocating, and telling their story to anyone who would listen were his strategies. Could he marry Deta by proxy? No, Washington clarified, this was not a valid route to a visa. In mid-October, he contacted the writer Sherwood Anderson, who forwarded Emil's letter to the YWCA's National Board Committee on Refugees. Since Deta was Christian, this organization referred her case to the American Committee for Christian Refugees in New York.

"Does an individual have the right, in the midst of the chaos [of current events], to seek his own modest good fortune?" Emil asked a German acquaintance. In the Rüb family, personal needs were considered secondary to the needs of others. Was it acceptable to think of marrying Deta while Europe was falling apart? Emil concluded that, this time, the answer was yes. If the Camera Shop was the route to his daily bread, he needed Deta to feed his soul—a need so strong it blinded him to reality. Compared to his parents' plight and that of Jews, socialists, communists, and ordinary citizens in Great Britain and Europe, the danger to Deta on the Isle of Man was far lower. Nevertheless, Emil focused on Deta.

21. ISLAND INTERNMENT,

PART 2 (1940)

Toward the end of summer 1940 the British Home Office revised its position on the enemy alien internees. Perhaps the threat of a fifth column had been exaggerated. On July 31 the Home Office published a report listing eighteen categories under which one could apply for release. Jews released from a German concentration camp were clearly fleeing persecution, and there were internees with talents and skills that could aid the war effort. With this mindset, the government organized tribunals in Douglas to review individual cases.

Deta certainly had no interest in overthrowing the British government. The only flag she carried was for Emil. She considered committing to a year's farm work in the Dominican Republic as a way to cross the Atlantic, but Emil thought farm work would be too difficult for her. Cuba might be a possibility, although visas had to be purchased and were costly.

Port Erin's breezy summer gave way to autumn rain, fog, and gray. Darkness came early, sunrise late, and there were days of high wind and bitter cold. In December, the wind on the Promenade was so strong that people had to hold onto railings built along the wall or the street to avoid being knocked down. On such days, the Belle Vue residents stayed indoors. Coal was scarce, and the cold was an issue. The internees were given two extra blankets, and the Belle Vue received an additional sum to heat the lounges and living areas.

Winter evenings were long and trying. Because their bedrooms were unheated, the internees stayed downstairs in the lounge until nine thirty, the women competing for a seat around two fires. A hot-water bottle was de rigueur for bed, as a poem in Deta's notebook attested:

> *Gehst des Abends du zur Ruh,*
> *Stelle dich an in eine queue,*
> *fuell' dir deine Bottel heiss*
> *Dann schmitzt selbst das dickste Eis!*

> When you go to bed at night,
> In a queue stand in line,
> Fill your [hot-water] bottle so hot
> That it would melt the thickest ice.

To amuse themselves, the women created entertainments. The more creative poked fun at their circumstances in mixed German English lyrics to the tune of familiar melodies. Deta did not perform the songs because she could not hold a tune, but with her dry sense of humor, she helped invent the lyrics and copied them in her notebook.

Internees with musical talent offered evening concerts. One program at the Belle Vue featured three musicians performing vocal and instrumental music by Corelli, Handel, Mozart, Mendelssohn, and Strauss. Another evening, a contralto sang Schubert Lieder. The first song *"An die Musik"* ("To Music") touched Deta's heart:

"Du holde Kunst, in wieviel grauen Stunden,"
O hallowed Art, how often, when depression
and life's wild circle had ensnared my space,
have you aroused my heart to love's compassion,
have you removed me to a better place!

The internees contended with uncertainty, monotony, and cold, but these difficulties were nothing compared to what Londoners endured. Starting September 7, 1940, the German Luftwaffe bombed London fifty-six out of fifty-seven nights. Over one million London houses were destroyed or damaged in the Blitz, and more than forty thousand civilians were killed.

Without news from her employers, Deta worried about Susan. Mrs. Marx explained her silence in a letter dated November 4. They had had "a terrible time in London and no . . . rest at all. Air raids the whole day and nights, and you know what it is to stay all day inside with a little child. . . . We had two bombs on our house, one oil bomb and one incendiary bomb. We had both times a very lucky escape . . . eight weeks we slept in deck chairs in the shelter, and the whole family was very worn out and overtired." The Marx family rented a house in Gerrards Cross, nineteen miles outside of London, where they remained for the duration of the war.

On November 11, early in the morning, Deta and seventeen detainees, under guard, boarded a bus.[60] Their destination was the Douglas Courthouse, where they had a 9:45 a.m. hearing. The tribunal would decide whether Deta and her companions would be released or remain on the Isle of Man. The day was cold, with frost on the meadows. The route the bus took ran along the sea, and the yellow-red sun rising over the water seemed a good omen.

---

60. Poem by internee Friedel Breslauer, found with Deta's Isle of Man notebook, about the women's trip to the Douglas Courthouse.

Under the watchful eyes of the policewomen, the detainees were led two by two into the Court House to wait for the daylong hearings to begin. "You will not receive the results of your hearing today," they were told. One by one, each woman was escorted to the courtroom to face a panel of three men. When it was Deta's turn, she stood and answered questions about her loyalty. Mrs. Marx had advised her to say she had left Germany because she was "very, very anti-Nazi." This Deta could do easily. She loved a Jew; how could she possibly be pro-Nazi? Two weeks later, Deta received word that she would be released.

German bombs kept coming. In December, the English cities of Manchester, Liverpool, and Sheffield were hit. On the Atlantic, British cargo ships and eleven ships of an allied convoy were torpedoed and sunk. Britain feared that Hitler would invade in the spring of 1941. One thing was certain: the war would not end soon.

❖ HANOVER, NEW HAMPSHIRE

*I*n May 2008, I spent five days in Port Erin on the Isle of Man. Retracing my mother's journey, I took the train from London's Euston Station to Liverpool, the ferry to Douglas, and, from the same redbrick Victorian station, the narrow-gauge train to Port Erin. There, a kind gentleman pulled my suitcase up the Promenade to the former Belle Vue Hotel, renamed the Port Erin Hotel. From the hotel, there was an expansive view of the bay, the beach, and the sea.

This was my first trip alone after my husband died. Looking out over the water, I struggled with grief and loneliness. My mother was much older when she became a widow. Perhaps her accumulated experiences, including internment, helped her survive widowhood.

How unsettled my mother must have been in May 1940, not really knowing where she belonged. In Port Erin, she was in limbo—far from home, a German who had said no to her country, now under suspicion by the British, longing to make a new home with her Emil.

My mother was a survivor, and I took courage from standing where she had been.

22. THE CLOCK IS TICKING (1940)

*"My dear ones, I thank you for your letter of
16 August and for the birthday wishes expressed.
I congratulate you, dear Papa, also sincerely for
your birthday and wish that you stay healthy
for many years so you can be pleased with my
successes and rest from a difficult life."*
—EMIL TO HIS PARENTS, SEPTEMBER 6, 1940

On Sunday, June 9, 1940, Emil was at the Camera Shop composing letters on the typewriter. To his Uncle Josef Schloesser, he described his current preoccupations: "Hede and Carl have received their visa, and I am compelled to search for passage money for them. Not to do this would be difficult to answer for. That is why my letter today is brief. Elisabeth was recently interned; I am trying everything in my power to bring her over. Lately I have to give my entire energy to the Camera Shop so that it doesn't owe me my salary longer than one or two weeks. I don't know if it would be better to let the store die. Otherwise, I am well."

Now that Hede and Carl had visas, which were valid until September 21, 1940, they needed transportation to the

United States. A telegram dated June 24, 1940, put this squarely in Emil's view: "Received visa—Please urgently have ready ships passage for Carl—regarding Hede notify Schloesser—cable when in order HAPAG [Hamburg America Line]." Despite Bertha's repeated requests that he raise money for the Hartogsohns' Atlantic crossing, Emil had incorrectly assumed that Hede and Carl were lobbying other relatives for their passages.

Why hadn't Hede asked him directly for help? After Carl's behavior toward David and Bertha, did his parents now expect Emil to "cut off a leg" for his sister? Emil needed his family to understand his situation: "From eight thirty in the morning till seven at night I stand in the darkroom, or I run up and down the stairs 150 times to wait on customers. Then I make my supper and write [letters] till midnight. I love my profession; I love my work; I just wish I didn't have a host of worries." With his limited funds, he had some pants refurbished and was saving money to buy his first pair of shoes in America. Once a week, he allowed himself to go to the movies. "Hede and Carl should not lose patience," Emil declared. If someone else could help the Hartogsohns, "it would be a tremendous load off my mind."

Fearing that the Camera Shop could go under and he would have to start over, Emil purchased equipment and was making monthly payments on a new enlarger, even when his wages were sometimes two weeks late. He also set money aside for a second hernia operation. What he saved—and had spent—could have brought one person across the Atlantic. Where was Emil to find the money for two ship fares in the three months before September 21, when the Hartogsohns' visas expired?

A trip to the United States via Russia and Japan, by then the only exit from Europe besides Lisbon, cost between $200 and $300 per person. The Russia portion had to be paid in marks (500 marks) and the ship fare in dollars. Regretting they could not help, the Hebrew Sheltering and Immigrant Aid Society (HIAS) in New York recommended Emil ask his uncle Emil Schloesser for the deposits on the tickets. However, Emil resisted asking, afraid that Uncle Schloesser would withdraw the affidavits of November 1938 that he had given with the expectation that Emil not request financial help. Although Uncle Schloesser had a thriving delicatessen store in Jamaica, Queens, the Schloesser brothers—Josef and Emil—refused to lend Hede money. There was, apparently, some bad blood between Hede and Josef.

Emil considered his situation at the Camera Shop more pressing than transportation for Hede and Carl. He had come to Hanover believing he would eventually participate in the Camera Shop's future as a partner. Mr. Carter had raised Emil's hopes: he would make Emil manager, give him a percentage of the sales, lease the business to Emil. By summer, however, Mr. Carter had not followed through on any of these proposals and in fact hardly spent any time in the store.

Emil was at an impasse. Should he stay in Hanover? Should he go? Should he set himself up independently? The last thing he wanted to do was compete with Mr. Carter. When Mr. Carter came to the store, Emil asked if they could talk.

"What is it, Emil?" Mr. Carter asked. He wasn't in a good mood.

"I wish to discuss my wages with you," Emil said.

"So you want more money," Mr. Carter replied.

"I want to have more of a say in the future of the Camera Shop, as you promised when I was hired. You know I work more hours than what you pay me."

Mr. Carter looked at Emil. He hesitated and then said, "The job isn't worth more than what I pay you."

Emil was silent. He retrieved a few items from his desk and walked out the door. Hurt, angry, his parting words to

Mr. Carter were, "I won't be in next week." He returned to his rooming house and took a nap.

The following day, Emil got up early. He resolved not to enter the store, but he would, as usual, go to the post office to check for mail. He was especially anxious to hear from Deta. On his way uptown that morning, Emil ran into Dr. Syvertsen. "Why aren't you in the darkroom?" Dr. Syvertsen asked, surprised to see him.

"Because I'm on strike," Emil replied.

"You are the last person who can allow himself to be on strike," responded Dr. Syvertsen. "What's going on?"

Emil quickly brought him up to date. "Tell you what," Dr. Syvertsen said thoughtfully, "how about I talk to Carter on your behalf?"

Emil thought for a moment. Dr. Syvertsen was a mentor to him, and Emil trusted him. "Thank you," he said. "Yes, please talk to Mr. Carter. He won't listen to me."

Emil spent the day resting, catching up on his correspondence, and going for a long walk. Walking out of the store was not his usual way of behaving. What if Mr. Carter decided he shouldn't come back? Had he been too impulsive?

That evening, Dr. Syvertsen came to Emil's room. After a long day at the Medical School, he was tired. Stretching out on Emil's sofa, he said, "Well, I talked to Carter this morning. Things don't look as bad as you made out. Carter doesn't want to lose you and is willing to discuss partnership. And he wants you to come to dinner at his house tomorrow."

A dinner invitation was an unusual way to conclude a resignation, but Emil accepted. At dinner the following evening, without resolving the question of partnership, boss and employee agreed to a "cease-fire." And Emil would help photograph the three to four hundred participants of the upcoming American Mathematics Congress at Dartmouth in early September.

Of course, Emil preferred to stay at the Camera Shop. If he built up the Camera Shop, he would make more money and be creditworthy. He would then qualify for a bank loan to pay for overseas passages for Hede and Carl and for his parents. It was a plan built on logical building blocks and on the assumption there was time to implement it. An expired visa, Emil told himself, wasn't a catastrophe. Surely Hede and Carl could reapply later. By then Emil would be in a position to send the money they needed.

By now, Emil knew about the restrictions on Jews in Frankfurt described in Ludwig Liebmann's letter, and as he told an aunt in New York, he had "no illusions how my people are faring. . . . If they could only survive so I could see them again." Yet laser focused on the Camera Shop and doing what he could for Deta, Emil ignored the repeated message from Seilerstrasse that "we have to get out now, before the visas expire."

In July 1940, after months of silence, Hede wrote her brother. "Although you don't want any thanks from us, we thank you for your efforts. We are not at all such terrible people [for you] to not be in good relations with us. I believe that once we are over there, we will understand each other better than ever. But till we get over!"

Hede reported that Carl had taken voice lessons for two years and could be employed as a cantor. "He is well-liked [in the Wiesbaden Jewish community], and everyone loves his voice. You will be amazed when you hear him. Perhaps you can organize an evening recital in Hanover for him. Regarding Orthodoxy, he has greatly changed. He doesn't need to be in an Orthodox congregation." Hede was taking additional training in cooking, had learned to make artificial flowers, and was willing to work as a housekeeper.

As September 21, 1940, neared, Carl wrote, "We want to start our journey as soon as possible; every day is time lost."

Although David and Carl again weren't speaking to each other, David begged Emil to borrow money from the New York relatives for Carl's fare. "It is high time," emphasized David, "and there is no time to lose. So try to do what you can; it would be a shame if the visas expire." If the visas expired, so would the affidavits of support, and there was no certainty Emil Schloesser would provide new affidavits.

Emil tried. He wrote to the refugee committee to find a position for Carl in an Orthodox congregation. Through other relatives, he sought to obtain addresses of persons connected to the Gimbel family, owners of the New York department store. Contacting the Gimbels, the relatives replied, was futile. Others had tried without success.

On September 1, he wrote Uncle Emil Schloesser, "I am sorry enough that at the moment I must use every penny for my operation [hernia] and for taking over the store. Without that, I could contribute something to at least one travel fare. So, the way things stand, I must ask you again for help." If Uncle Emil could provide half the money for the trip, perhaps HIAS would contribute the other half. "But do it soon, for Hede's visa expires on September 21."

Emil faced competing priorities: the Camera Shop, Hede and Carl's emigration, getting Deta released, and his health. To his parents, he explained: "Here at the moment I can't strain the people's goodness, I mean the willingness of the Americans around me to help. I will need them myself shortly, as in a few weeks I will probably take over at my expense the working of the business. . . . The Camera Shop earns a lot of money based on my good reputation while I live more from this honor than from the result of my work. . . . I will do everything to help Hede and Carl at a later time . . . I urgently and sincerely beg for your understanding."

September 21 came and went, and the Hartogsohns' visas expired. Now they had to send another application to the American consulate in Stuttgart, obtain a new affidavit of support from an American relative, and find money for their travel fares. There was little to celebrate during the Jewish holidays in early October. Hede and Carl were "bitterly disappointed"; they thought Emil could help with at least one overseas fare. "A telegram with the invoiced ships passage," Hede wrote, "would probably help make a new visa possible, that is, when the sponsorship is renewed. Do ask about this. Again, all the best!"

But Emil had other concerns. Mr. Carter refused to discuss partnership, and on September 15, Emil left the Camera Shop a second time. "No matter what, this week I will decide what to do," Emil wrote his parents—whether to remain dependent or to begin modestly on his own. "You see, for the time being I am safe from bombs, but the fight for advancement is not easy and takes a lot of energy."

He assured his parents he was confident about his future. His English and his technical knowledge had improved and people treated him well. "Take from this letter," he continued, "the message that on my life's journey I have arrived at a new stage. From the time of my departure from the old homeland till today it has been steadily upwards, so that this time I believe in my own advancement."

"In our thoughts, we are with you," replied David on October 20, 1940, "especially since you have such important decisions to make, and we hope for the best."

By mid-October Emil returned to the store, expecting to reach an agreement with Mr. Carter by the end of the month. "It will be very difficult at first," he alerted his parents, "and require countless hours to keep the ship afloat." A professor offered to lend him around $500, and Emil hoped to earn enough from the business to repay him.

It took until November for Mr. Carter's lawyer to deliver a memorandum of understanding. The agreement was reached with the help of several mentors: Professors Rosenstock-Huessy and Silverman, Dr. Syvertsen, and Mr. Williams in whose home Emil lived when he first arrived. The Camera Shop would now become the Camera Shop of Hanover Inc.

The undersigned declares that the article described on the other side was duly delivered
Le soussigné déclare que l'envoi mentionné d'autre part a été dûment livré

on **29 November**, 19**40**
le

SIGNATURE[1]

Postmark of the office of destination
Timbre du bureau destinataire

of the addressee:
du destinataire

of the agent of the office of destination
de l'agent du bureau destinataire

[1] This receipt must be signed by the addressee, or, if the regulations of the country of destination so provide, by the agent of the office of destination, and returned by the first mail direct to the sender.
Cet avis doit être signé par le destinataire, ou, si les règlements du pays de destination le comportent, par l'agent du bureau destinataire et renvoyé par le premier courrier directement à l'expéditeur.

U.S. GOVERNMENT PRINTING OFFICE   5—11654

Hede's signature on a registered letter delivered November 29, 1940.

Preoccupied with the Camera Shop, Emil still advocated for his sister. On November 29 Hede "Sara" Hartogsohn signed for a registered letter from Emil Rueb. The letter contained new affidavits of support from Uncle Emil Schloesser. "Whether we will have luck with it? . . . We will write when we have an answer from Stuttgart," replied Hede.

"Hopefully it will work this time," wrote David on December 10, 1940. "We will keep you posted."

The Rübs didn't mention the June Royal Air Force (RAF) bombing in Frankfurt nor the nightly air-raid alarms. Listening to the evening radio broadcasts from Berlin, Emil worried about his parents' safety. "I wish that a kind fate will keep you until I can bring you over," he wrote them.

For Emil the holidays were depressing without Deta, still detained on the Isle of Man. Printing Christmas cards for Camera Shop customers kept him so busy that on December 23, his landlady, Mrs. Gerard, had to remind him that the following day was Christmas Eve. (Emil now rented a larger room with his own bath in a rooming house near the Catholic Church, a five-minute walk to the Camera Shop.) On December 24, 1940, on his way to work, Emil stopped at the Hanover Post Office to mail his Christmas letter to Deta. "Let us hope," Emil had written, "this might be the last time we have to celebrate a holiday living in different countries." In the evening he would cable her to say, "All my thinking is with you." Emil's Christmas letter reached Port Erin two months later.

On the evening of December 29, the Germans fire-bombed London, the most devastating air raid of the blitz. In his fireside chat earlier that evening, President Roosevelt spoke about the failure of appeasement, the flaws of isolationism, and the fate of German-occupied countries: "The people of Europe do not ask us to do their fighting. They ask us for the implements of war, the planes, the tanks, the guns, the freighters, which will enable them to fight for their liberty and our security. Emphatically we must get these weapons to them, get them to them in sufficient volume and quickly enough so that we and our children will be saved the agony and suffering of war which others have had to endure. . . . We must be the great arsenal of democracy. For us this is an emergency as serious as war itself."

On December 30, 1940, Emil and Mr. Carter signed an agreement. The Camera Shop was now a corporation. Of the one hundred shares of capital stock, Emil and Mr. Carter each held forty-eight shares, with the remaining four going to Mrs. Muriel Carter. As general manager, Emil would receive a salary of $35 a week. Emil would also pay $41.67 per share into an escrow account for his forty-eight shares and later $2,000 in monthly installments of $75 for Mr. Carter's stock. With a loan from Dartmouth Professor Rosenstock-Hussey, Emil could start purchasing shares.

How proud he was to read that he held "one half interest in stock, fixtures, furniture, machinery, equipment, accounts receivable lists, goodwill, including all the assets and property of every description and the business of the Camera Shop of Hanover Inc. in Hanover, New Hampshire." He was on his way to owning his own business. There was an additional bonus: two hours after signing the Articles of Agreement, Mr. Carter's lawyer brought Emil an affidavit for Deta, a significant step toward her visa. But how much longer would it take for Deta to come to Hanover? And what of the residents at Seilerstrasse 9 parterre and the Hartogsohns' expired visas?

23. UNDER PRESSURE (1941)

Emil's New Year resolutions for 1941, just as in 1940, were to make the Camera Shop profitable, to help his family exit Germany, and to marry Deta. What changed was that each individual goal had become more urgent, requiring focused effort and attention. Handling them one at a time might have been manageable. Together, they created an overwhelming perfect storm.

The formal transfer of Camera Shop ownership was scheduled for February 15, 1941. Afterward Mr. Carter would return to Patterson, New Jersey, and to Wright Aeronautical Corporation, where he had worked before, to be the corporation's liaison with the Air Force. When Mr. Carter left, responsibility for the store would rest entirely on Emil's shoulders.

Becoming part owner of the Camera Shop of Hanover Inc. was a milestone for Emil. In Guntersblum, he had depended on his parents and avoided making commitments, always keeping open what Deta called "a back door." At thirty-four years old, it was high time to set his own course, although he admitted, "It was Hitler, not I, [who] did this job." Had Hitler not come to power, Emil might have still been living at home and working in his father's business. Now he was on his own.

When 1941 began, Deta's whereabouts were unknown to him. Emil had last heard from her before Christmas. Had she been released, or was she still on the Isle of Man? Was she ill—or worse? Just when Emil's anxiety was intolerable, a cable arrived on January 25, 1941: "Arrived Safely in London Elisabeth Bickel"; three letters followed. On January 24, Deta had been released from internment as a "non-refugee" who "did not wish to be repatriated."

In mid-February, Deta took a temporary position with the da Casa family in Bovington, Hertfordshire, in southern England. Mr. da Casa, former agricultural attaché and member of the Spanish diplomatic corps in England, had resigned when General Francisco Franco became dictator of Spain in 1939. Mrs. da Casa was unwell after her youngest child was born, and the baby had some medical problems. When Deta was released from Camp Rushen, Dr. Marx, Mrs. da Casa's obstetrician, offered to "lend" Deta to the da Casas. The da Casas had three children and lived in a Victorian house with a large garden. They were warm and kind, and Deta soon felt at home. Emil was relieved that Deta was out of London.

At Seilerstrasse 9, the Hartogsohns' departure was top priority. "We are all nervous about the ship tickets, and it is the main topic of discussion the entire day," wrote Bertha. Of course, Emil shouldn't pay for the Hartogsohns out of his own pocket, but surely he knew people to ask for a loan. Hede and Carl submitted the new affidavits to the American consulate in Stuttgart, and, once they verified their travel arrangements, they would be called to Stuttgart for their visas. "Can't you ask your acquaintances for one ticket? The visas must not expire again," begged Bertha. It would be lonely when Hede and Carl left. With tickets in hand, they could be gone in six weeks.

Regarding the Camera Shop, David and Bertha congratulated their son on his promotion to general manager and his future as a partner in the business. "In my opinion," wrote David, "you have handled the matter correctly." But Emil's pride in his new status was short-lived. His successes, he told Deta, seemed "so little compared with the fact that I have not succeeded yet to have you here." To his parents, he stated, "If I don't say a lot about myself, it is because I am ashamed that I can't do anything for you, that I am so much better off than you, and that I still can't tell you I have a handsome bank account."

Hoping to expedite Deta's and the Hartogsohns' immigration, Emil went to New York City in early January 1941. At HIAS, where hundreds of people came for help daily, Emil waited over five hours. Unfortunately, the Hartogsohns' file had been misplaced, and the visit yielded no results. In a February 3 follow-up letter to Emil, HIAS explained the file was unavailable because a worker was attending to it.

HIAS enclosed a statement from the Hilfsverein, the Frankfurt Jewish Aid organization: because the Hartogsohns' visas had expired, the American consul declared their initial application documents invalid. The consul required a $5,000 irrevocable trust fund to be established before he would consider the case. Once in the United States, the immigrant would receive "a stipulated amount in monthly installments." This requirement put visas well out of reach.[61] A few days later, two telegrams from the Frankfurt Jewish Aid Agency ratcheted up the Hartogsohns' predicament. A telegram to Emil requested that money for Carl's ship passage be paid to the Joint Emergency Committee for European Jewish Affairs in New York. The other telegram with similar content on Hede's behalf landed with Cousin Erich in New York.

On receipt of his telegram, Cousin Erich contacted the Schloesser brothers. Uncle Emil Schloesser agreed to give

---

61. See Michael Dobbs, *The Unwanted: America, Auschwitz, and a Village Caught in Between*, Alfred A. Knopf, New York, 2019, Chapter Two "Visa Lines," pp. 19–41 and 81–82. It seems some consular employees took advantage of Jewish applicants.

$100 and Josef Schloesser $50; Cousin Erich and his parents, newly arrived from Germany, offered $50. Emil would have to raise the balance—$50 to $100—for Hede. According to Cousin Erich, the consul's request for a $5,000 deposit was madness; one could probably circumvent this requirement by presenting a ship ticket.

```
Schiffskarte Lissabon-New York        $350.- (3. Klasse!)
Eisenbahnfahrt von der deutschen
Grenze bis Lissabon (seit neu-
estem in Devisen zu zahlen!)          120.-      (bisher $42.-)

Portugissische Hafensteuer            20.-     (   "    $ 8.-)
Amerikanische Kopfsteuer               8.-
Kabelspesen der Schiffahrtslinie      10.-
                       Summa:        $508.-
```

Letter from Cousin Erich to Emil (Feb. 23) with a breakdown of travel costs:

$350:   third-class ship ticket from Lisbon to New York
$120:   train ticket from the German border to Lisbon
        paid to the German foreign exchange (a new
        requirement, increased from $42)
$20:   Portuguese Harbor Tax
$8:   American head tax
$10:   Cable expenses
TOTAL: $508

The Schloessers' offers came with assumptions and judgments. The New York relatives assumed that only Hede's passage was required; once Hede was settled and working in the United States, Carl would follow. The judgment was that Emil was letting others wrack their brains for Hede's immigration and did nothing himself. In effect, they said they wanted to see what Hede's next of kin—her brother, Emil—would contribute. Uncle Emil Schloesser demanded that Emil obtain a loan from a loan company. The Schloesser brothers would help, but Emil needed to do his part. Surely by now he had a secure salary and could contribute toward Hede's ticket.

That Emil hadn't done more to help his sister was, according to the New York relatives, a character flaw. "Where there is a will, there is a way," wrote another uncle. "If one has been in this country for two years, then raising $50 for one's sister must be a small thing. . . . One would think you were a native-born American and hadn't experienced anything in Germany. You must know exactly that all our relatives are in constant danger, and I expect that one must do one's all if one wants to save someone."

Note to Emil, perhaps from Cousin Erich, with name and address of the Hebrew Free Loan Society, and the question "Should I go there for you?" This organization, founded in 1897, followed the Torah mandate of interest-free lending. The back of the note says that one can borrow interest-free with a $10 monthly payment required. Only two guarantors are needed. "(Carter, Silvermann (sic), Levy?)" There are no documents showing Emil tried this option.

The family's expectation that Hede would travel first was incorrect. Hede and Carl wished to leave Germany together, which required immediate payment to the American Jewish Joint Distribution Committee of $1,016. This information made Cousin Erich's agreement with the Schloesser brothers obsolete.

At this point, Cousin Erich washed his hands of the matter. He refused to spend time he did not have contacting

HIAS, the National Refugee Service, or the Council of Jewish Women—organizations he claimed were ineffective. According to reports in the *Aufbau*,[62] Erich thought the consulate was now more likely to award visas. Perhaps Emil could find someone in Hanover to contribute. "The life of your sister must be worth the repression of your feelings of revenge" against Uncle Josef, urged Cousin Erich.

Shamed, Emil defended himself. He was repaying loans from relatives, supporting his parents, and purchasing equipment to establish some security for himself. For two years he hadn't eaten breakfast; for weeks he had not received his wages and gone hungry because he did not want to freeload; he sent money to Deta while she was interned. Compared to other immigrants, perhaps he had not accomplished as much, but he was doing his best. Had he not arrived in New York penniless and without his photo equipment, he might have had a faster start and saved more money.

Emil also acted, asking HIAS if they could loan the remaining $250 for one ship passage "to bring out one person who could help afterwards to free the other one." He would immediately pay $10, he informed the uncle who had criticized him, and the additional $40 in monthly installments. HIAS again denied assistance, explaining they did not have money for this purpose, and even if they did, it would be illegal for them to give a loan.

The Seilerstrasse residents were desperate, their desperation exacerbated because Emil's letters arrived so infrequently. "You can imagine that we wait daily for mail from you, especially since we want to know how things are going for you with the store and, besides that, how things stand with Hede's passage," wrote David. "Couldn't you at least raise a portion of the fare from your friends? . . . Do it for us, do your part. . . .

---

62. Founded in New York City in 1934, the *Aufbau* (*Reconstruction*) was a weekly newspaper for German Jewish immigrants with articles in English and German.

We know you don't have the means to afford the fare, but perhaps a couple of your friends could give $50 to $100, which you know is not at all a risk."

While the New York relatives judged him, his parents pleaded, and the Camera Shop required his attention, Emil faced another hernia operation. This problem developed when he first arrived in New York. A truss might have helped, but purchasing one was beyond Emil's means. Climbing up and down the Camera Shop stairs between the basement darkroom and the main floor made the rupture worse, causing great discomfort. As a condition for helping Emil resolve his status at the Camera Shop, Dr. Syvertsen insisted Emil consult a surgeon.

The surgeon recommended surgery, which took place on February 4 with Dr. Syvertsen in attendance, and it went well. Not wanting anyone to worry, Emil informed his family and Deta afterward. He told his parents he was well-treated, had visitors daily, and received flowers, fruit, and letters from those unable to come. He shared a room with a young man whose German grandmother was from Hessen-Cassel. When she visited her grandson, she spoke to Emil in German. She resembled, Emil said, *"die selige Grossmutter"*—Emil's blessed Oma Dina. Other than two postcard greetings from New York family, this was the only touch of home he had while in the hospital. After seventeen days in the hospital and three days resting in his room, Emil was back at the Camera Shop. Mr. Carter, who had postponed his departure, picked him up in the car and brought him to the store every day for two hours.

News of Emil's surgery caught the Seilerstrasse residents by surprise. They regretted not being present to take care of him and hoped he remain healthy to help the business grow and be successful. Emil replied, "I am preparing myself that your [quota] number will come up soon. . . . If the store does well, I will probably then not lack possibilities to obtain money for your trip."

Besides working on the Hartogsohns' transportation, undergoing surgery, and taking over the Camera Shop, Emil pursued a visa for Deta. His previous strategy, that she would come on a tourist or student visa and become a legal resident through marriage, was outdated. Now Deta had to register at the American consulate for the regular quota and wait her turn. Coming outside the quota was impossible; Deta was ineligible for a preferential quota number. For the regular quota, an American citizen had to guarantee Deta's character and confirm that she would be of value to the United States. As a stateless person with only his "first papers" toward citizenship, Emil could not sponsor her. He needed to find a sponsor.

Before going to the HIAS office in New York for the Hartogsohns, Emil visited the American Committee for Christian Refugees and saw Miss Shaw on Deta's behalf, efforts with little result other than moral support. While waiting at the HIAS office, Emil started a letter to Deta. The hope she would come soon gave him strength to "ask people for help I never would have asked before." For a sponsor to guarantee someone they had never met was asking a lot. The sponsor had to show proof of American citizenship, yearly salary, bank accounts, and market value of assets and to swear that the applicant would not become a public charge. Nevertheless, Emil asked.

Emil thought that Deta could come on the regular quota within the year, perhaps even that summer, despite the dangers of crossing the Atlantic and the lack of civilian passenger ships. Bringing Deta from England had to be easier than getting the Hartogsohns out of Germany. In short order he obtained affidavits from several local doctors and a Dartmouth professor. They were good, "so nicely done," Emil wrote Deta on February 3, "that the consul will admit you." He prepared her for questions the American consul might ask: "How many states are in the United Sates? Why don't you like Germany? Do you prefer democracies to dictatorships?"

The transfer of Camera Shop ownership was rescheduled for March 15, 1941. It had been three and a half years since Emil stepped off the SS *Hansa* as a refugee, almost two years since his Hanover arrival. The road he had traveled had many difficulties, and more challenges lay ahead. But now he would survive, for even in the worst month, the business brought in enough for his food and shelter.

Despite his belief to the contrary, Emil did have something to show for himself. On January 2, 1941, Emil signed an affidavit on Deta's behalf as general manager and part owner of the Camera Shop of Hanover with a share in the store's profits. He had "the means to support and maintain Miss Elizabeth Bickel if she were permitted to come to this country" and could guarantee she would not become a public charge. He had earned the respect and trust of professors, doctors, students, and local residents. From Professor Rosenstock-Hussey, he received an unsolicited offer of a $250 interest-free loan toward the Camera Shop partnership and a similar loan later. These were major accomplishments for the modest young man from Guntersblum, personal victories that he had a right to be proud of.

Recovering from surgery and with the Camera Shop on his mind, Emil may have missed the news that leaving Europe via Lisbon was no longer possible. As reported by the *New York Times* on March 15, 1941, "The last remaining regular passenger service on which refugees by the thousands escaped from Europe directly to the United States has been indefinitely closed by an order issued yesterday of the American Export Line." There weren't enough ships to transport the estimated backlog of over ten thousand passengers. How would the Hartogsohns get to the United States now?

❈ HANOVER, NEW HAMPSHIRE

*F*acts I can't avoid: My father failed his sister. He failed his parents, who asked him to help Hede on their behalf. Had my father found the money for his sister and brother-in-law, they might have made it to the United States. But it appears he put more effort into the Camera Shop and Deta's visa than the Hartogsohns' ship passages.

Was holding Deta in his arms more compelling than seeing his sister and brother-in-law again? Why did he believe there was still time to help his family? Why couldn't he hear the pleas from Seilerstrasse?

My father thought he had to make a choice: overseas passage for his sister or partnership in the Camera Shop. In choosing the Camera Shop, he voted for himself and his future. But were the Camera Shop and Hede's passage mutually exclusive? Would he really have strained "the goodness" of his Hanover supporters if he asked to borrow money for the Hartogsohns' travel? The people he met in Hanover were sympathetic to the plight of German Jews. Did he fear that soliciting for Hede and Carl would jeopardize his chance for partnership in the Camera Shop?

Had my father truly understood how bad things were in Germany, would he have acted differently? Was blocking out the dire news from Frankfurt a defense so that he could get up every morning and function?

It is not my place to judge my father but knowing that he didn't help his sister is painful. Sadness and disappointment stay with me along with questions no one is alive to answer.

24. STANDING ALONE
(MARCH–SEPTEMBER 1941)

The Carters' departure from Hanover was a personal loss for Emil. "I had a hell of a time the first week," he informed his former boss. "Business was not good. But much work came in, and I had to run upstairs often." Running up and down stairs after hernia surgery was not ideal, but Emil had no choice. There was much to do: photograph a play at the college, take a passport photo, mix chemicals, copy documents, retouch prints, and undergo a physical for the army ("I couldn't send anybody else," for the physical, he joked). With Mr. Carter gone, Emil needed an assistant. Money was tight, but he paid the February and March rents, and there was $100 in the store account.

Sleep was a luxury. For several nights, Emil worked until three in the morning. During the day he supervised the employees, dealt with delivery men, and sought to obtain credit from suppliers. "It is incredibly difficult," Emil commented, "but [the store] goes slowly and certainly upward."

Some of Emil's lost sleep was due to Deta's visa application, a process full of hurdles. First, the American consulate in London required verification that Emil could support Deta and would marry her when she arrived in the United States. This barrier was cleared in late April when the consulate determined Emil's financial evidence and the affidavit from a supportive Dartmouth professor were satisfactory.

Second, the consulate required proof that Emil had been legally admitted to the United States. This involved having the United States Department of Justice forward Form 575 to the State Department, a step Emil had already completed. Furthermore, on January 24, the Department of Justice had sent Form 575 to the State Department to transmit to the American Consul in London. Why was the consulate still asking for this document?

On May 8, almost four months later, the American consulate in London informed Deta that they had received Form 575 and that she qualified for an immigration visa. Once Deta confirmed steamship passage, her application would receive further consideration. Money was not an issue because Deta had saved enough to pay her own way. The problem now was that no English passenger boats had left England for over two months, and no sailings were scheduled. "But leave it to me," Deta consoled Emil. "I shall try everything to get a passage."

Deta reached out to Mr. da Casa, who, as a former diplomat with connections, contacted the Cunard line on Deta's behalf. Perhaps Deta could get to the United States via Uruguay. Through Mr. da Casa's influence, the manager of the Cunard White Star Line promised Deta a ticket to Montevideo for August. But Deta and Emil were in the land of circular reasoning: no visa without a ticket, no ticket without a visa. How did one exit this roundabout?

At the same time, from Frankfurt, Carl urged Emil to do everything in his power so he and Hede could leave. There was no time for delay. For $450 (almost $7,000 today) they could travel on a freighter in August or September. If, however, Hede and Carl couldn't leave together, they would remain in Frankfurt.

If Emil found him a cantor position, Carl would sing with either organ or harmonium accompaniment, and with his recent vocal training, he could fulfill the standards of any small congregation, Orthodox or Reform. "A few days ago . . . Hede was with me in W. [Wiesbaden]," Carl recounted. "There I sang for an audience of five hundred with, it was said, success."

"I must close," Carl ended his letter, "because in a few hours I must officiate [as a cantor], [and] still need to change and shave, then depart." Carl was fortunate if he had shaving cream; by the end of June, the supply of soap and shaving cream for Jews was discontinued.[63] The welfare department of the Frankfurt Jewish Community maintained a hairdressing site at 8 Seilerstrasse, across the street from where the Rübs and Hartogsohns lived, and offered a dry shave.[64] Did Carl and his father-in-law have to resort to this service?

The letters from Seilerstrasse omitted that beginning March 4, Jews were ordered to work, sometimes under severe conditions, at jobs left vacant by able-bodied men drafted into the Wehrmacht. Jews who weren't called up feared they soon would have to do forced labor. By April, Jews could no longer receive packages from abroad. Most Jews had to move into cramped quarters in so-called *Judenhäuser*, of which there were two on Seilerstrasse. As Jews living in an "Aryan" apartment building, the Rübs feared they were being watched. In August, as people planned how to heat their apartment that winter, Jewish households could buy coal only after "German" households were fully accommodated. Because it was strictly forbidden for coal dealers to deliver to Jews, they would have to obtain their own transport.

---

63. Inge Geiler, *Wie ein Schatten sind unsere Tage: Die Geschichte der Familie Grünbaum* (Schöffling & Co., 2021) p. 150.
64. Geiler, p. 159.

Denunciations of Germans who occasionally helped Jews—a baker or a butcher secretly adding food to a Jew's purchase—were increasing. Shopping hours for Jews were reduced to one hour, from four to five in the afternoon, and their ration cards were more limited than those of other Germans. Jews got less butter, no cocoa or rice; chicken and fish could not be sold to Jews.[65] The Rübs told their son none of this. What they said was, "We are waiting—waiting to hear from you, waiting for Hede and Carl's tickets, waiting for new affidavits, and we need your help now."

There was another development Emil didn't know. In the spring of 1941, the Gestapo required the leadership of the Frankfurt Jewish community to submit a card, in triplicate, listing the members of each Jewish family.[66] Although Jewish community leaders were instructed to deny the ensuing rumors, many thought the lists were for deportations. With the increasing isolation, food scarcity, and fear, the Rübs and Hartogsohns became even more desperate.

Although letters from Frankfurt came less often, the request for help was repeated without letup. Waiting to hear from Emil, sometimes for five or six weeks, was harder to bear as the Seilerstrasse residents needed news about travel money and affidavits. For them, mail was a lifeline. Had Emil written to the relatives Bertha mentioned? Why hadn't he asked his acquaintances and other family members to contribute to Hede and Carl's tickets? Other family and acquaintances received mail and managed to leave—why not them? The letters reiterated the same questions over and over again, as if Emil had not "heard" them, as if he were deaf.

In May, Bertha wrote, "For five weeks we have been awaiting news from you with no result. . . . I now have a lot

---

65. Geiler, p. 108.
66. Wolfgang Wippermann, *Das Leben in Frankfurt zur NS-Zeit: Die nationalsozialistische Judenverfolgung* (W. Kramer & Co. 1968) p. 132.

to do in the household because dear Hede is employed." Was Hede doing forced labor?

On May 26, David pressed, "We have so many relatives and friends that we believe if you go ask them, it has to work. It is really high time that Carl and Hede travel. It would be a personal favor to us; of course, you should not cut your finances in any way, in no circumstances do we want this."

Bertha was more direct. "Dear Emil, I am astonished that you still haven't had our sponsorship renewed. Perhaps you haven't done it yet; we hope that you have finally done it. I also can't understand that you haven't turned to all relatives and friends. We know that you can't provide the passage on your own."

On June 16, 1941, David wrote, "There is still nothing regarding Hede and Carl's ship tickets, and you can well imagine they are beside themselves. Regarding our sponsorship, we want to telegraph Schloesser this week, as we are waiting daily for mail with no results. You can imagine what it is like when one waits daily for mail."

Perhaps Emil wrote, and the letters did not get through. Perhaps he wrote less often because running the Camera Shop took all his time. Through the American Committee for Christian Refugees, Emil hired Mr. Roth, a fifty-year-old Austrian refugee, as a darkroom assistant. By the end of May, however, it was apparent that Mr. Roth did not meet Emil's expectations and had to be discharged. The situation became adversarial: Mr. Roth threatened to hold a client's film to prove Emil's ineptitude as a photographer.

Emil telegraphed the refugee committee: "Regret necessity giving notice Mr. Roth. His presence threatens to ruin my business. Will withstand any amount of criticism necessary to terminate his employment here because of his attempts to discredit me with my clients. Please telegraph Roth to desist otherwise shall be forced have him expelled by police. Letter follows."

In his two-and-a-half-page follow-up letter to the committee, Emil wrote, "Please understand that I am not just a refugee, but a man who worked through two years of difficulties and even hunger to gain this little bit of success and also a reputation—a man who is much ashamed that he had to bother you with this trouble." Left unsaid was that he was a man dependent on the committee for help with Deta's visa.

Terminating Mr. Roth meant more work and less sleep. Tired and lonely, Emil still hoped Deta might come in August or sooner: "Life will begin when you are here." But another barrier arose. On July 2, 1941, Deta cabled Emil that American immigration rules had changed. Applicants with family in Germany would not qualify for a visa, regardless of whether the applicant had transportation to the United States. The American consulate in London informed Deta there was no point in giving her application further consideration. "Can do nothing," Deta cabled, "very depressed." Having been so close, this was a huge setback.

The new regulations were instituted to weed out Axis spies, subversive agents, and propagandists. Apparently, the State Department had discovered cases where close relatives in Germany were held hostage in exchange for information on American defense activities. Yet no information on these cases was publicized.

The new restrictions were not ironclad. According to the American Committee for Christian Refugees, each case would be considered on its merits, and if the State Department decided admission of an applicant was not contrary to public interest, a visa would be granted. Two Washington committees were now working on a backlog of five hundred thousand applicants. As one of these applicants, Deta's case would now be reviewed by representatives from the State, War, and Navy Departments; the FBI; and the Immigration Service of the Justice Department.[67]

"Keep faith," Emil cabled Deta, requesting a list of all her relatives in Germany. Certain that Deta's case had merit, Emil returned with renewed intensity to his letter campaign. Surely the American public's complaints about the new restrictions would influence the State Department to make exceptions.

Knowing that the Nobel Prize–winning author Thomas Mann lived in the United States and actively opposed the Nazis, Emil sent him Deta's "life story" in August. The writer acknowledged Emil's letter a week later from his home in California: "As you know, the conditions under which an American visa can be obtained are very severe at present, and the number of applicants very great. As I have many obligations in this respect, I regret that I cannot help you with your problem."

The State Department sent Emil a new set of application forms, but by now Emil's patience was running out. Why should he spend time completing forms and finding sponsors if the situation were hopeless? Perhaps he should give up the Camera Shop if that was the only way to join Deta. He certainly wouldn't become a soldier for a country that was so unsympathetic to their difficulties.

In July, a recently arrived German cousin in New York wrote Emil: "Hede complains bitterly that you haven't bothered energetically enough that they can emigrate, and I hope that you have tried everything. The circumstances over there are now so acute for us that any day there can be trouble. Everyone is very frightened and upset."

---

67. On July 1, the State Department centralized the processing of visa applications and formed the Interdepartmental Visa Review Committee, here called the visa review committee.

The same month, the German government ordered all United States consulates closed. At the end of October 1941, emigration by Jews for the duration of the war was forbidden. Short of a miracle, the exit door out of Germany was now tightly shut.

❄ HANOVER, NEW HAMPSHIRE

I wish I knew more about Carl's Wiesbaden concert. Did he give a solo recital, or were there other artists? Did he perform "Within these hallowed halls" from Mozart's *The Magic Flute*, one of Sarastro's arias that my father told me Carl used to sing?

At the line about wandering "Cheerful and happy into a better land" ("*Vergnügt und froh ins bess're Land*"), I imagine Carl singing with great feeling. Surely such a land, a place Hede and he desperately wanted to reach, existed far from Nazi Germany.

The aria's last stanza speaks of love and forgiveness. Would Carl and my father have forgiven each other? This is another unanswerable question.

In diesen heil'gen Hallen
Sarastro's aria from *Die Zauberflöte*

In diesen heil'gen Hallen	Within these hallowed halls
Kennt man die Rache nicht.	One knows not revenge.
Und ist ein Mensch gefallen,	And should a person have fallen,
Führt Liebe ihn zur Pflicht.	Love will guide him to duty.
Dann wandelt er an Freundes Hand	Then wanders he on the hand of a friend
Vergnügt und froh ins bess're Land.	Cheerful and happy into a better land.

In diesen heil'gen Mauern,	Within these hallowed walls,
Wo Mensch den Menschen liebt,	Where human loves the human,
Kann kein Verräter lauern,	No traitor can lurk,
Weil man dem Feind vergibt.	Because one forgives the enemy.
Wen solche Lehren nicht erfreun,	Whomever these lessons do not please,
Verdient nicht ein Mensch zu sein.	Deserves not to be a human being.

—Literal translation by Lea F. Frey

Carl and I have music and singing in common. Had things been different, we might have sung together.

25. "EVACUATION"

(NOVEMBER 1941)

Frankfurt, October 7, 1941:
   Letter from the Rübs to their son:

> *"So if not now, hopefully we will*
> *see each other later."*
> —DAVID

> *"Stay healthy, may things go*
> *well for you, think of us."*
> —BERTHA

*S*ummer was ending in Frankfurt. Once the morning fog lifted from the River Main, the early autumn days were often warm and sunny, the sky a rich blue. In September, David's thoughts wandered west, across the Rhine to Guntersblum, to the grapes ripening in vineyards once his. Soon the grape harvest would begin. But David wouldn't oversee the laborers picking the grapes, and Bertha wouldn't make potato soup and *Zwetschgenkuchen* (traditional plum cake) to feed the workers. Neither David nor Bertha participated in the harvests after 1938. Their vineyards, sold below value at forced auction, now belonged to neighbors. Proceeds from the sale went into a locked bank account that the Rübs could not touch.

Beginning September 19 all Jews from the age of six on up were to wear a yellow star. The six-pointed star had to follow exact specifications: palm-size, outlined with black, labeled "Jude," and attached on the left side near the heart. It was to be worn in public and to be visible at all times. The regulation admonished Jews "to always look after their badge with care as well as to wear it in clean condition." (*"Die Juden sind anzuhalten, ihre Kennzeichen stets sorgsam und pfleglich zu behandeln sowie in sauberem Zustand zu tragen."*)[68] Public identification of Jews meant they could be further singled out and victimized.

Did Emil know about this discriminatory practice? An Associated Press report in the *New York Times*, September 7, 1941, page 14, and an article in the September 26 *Aufbau* described the new requirement. But when did Emil have time to read a newspaper? And if he knew, what could he have done?

Over the summer of 1941, few letters from Seilerstrasse reached Hanover, and few were sent from Hanover to Frankfurt. A June 3 registered letter from Emil enclosed a new sponsorship for David and Bertha from Uncle Emil Schloesser. In his June 20 letter, Emil described walking to the Camera Shop at five or six in the morning. David, an early riser, replied on July 17, "I could accompany you every morning since at that time I am also up; Mama gets up around seven, and at that time Hede is already over an hour out of the house." Their emigration, David noted, was at a standstill, his offer to keep Emil company wishful thinking.

For Emil's thirty-fifth birthday in August, David asked that God keep his son healthy and hoped the Camera Shop's future would be successful. Bertha too wished Emil good

---

68. *Dokumente zur Geschichte der Frankfurter Juden* 1933-1945) Verlag Waldemar Kramer, Frankfurt am Main, 1963, p. 435.

health and "for the store, much good luck, all the very best that only a mother can wish. It is already the third birthday that you spend away from us, and I believed that surely for this birthday I would bake the customary birthday cake, but sadly, sadly, that is not the case." That they might have been together had Emil written the people she repeatedly mentioned, had he asked each relative and acquaintance for $50, if Uncle Emil Schloesser had helped financially—Bertha couldn't relinquish these recriminations.

Although the Jewish congregation of Guntersblum had dispersed, David still fulfilled his responsibility as *Vorsteher*. On September 24, 1941, Franziska Mayer, formerly of Guntersblum, died in Frankfurt. The following day, David presented himself at the Frankfurt civil registry and, after verifying his identity with his *Kennkarte* (official ID), registered the death. The death certificate was issued with his signature—David Israel Rüb.

On October 3, answering Deta's question about his parents and Hede, Emil replied, "I think and hope they are well." Emil was preoccupied with the Camera Shop and the difficulty of obtaining chemicals and paper for printing photos. The same day, David confirmed that Emil's September 22 birthday cable for David's sixty-third birthday had arrived. "For your good wishes I thank you sincerely, and we shall hope they come true."

"On October 11, we are moving," David added. "Unfortunately, I can't give you the new address yet; still write to the old address until you have our new address. I will give the post forwarding information. Isidors moved yesterday, also to one room." Were "Isidors" Georgine and Isidor Wolf from Guntersblum? Formerly living at Liebigstrasse 50 in Frankfurt, Georgine and Isidor Wolf moved to a *Judenhaus*, an apartment building where Jewish residents were concentrated. Were the Rübs and Hartogsohns also being evicted to a *Judenhaus*? David does not say.

"I can tell you that we are, thank God, still well," David reassured Emil, the "still" a deviation from David's usual statement that, "Thank God, we are well and hope the same for you." Did "still" mean that despite everything—hunger, fear, moving without knowing where, needing to dispose of their belongings, they were alive? How could the Rübs and the Hartogsohns be "still well" under such conditions? Perhaps, understanding the pressures on his son, David didn't want him to worry. "Our care and good wishes are always with you," David continued. "I am also convinced you are doing what is in your power to bring us or at least Hede and Carl over there."

"Hede is mostly not at home," he continued, "so dear Mama must manage the household, which is extremely complicated, and I help as much as possible." David now did the shopping. Keeping a kosher household when there were no Jewish butchers was impossible but also irrelevant since the Seilerstrasse residents hadn't eaten meat since Emil's last food package. Perhaps the "complication" was the difficulty of obtaining food during the single hour the shops designated for Jews were open. Mention of Hede brought David back to his main point: "I can assure you it would be advisable if at least Hede and Carl could leave." There was no mention of Carl's activities. Given the tighter restrictions on mobility and the imposition of forced labor on able-bodied Jews, Carl presumably no longer commuted to Wiesbaden's remaining Jewish community.

If the store were not profitable, David had counseled in August, Emil should not "bleed to death there" and as best as possible divest and start smaller on his own. In his October letter, however, David moderated this advice: "My last letter was not meant as a reproach, only as an admonition, since from here I can't form any opinions. Besides, today you are old enough to know what is best for you. It was just my idea viewing the matter from here."

David hadn't learned bookbinding as he had hoped; he lacked money for the training and was behind paying rent. "You write about a helper—wife—and for that I also have understanding," David continued, "though we thought you would first have a secure livelihood, and besides we hoped to be there and believed that it would still work out with Lotte [Emil's cousin]." Did David still wish that Emil would marry Lotte? Might he accept a Gentile wife as a daughter-in-law? Emil longed for his father's blessing and approval.

Unlike David, who seemed reconciled to facts he couldn't change, Bertha was angry. "Dear Emil, unfortunately I have to contradict you. In your letter you write that for our emigration you have made an effort for all of us. You haven't written to a single address that I gave you. . . . I don't know why you have concerned yourself so little. Every son and brother would do this. . . . I must urgently beg you to write to all, but please immediately. . . . Can't your boss do something for us? We now have a fine job here: moving. You have been over there for three years. Hopefully, you won't let us wait so long for an answer. You know that one always longs for that. . . . So stay healthy, be warmly greeted and kissed from your Mama."

Emil did write, and his letter reached Seilerstrasse on November 4. The store had grown, he reported, and, in his November 7 reply, David hoped the income had grown accordingly. The Rübs had sent Emil a telegram, but whether Emil received it is unknown. From David's letter, however, it is clear the telegram confirmed that the Rübs were moving. "I already figured," David stated, "that before the war ends, that it [emigrating] was futile." Indeed, as of October 23, 1941, the Nazis had forbidden further emigration. Should Emil renew his efforts for their emigration, David cautioned, "Don't do anything rash, and don't pay anything in advance until I telegraph agreement. So if not now, hopefully we will see each other later. . . . I still can't give you our new address. Let us hear from you soon, and for today be warmly greeted from your Papa."

"My dear Emil," added Bertha on November 7, "in haste I want to write you a few lines. You will have received the telegram. We thought given our circumstances the relatives would do something for us, the way so many relatives now do. . . . Stay healthy, may things go well for you, think of us. Be well for today and be greeted and kissed from your Mama."

At the end of his note, David had written, "More next time." But there was no next time. The hastily written letter of November 7 that Emil received a month later was the last communication from his parents.

The Seilerstrasse residents surely knew that on Sunday, October 19, the Nazis had carried out the first deportation of Jews from Frankfurt.[69] That day, between six and seven in the morning, the SA entered Jewish residences in Frankfurt's West End and gave the inhabitants two hours to pack some belongings. Each person had to wear a cardboard sign with their name, date of birth, and identity card number. An eight-page declaration listing all property and valuables had to be completed. The family then had to wait for an official to escort them to the collection point. There would be severe penalties, they were warned, if orders were not followed to the letter. On October 20, 1941, 1,078 Jews were transported from Frankfurt to the Lodz ghetto in Poland, among them Isidor and Georgine Wolf from Guntersblum.

Starting the deportations in the West End was deliberate. The West End was a prestigious section of Frankfurt, and the Nazis had their eye on the accommodations of remaining Jews. There was also the need to house "Aryan" Germans who had become homeless due to RAF bombings. However,

---

69. Monica Kingreen, *Nach der Kristallnacht: Jüdisches Leben und antijüdische Politik in Frankfurt am Main* 1938–1945) Campus Verlag, Frankfurt, 1999) pp 358–361.

the larger rationale for the deportation, formulated as official policy at the Wannsee Conference in January 1942, was "the final solution of the Jewish question in Europe," a euphemism for genocide.[70]

On November 7, the date of their last letter to Emil, the Rübs and the Hartogsohns received written notice they were being "evacuated" in three days, with no mention of their destination. As required by the Gestapo, the leadership of the Frankfurt Jewish community selected the names for the November 11 deportation. Initially planned for November 2, the Gestapo postponed this second deportation, presumably influenced by protests from armament factories not wanting to lose their Jewish forced laborers.

The form letter began, "Sir/Madam/Miss: By order of the authorities we inform you that as of November 11, forenoon at eight o'clock you are to be prepared to leave your residence and hereby hand you the declaration of property to be completed. With the completion of the property declaration, your entire assets are seized. . . . You are especially forbidden to give away, sell, or entrust any objects found in your possession."

According to the instructions, each person was allowed to bring no more than 50 reichsmarks. Valuables were not allowed, and, other than a wedding ring, gold and silver items were forbidden. Warm clothes and sturdy shoes were strongly recommended. Allowed luggage was a small hand suitcase or backpack containing only the most necessary items: a food bag or handbag with travel provisions for three days along with eating utensils, but no knife, and a drinking cup.

The need to pack and to complete the property declaration explained the brevity of the Rübs' last letters. Violating orders, they and the Hartogsohns entrusted valued possessions to neighbors and acquaintances for safekeeping until their return. Among these items were a small wooden box

---

70. Transcript of the Wannsee Conference, 1942.

containing Hede's costume jewelry, monogrammed linen (perhaps from Bertha's trousseau), some silver, a small bronze figure, a book, and Hede's two photo albums. There were also a few gramophone records of Hebrew songs, a brass candleholder (possibly a menorah), and two small boxes of Emil's glass plate negatives and film. Remaining jewelry and objects of value were entrusted to a young woman, a friend of the Hartogsohns, who often visited. There was also a small amount of cash—750 reichsmarks (about $45, or $690 or so today). To a neighbor who assisted with packing and had been helpful to them, the Rübs and Hartogsohns left the contents of their cellar storage area as thanks. Before their departure, Hede visited their upstairs neighbor, who noticed Hede showed signs of being pregnant. "Even if I survive," Hede told her, "I shall never put my foot on American soil because my brother did nothing for us."[71]

Some of the Jews scheduled for the November 11 deportation chose suicide. Despite feeling that the world had given up on them, both the Rüb and the Hartogsohn families had been clinging to life and to hope. But those hopes—for the Rübs to join their son, for the Hartogsohns to start a family in America—disappeared into the gray and damp of November 11, 1941.

When the time came, David, Bertha, Hede, and Carl were composed, leaving the Seilerstrasse building, their home for the past two and a half years, as a crowd looked on from the street.[72] Each wore a cardboard identification sign around the neck, making sure the sign didn't cover the yellow star. Suitcases in hand, they walked under police guard, in procession with other evicted Jews. Their destination was the Grossmarkthalle, the city's main wholesale market for fruit and vegetables on the right bank of the Main, a twenty- to

---

71. As reported to Emil in 1954 by an upstairs Seilerstrasse resident who thought Hede was pregnant.
72. Ibid.

thirty-minute walk. As Jews were forbidden to use public transportation, taking the streetcar was out of the question. Crowds gathered along the way. Some yelled insults; others stood in silence.

The Grossmarkthalle, built in 1928, was the largest building of its time in Frankfurt and served the city and the entire Rhein-Main region. It had two eight-story wings at either end, one housing offices and storage areas for wholesalers and shipping companies, the other containing additional stalls and cold storage rooms. Next to the south side of the hall were railway tracks so that goods could be delivered by train. The basement of the east wing was made available to the Gestapo as a collection point because of its proximity to the rail network. This part of the building was now cordoned off.

Arriving at the Grossmarkthalle, the procession stood outside in the light rain. It was cold and damp, typical November weather. The Rübs and the Hartogsohns were four people among 1,042 (including elderly and children) whom the Gestapo had rounded up. All 1,042 were to be processed and accounted for. Waiting their turn, the Rübs and the Hartogsohns stood in the crowd while guards barked orders and insults at them. Nearby was a shed with a large inscription, "Protect the animals."

As they waited, the former Seilerstrasse residents must have asked themselves questions. *Why didn't Emil get us out? What if we need a toilet? Where are they taking us? How will Emil find out where we are going?* Hede was especially terrified for her unborn child. With insufficient nourishment for several months, they had little stamina to draw on.

After what seemed an eternity, the Rübs and the Hartogsohns entered the basement by a wide ramp and walked a short distance past a large storage area.[73] Again, they waited,

---

73. *"Und Keiner hat für Uns Kaddisch Gesagt..."*: *Deportationen aus Frankfurt am Main* 1941–1945, Jüdisches Museum der Stadt Frankfurt, Georg Heuberger, ed., 2004, pp. 116–125.

now in groups of fifty cordoned off by ropes. When their turn came, they passed through a control station, where their names were checked off a list. Their luggage was searched, and men and women were separated for a brutal and degrading body search. Next, they stood before an official from the finance authority, where they handed over their list of possessions and their apartment key, properly labeled. Fifty RM was collected for the cost of deportation along with ration cards, identity cards, and any remaining cash. Each identify card was stamped "evacuated." Finally, the Rübs and Hartogsohns entered a large room laid out with mattresses. The room was dark, stuffy, and crammed with people.

Processing 1,042 people individually took hours, and it was not done with kindness. Most likely David and Bertha did not say anything about the rough treatment they received, for they were raised to respect authority and to do as they were told. Hede certainly remained quiet, not wanting to draw attention to her pregnancy. But if Carl, defensive about his rights, spoke out and complained, he would have been roughly put in his place.

Among the people pushed into the cellar, although not necessarily seen by the Rübs or the Hartogsohns, were Carl's sisters: Bertha (age 49), Therese (age 47), Emma (age 46), and Adele (age 41). There were also two families from Guntersblum: Betty (age 44) and Erwin Lichtenstein (age 51); Johanna (age 46) and Eugen Wolf (age 48) and their nine-year-old daughter, Marianne, whom Deta looked after when Marianne was born. All the while, the normal activities of the Grossmarkthalle were continuing around them as on any ordinary Tuesday.

Crammed into a cold, damp basement meant for storing fruit and vegetables, the former Seilerstrasse residents hardly slept. Throughout the night, people were processed, harassed, and mistreated. The Gestapo did not miss the opportunity to trample over people lying down.[74] "Think of us," Bertha had written her son. But Emil was thinking about the Camera Shop and Deta's visa application. In Hanover, November 11 was Armistice Day, the end of the Great War (1914–1918) to end all wars. Emil had no idea what was taking place in Frankfurt.

The next morning, November 12, a secretary for the Grossmarkthalle arrived at work and observed closed railroad cars guarded by the Gestapo on the tracks. While crates of vegetables were unloaded and sold in the Grossmarkthalle, over a thousand Jews—men, women, the elderly, and children—were herded outside to the nearby Frankfurt Ost station. The deportees with their meager belongings had to wait outside, still unaware of their destination and the length of the journey. Once all had boarded the third-class passenger cars, the doors were locked, the signal given, and the train, assigned number Da 53 by the State Railway, departed Frankfurt for Minsk.

The German Wehrmacht had bombed and then taken the city of Minsk in June 1941, four days after invading the Soviet Union. Minsk, the capital of Belarus, was an industrial city of three hundred thousand. The Nazis administered their occupation of the Baltic states, northeastern Poland, and western Belarus from Minsk. Prior to the German occupation, fifty thousand Jews lived in Minsk. After taking the city, the Germans began persecuting the Jewish population and on July 20 established a ghetto for Soviet Jews.

Train Da 53's journey from Frankfurt took six days, through Berlin and Warsaw, reaching Minsk around November 17. No food or water was distributed during the trip. What little food the Rübs had brought with them could not have lasted, and they had nothing to drink. Temperatures dropped to zero, and there was no heat. Many passengers died on the way.

---

74. Monica Kingreen, *Nach der Kristallnacht; Jüdisches Leben und antijüdische Politik in Frankfurt am Main* 1938-1945, Campus Verlag, 1999, p. 363.

At the Minsk train station, the still-living deportees were ordered to leave their luggage; guarded by German and Latvian SS, they walked through the destroyed city to the ghetto. The previous residents, Belarusian Jews, had been shot to make room for the German arrivals. The newly vacant area was labeled *Sonderghetto*—"Special Ghetto"—for German Jews. Soviet Jews called this section the "Hamburg Ghetto" after Jews from Hamburg and Düsseldorf were herded there a few days earlier. The *Sonderghetto* was separated from the ghetto housing Soviet Jews; transit between the two sections was prohibited. Later transports came from other parts of the German Reich—Berlin, Brunn, Hamburg-Bremen, and Vienna. The newly arrived Frankfurt Jews would have been sent to the "Hamburg Ghetto."

If life in Frankfurt was difficult, Minsk was hell. "Housing" for the deportees was small wooden huts into which four to six families were crammed. The new arrivals had to remove the corpses of recently murdered Belarussian Jews; dead bodies also lay outside. The huts had no electricity or running water. Because there was no light, inmates "retired for the night" at four in the afternoon, sleeping on the floor as there were no mattresses. The sounds of indiscriminate and arbitrary shootings by the SS in charge were heard during the night.

Cold, little food, hunger, and illness were daily conditions, along with forced labor. David may have had to shovel snow or unload railroad cars; if Bertha were lucky, she was assigned to work inside a factory, sorting and repairing clothes from the deportees' suitcases.

Early in December 1941, a postcard from Germany sent to Uncle Schloesser's New York address was forwarded to Hanover. Postmarked November 12, the same day the Rübs and Hartogsohns were "evacuated" east, it was mailed from

Rastatt, one hundred miles south of Frankfurt. "Dear Emil," the writer began. "You will be amazed to hear from me again. Your relatives have gone away so that I feel very alone. Have you heard from Lotte? Next time I will write with more details, because today I have little time. I would be happy to hear from you very soon. My parents send greetings. Many greetings from your Erika." The postcard was signed "Erika Krone." The return address was a town outside of Frankfurt—Büdigen, Obergasse Strasse 21.

Who wrote the postcard, who mailed it, and who was Erika Krone? The Rübs had a cousin, Elise "Liesel" Kulp, now living in Frankfurt, whose former address was Obergasse Strasse 36 in Büdingen.[75] Liesel often visited the Rübs with her little boy.[76] But the handwriting strongly resembled Hede's, and the first sentence—"You will be surprised to hear from me again"—sounded like Hede. Only Hede would have referred to Cousin Lotte. The postcard alerted Emil that his parents were no longer living in Frankfurt.

Did Hede ask her cousin Liesel Kulp to mail the postcard? Did Liesel find someone to mail it far from Frankfurt so as not to arouse suspicion? Could the last name Krone refer to the city of Krone in northwestern Poland, suggesting that the Rübs were sent to Poland? From the postcard, Emil understood that his parents were deported, possibly to Poland, and that Hede had stayed behind to do forced labor.

---

75. There is no evidence that an Erika Krone lived at Obergasse 21, Büdingen. Researched by Fred Trumpler, member, Stolpersteine Gruppe, Guntersblum.
76. Elise "Liesel" Kulp moved to Frankfurt from Büdingen in 1937 after marrying. She and her little boy were deported in 1942 and presumably died in a concentration camp in Poland.

Postcard mailed November 12, 1941,
the day the Rübs and Hartogsohns were deported.

Sample handwriting comparison—
birthday greetings to Emil from Hede.

In late November, the Gestapo removed the remaining furniture and objects and sealed the empty Seilerstrasse apartment. The Hartogsohns' bedroom set and dining room furniture were auctioned off. The Rübs' glass cabinet and other items were sold privately, their linen and clothing sold piecemeal[77]. Nothing in the empty apartment showed that Bertha, David, Hede, and Carl once lived there. Soon another family moved in. The new residents knew only that the previous tenants had "moved out," but not their names nor where they went. The fate of these former tenants did not concern them.

Nazi bureaucracy, however, did follow up. Data cards of the Frankfurt Foreign Exchange were updated for the Rübs and Hartogsohns on November 20, 1941, and December 14, 1941, respectively. The revised cards read: "As ordered. 1. Registration 'Evacuated' to be noted on the index card. 2. The Safeguard order is carried out. File to be put away." The files were then archived.

---

77. Information obtained by Jakob Bickel, Deta's father, after the war.

❈ Hanover, New Hampshire

In 2017 I rode the streetcar from Seilerstrasse to the site of the Grossmarkthalle, unlike my grandparents, my aunt, and her husband in 1941, who had walked. In my mind I saw them—the Rübs and the Hartogsohns leaving Seilerstrasse 9, silent and dignified.

The Grossmarkthalle has been replaced by the modern European Central Bank, but a section of the former building remains, a memorial to those deported from there. Here, the mental pictures I've been creating stopped. Hard as I tried, I couldn't imagine my family and the over one thousand people who were processed that day. The ramp they descended to the large cellar is there, but to enter, one must take a scheduled tour. As I stood there, I already knew I wouldn't go inside. And the long journey on the train to Minsk? At least the trains weren't cattle cars, a small mercy.

I hope that the Rübs and the Hartogsohns remained together; that they were dressed warmly; that if they prayed, their prayers sustained them. It is unbearable to think of them otherwise. And Minsk? My mind refuses to take me there.

26. DARKENING DAYS

(SEPTEMBER 1941–JANUARY 1942)

*"I am very homesick for you. I do not
think that my present life is a life at all.
It is not normal enough to be true life."*
—EMIL TO DETA, JANUARY 1, 1942

In the fall of 1941, Deta wrote to Emil, "Nowhere is a bit
of light—everywhere it is dark." Deta's chance of sailing
to America, to Cuba, or elsewhere was zero. And with
American immigration policies excluding anyone with family
in Germany or in a German-occupied country, Deta had to
face facts. Joining Emil would not happen soon, indeed not for
the duration of the war. She cabled Emil with this information,
reminding him to be strong and not to despair.

If the war prevented their reunion, she counseled Emil,
"Please let us keep our character—we won't get bitter and be
against everything!" Looking ahead, she continued, "Darling,
once we are together, we won't separate us for one minute
and make up for many years we lost."

But Emil couldn't accept the status quo. Despite the war, the denial of Deta's recent visa application, and the need for new affidavits—the ones he had so painstakingly obtained were now invalid—Emil soldiered on, intent on making his case before the visa review committee of State and Justice Department representatives, military intelligence, and FBI personnel. Bureaucrats, Emil thought, were also human beings; once they knew the story behind an application, they would act accordingly.

Emil tried to stay optimistic that Deta would join him soon. Without optimism and hope, he could easily fall into depression. Giving up—letting the Camera Shop fail, letting go of Deta—was not an option. Neither was accepting that his parents had been deported and might not survive, for this would have plunged him into darkness.

With so much on his mind, Emil wasn't following the situation between the United States and Japan. On Sunday, December 7, 1941, Emil was in the Camera Shop darkroom catching up on developing; except for classical music on the radio, the darkroom was quiet, and he could concentrate without interruptions. Even with four employees, Emil handled all the photo finishing because no one met his standards. This meant extra hours in the darkroom in the early morning, at night, and on weekends to keep up with the demand. Work was Emil's solace, an escape from loneliness and anxiety. In the darkroom he was in charge, and his efforts produced results.

Sunday, December 7, 1941, however, was different. At two thirty in the afternoon, as Emil prepared to develop a film, an announcement came over CBS radio: "We interrupt this program to bring you a special news bulletin. The Japanese have attacked Pearl Harbor, Hawaii, by air, President Roosevelt just announced. The attack also was made on all naval and military activities on the principal island of Oahu. We take you now to Washington. The details are not available. They will be in a few minutes." The announcer then read a statement from President Roosevelt.

Emil stopped what he was doing. Had he understood correctly? Alone in the darkroom, illuminated only by the red laboratory lamps, he felt claustrophobic and needed air. He put the film he planned to develop back in its cannister, locked up the store, and returned to his rooming house. He wanted to be with people and to make sure his landlady, Mrs. Girard, and her husband, Fred, had heard the news. The rest of the afternoon, he listened to the radio in the Girards' parlor, grateful for their company. Together they learned of a second Japanese attack on Manila. That night, Emil slept badly.

On Monday, December 8, President Roosevelt asked a joint session of Congress to declare war on Japan; three days later, following declarations of war by Germany and Italy on the United States, the US also declared war on them. With the country now at war, the president proclaimed that all unnaturalized natives fourteen years or older of a hostile nation "shall be liable to be apprehended, restrained, secured, and removed as alien enemies."[78] Just as Great Britain took action against a supposed fifth column of spies and saboteurs inside the country, the United States was going to round up Germans, Italians, and Japanese considered dangerous to American security.

Despite his frustration with American immigration policies, Emil's loyalty to the United States was unwavering. It never occurred to him that he might have difficulties. Given how well Hanover had accepted him, a stateless Jewish refugee from fascism, and that in two years he would be an American citizen, he didn't consider himself "an enemy alien."

More restrictions followed. Enemy aliens were forbidden to leave their town of residence without applying to federal authorities one week prior to a planned trip. The application, in triplicate, had to show purpose of the trip,

---

78. Presidential Proclamation No. 2526.

destination, date of departure and return, route to be followed, and mode of transportation. Enemy aliens were not allowed to possess or use firearms, ammunition, explosives, shortwave radios, signal devices—or cameras. The Justice Department warned that "any Japanese, German, or Italian citizens found in possession of a camera, regardless of the use to which it was put, faced loss of his equipment and possible detention."[79]

Unaware of these restrictions, on Christmas Day 1941 Emil took the train to New York City to visit cousins Lotte and Erich. When he arrived at the Haven Avenue apartment, they greeted him with astonishment. "How did you manage to get here?" they asked.

"Why, by train, of course," Emil answered.

"But did you get permission?" Erich asked.

Emil was puzzled. "Permission for what? From whom?"

"Permission from the town officials," Erich explained. "President Roosevelt said that enemy aliens need special permission to travel. Didn't you read the newspaper?"

Emil usually did read the newspaper, preferring *PM*, a left-leaning New York daily with photos and less text, which was easier to read than the *New York Times* or the *Herald Tribune*. But for the month of December, Emil had been occupied printing hundreds of Christmas cards for his customers. War or not, Americans would celebrate Christmas, and Hanover residents were no exception. Working long hours, Emil had been too exhausted to read the newspaper.

Now in New York, Emil couldn't rectify his mistake, so he tried to enjoy this much-needed break while Cousin Lotte did her best to feed and entertain him. "The holidays were no holidays, to me," he wrote Deta on New Year's Day 1942, "because you were not here. Mostly I worked or slept or read." Worry for his parents added to his gloom. "Detalein,

---

79. *New York Times*, December 13, 1941, p. 8.

let us hope that my parents survive this war. I am quite pessimistic about it and have hard times often." With his parents' whereabouts unknown and the United States and Germany at war, Emil was now completely cut off from his roots.

In early January 1942, shortly after returning to Hanover, Emil was called out of the darkroom. Waiting to speak with him were Hanover Police Chief Andrew Ferguson and two unknown men. Chief Ferguson was in uniform, the two other men in civilian clothes and trench coats.

"Emil," said the chief sternly. "These men are from the FBI. We need to talk to you in private." Emil asked the employee who had been with him to go upstairs.

"Mr. Rueb," said one of the FBI men once they were alone, "we understand that you left town and went to New York without official permission."

"And we see that you have photographic equipment, which should have been turned in to Chief Ferguson here at the police station," said the second man, nodding at the police chief.

"Sir," Emil replied, hoping his German accent wasn't too pronounced, "Mr. Murchie, the district attorney in Concord, told my lawyer that I will receive a temporary permit to use my camera in New Hampshire while I am investigated. Mr. Murchie said that I can use my camera until the permit comes through. I need my equipment. It is my livelihood. I use it to take passport photos and baby pictures for customers. And the rest of the cameras belong to the Camera Shop Corporation."

"You were required to turn in your photographic equipment three weeks ago," answered the first FBI man menacingly. "You know, in this country we also have concentration camps."

"If you don't turn in your equipment to the police immediately," continued the second man, "you will be on your way to one of these camps. You already disobeyed orders traveling without prior permission to New York."

"I'll expect you at the station by the end of the day, Emil," Chief Ferguson said curtly. With that, the three men left.

Emil was rattled. The FBI agents reminded him of the Nazi authorities who made him feel small and powerless. He was also angry. How would he carry on without cameras?

Remembering he had many supporters, he telephoned his lawyer and Mr. Carter. Then, after explaining the situation to the staff, he gathered up the store cameras, along with his own camera and lenses, and walked the short distance from the store to the Hanover Police Station. There, he turned everything over to Chief Ferguson.

Returning to the Camera Shop, he started to worry. Would he be arrested and languish in a concentration camp? Had someone in Hanover accused him of spying? Yet nobody connected to him had been questioned. Nothing made sense. For the second time in his career, he was without his camera, and now the business was endangered. It occurred to him that confiscating equipment belonging to the Camera Shop, an American corporation, was illegal because the partial owner, Mr. Carter, was an American citizen. Feeling violated, Emil decided he would sue those responsible for any losses the corporation might suffer.

The two FBI agents didn't know Emil or care about his story. They saw only a German with an accent who had several cameras in his possession. They probably hadn't heard the January 4 radio address "Aliens and the War Emergency" by Ugo Carusi, executive assistant to U.S. Attorney General Francis Biddle, who stated that most of the aliens living in the United States were not enemies of democracy and should not be discriminated against. Bullying and mistreating minorities was what America's enemies did. Mr. Carusi was confident that Americans would not abandon "the very principles upon which their country was founded while fighting an all-out war to preserve them."[80]

---

80. *New York Times*, Jan. 5, 1942, p. 11.

But the FBI was charged with identifying and separating the so-called good aliens from bad. As the newspaper *PM* noted, "Lots of interesting fish have turned up in the net cast from fifty FBI offices throughout the USA." In the process, there were some sad stories and hardship, "but this is war, and some time will lapse before the innocent are separated from the suspected and real Axis agents."[81]

With Mr. Carter's help, Emil found out more. The required permit was delayed when New Hampshire district attorney Alexander Murchie learned of the FBI investigation. The New Hampshire attorney general's office was unfamiliar with the procedure for issuing permits, and Emil was the only refugee photographer in New Hampshire. Some refugee photographers in New York, stateless like Emil and applying for U.S. citizenship, received their temporary permits easily. Mr. Carter may have been correct when he said that the "small town" factor and local "busybodies" were at work. There was apparently a power struggle between Chief Ferguson and the local judge, with the chief flexing his muscles to demonstrate his power to the judge. Emil had fallen in the middle of this disagreement.

Fortunately, Emil did not have to sue. On January 29 District Attorney Murchie authorized Chief Ferguson to return the Leica camera and other equipment to Emil and granted Emil permission to photograph inside the Camera Shop and inside homes in Hanover.

Marked by this experience, in February Emil wrote the editor of *American Photography*, upset by their editorial about severe penalties for an unnaturalized enemy alien with a camera. Such statements were "wrong, careless, and apt to bring worries to the many refugee photographers," prospective citizens like himself who were against Hitler and had suffered very much. According to Emil, the writer should have added that the government made exceptions and allowed

---

81. *PM*, December 10, 1941.

"prospective citizens to keep cameras at least for indoor use when they have proved their loyalty and good will." He would therefore no longer sell that magazine in his store.

For Emil, the end of 1941 and the beginning of 1942 were especially trying, and he felt the most alone he had ever been. He wrote Deta on New Year's Day, "You are my only hope for the future. You will help me to carry on, despite all the mistakes I have made." Deta was the one person left who knew him well, with whom he had a history.

If only he would hear from his parents and could write to them at their new address. If only Deta's visa could be resolved. If only he remained healthy and could keep the Camera Shop afloat. With the United States entering the war, the equilibrium Emil had found in Hanover was shaken. Rules, regulations, hopes, expectations, life and death—war changed everything.

❈ HANOVER, NEW HAMPSHIRE

In my father's papers is a copy of a letter, dated February 4, 1942, to the American Red Cross in Washington, DC. "I would greatly appreciate it," my father wrote, "if you could try to find out if my parents are still alive, where they are now living, and if I am allowed to do something for them." If there was a reply, that document has disappeared. The Red Cross must have received countless letters just like it.

In Deta's case, there was always someone or some institution to contact—a consulate, an ambassador, the London Home Office. Most of these had the courtesy to respond. But, to whom could Emil have appealed in Germany on behalf of his family? To the Third Reich, a Jew was a nonperson to be eradicated. Money, if Emil had had it, might have made a difference. Without money, he was powerless to help his family. Having the opportunity to do something, even if it turned out to be fruitless, is perhaps another explanation for why he appeared to do so much more for Deta than for his family.

27. WAR PREPARATIONS
IN HANOVER (1942)

*"You, you, and you again are my main thinking
... I have only you and us in my mind and my
poor parents, when I work hard and think how to
proceed and keep the business running."*
—EMIL TO DETA, JUNE 13, 1942

For Emil, war had begun in 1933 when Hitler assumed power in Germany. For Hanover, New Hampshire, war started on December 7, 1941, with the bombing of Pearl Harbor. The residents of small-town Hanover adapted to the new situation.

Town leaders discussed financing local civilian defense and protecting the public.[82] In early January, highway agents provided Hanover households with sand, in case an air raid caused a fire. Residents were advised to empty their attics of any combustible material and replace it with "a pail of sand, a shovel, an axe, eye shields, leather gloves, and a snuffer," in

---

82. Information about Hanover's response to the war from the *Hanover Gazette*, January 29, 1942.

the event an incendiary bomb penetrated the roof. Air-raid wardens were appointed for each neighborhood with a private home designated an airplane-spotting station, and blackout information was circulated.

Hanover merchants also adjusted to the war. Offering to advise residents on their individual blackout needs, a local store advertised blackout cloth and window shades. Grocery stores informed their customers that wartime conditions required cutting grocery deliveries to two per day. Dartmouth shortened the college year by five weeks and offered a summer session to speed students through their courses prior to entering the military.

War brought some drama to the train station in White River Junction, Vermont, where Emil had arrived from New York in 1939. Near midnight on January 1, 1942, a local resident posting letters at the station noticed a train pull in that was staffed with Army and Secret Service officers. Everyone had to remain inside the station until the train departed. It was rumored, and later confirmed, that Prime Minister Winston Churchill was on board, en route from Washington to Canada. "Our informant tells us that the atmosphere seemed to be full of secrecy and tension, prosaic as this incident may seem to be."[83]

On January 23, the *Hanover Gazette* alerted German, Italian, and Japanese aliens to apply for a Certificate of Identification. For Emil, this required crossing Main Street from the Camera Shop to the post office, being fingerprinted, completing an application, and providing three passport-size photos. A Camera Shop employee took the photo, which Emil printed. "Very unshaved, I greet you," he commented on the back of a copy for Deta.

---

83. *Hanover Gazette*, January 1, 1942.

Emil's photo for the required
Certificate of Identification.

On January 30, Emil received his permit to use his camera. The permit, he gratefully wrote District Attorney Murchie, allowed the Camera Shop to continue operating and to keep two assistants and two part-time workers employed. Thus began a cordial correspondence between Emil and Murchie in Concord, New Hampshire.

With the war curtailing the manufacture and sale of photographic goods, Emil supplemented his income by photographing children, babies, animals, and college students. Some of his subjects lived across the Connecticut River in Norwich, Vermont, within walking distance of Hanover. To cross the river, first Emil had to request permission to exit Hanover a week before his appointment and second, approval from the Vermont attorney general to enter the state.

This was a burdensome requirement. As Emil explained in a letter to District Attorney Murchie, a photography shoot depended "on the dispositions of the babies and animals." He suggested that Murchie allow him to simply alert Hanover Police Chief Ferguson twenty-four hours prior to a Vermont assignment. Murchie's assistant replied promptly. Yes, Emil could photograph in Vermont, but he must still file the requisite forms a week in advance in Concord, New Hampshire.

Another time, unable to make a permitted trip across the river, Emil wrote Murchie, "The writer of this letter feels very sorry to bother you again. . . . Due to the indisposition of the babies he was to photograph, he would . . . appreciate an extension of the permit." Weather and the gasoline shortage also affected Emil's plans, requiring yet another extension. Murchie must have been a reasonable man because Emil's petitions were easily granted. In May, short on time, Emil telegraphed his request to photograph the Dartmouth College Commencement Procession. The answer was positive, "provided it is agreeable to the authorities of Dartmouth College."

Another concern was the draft. On Monday, March 30, 1942, Grafton County Local Board No. 6 required Emil's presence for a physical examination. Consequences for not appearing included a fine, imprisonment, loss of rights, and being immediately inducted into military service. But surely "Uncle Sam" would not draft an "enemy alien."

If Emil were drafted, what would happen to the Camera Shop? Even Mr. Carter could not say what recourse Emil might have. "There is no question in my mind," Mr. Carter wrote on May 3 from New Jersey, "that many civilians are going to be called for service of one kind or another, and even those who are physically unfit will have to perform some kind of service for the war effort."

Emil appealed to Board No. 6; drafting him would destroy any hope he had of rebuilding his life, having tried twice in Europe and now in Hanover. On May 30, Board No. 6 determined that his alien status made him "not acceptable for training and service in the armed forces of the United States." Emil was relieved. Now he could concentrate on the store and on Deta's visa.

Hearing through the Red Cross that her parents and siblings were well, Deta encouraged Emil not to lose hope for his parents. But Emil prepared for the worst. Not knowing whether they were dead or alive was torture, made worse by his New York relatives insinuating he was responsible for his parents' fate. The relatives needn't have bothered, for Emil was skilled at self-flagellation. Running the Camera Shop, however, did not allow him to indulge his feelings, so he kept them inside. This was the only way he could get out of bed in the morning and go to the store. Working was how Emil avoided thinking about his parents.

The store required his full attention. There were bills to pay, inventory to be taken, stock to order, and staff assignments to prepare. Finding and managing employees who met Emil's standards was another challenge.

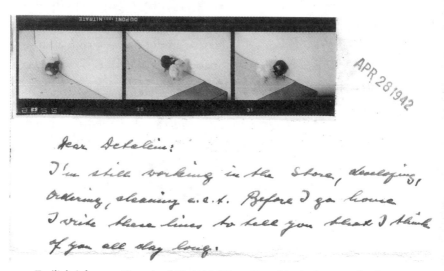

Emil's brief note to Deta, April 28, 1942. "I'm still working in the store, developing, ordering, cleaning, [etc.]. Before I go home I write these lines to tell you that I think of you all day long." Emil made a 26 x 20-inch enlargement of the chicks for Easter.

After his experience with the FBI, Emil was anxious to prove his loyalty to the United States. In July he donated money to the Loyalty Committee of Victims of Nazi-Fascist Oppression to purchase the Loyalty fighter plane. Members of this committee, whose names would be presented to

President Roosevelt, wanted to show their loyalty and gratitude to the United States for taking them in. Prominent committee members included Heinrich Mann (brother of Thomas Mann), author and playwright Franz Werfel, former cabinet members, scientists, writers, artists, and businessmen.

Evidence that Emil was against fascism and loyal to the United States.

In September, anticipating the visa review committee would ask about his contribution to the American war effort, Emil requested a statement from Mr. Carter confirming his loyalty and "that my preparedness for managing this store gave you the chance to take over your defense job." Emil also contacted the Department of Justice regarding his Certificate of Identification; deprived of German citizenship by the Nazis, Emil wanted the records to show he was no longer German.

In August 1942 Emil would be thirty-six years old. How many birthdays would he and Deta have to celebrate alone?

Deta wrote, "We only can pray and hope, that it will be the last one and that we will have strength enough to go on with our daily struggles."

"All my best wishes and a long long birthday kiss
from yours ever loving Detalein" (July 9, 1942).

Deta and Emil had now known each other for ten years. For over a third of this time, they had only communicated through letters. It had been four years since they had heard each other's voices.

Emil continued networking and advocating for Deta. He asked Dartmouth student Bob Blood, son of New Hampshire governor Robert Blood, if his father might help. At his son's request, on August 18, 1942, Governor Blood wrote former New Hampshire governor John Winant, now American ambassador to England, saying, "This is a deserving case, and [Emil and Deta] would make desirable American citizens."

Ambassador Winant wished he could be helpful. Until the State Department approved Deta's application and Deta obtained transportation, immigration law prohibited the embassy from intervening further. Once Deta was approved and had transportation, Ambassador Winant promised, ". . . we will make the question of a visa for her just as easy as possible."

In Hanover a naval training school for officers started at Dartmouth in July, and on Saturday mornings the officers paraded on the green. Emil saw this as an opportunity to photograph the officers, who could then send the pictures to their family. Since enemy aliens weren't supposed to photograph outdoors, especially not anything military, Emil sent his assistant to take pictures; he wanted to avoid another encounter with the FBI. One morning, however, the assistant called in sick. What was to be done?

Emil decided to take the photographs himself. After the parade, he asked to speak with the captain. "Sir," Emil began, "I need to inform you that I took pictures of the parade without permission. Would it be agreeable if I develop the pictures, make proofs, and bring them to you?"

"Of course," answered the captain. "And from now on, Mr. Rueb, you will consider me the person in charge of my troops. Whoever photographs them is my business and not the FBI's. When you take pictures of my troops, you are under my command, and my order is that you take as many pictures as you want. Just show me the proofs before you make them public." This arrangement was satisfactory to Emil and continued for the duration of the war. In his letter of support for Emil to the visa review committee, the local judge noted that "with a Naval Officers Training School located in Hanover, [Emil] is doing much to help the morale of the trainees by seeing that they have good pictures to send home, and otherwise serving their photographic needs."

As the weeks and months passed, Emil and Deta's longing for each other grew more intense. Life was incomplete, and precious youth was slipping away. "I love you more than anything else in this world," wrote Emil, a love that Deta reciprocated. At the mercy of the State Department, strangers who did not know them, their lives were on hold. How does a relationship survive in such circumstances? How does the beloved remain flesh and blood, instead of an idealized image becoming more perfect as the longing intensifies?

Emil standing in front of the Camera Shop,
undated photo taken by a student.

Deta in London photographed by a
professional photographer to send to Emil.

Of course, they had photographs of each other. Emil carried Deta's most recent letters with him. The dressing gown Deta gave him in England was a talisman to see him through the night. Deta had Emil's photo and the note, "All for you," that he slipped into her hand at the Mainz train station. She kept him present by talking to little Susan about kind and loving "Uncle Emil." Even seeing the same movie as Emil was a connection to him.

After so much time apart, were Deta and Emil the same people who had fallen in love in Germany? And, with their letters censored, how open were they with each other? "Detalein, often I think we do not know enough of the other one's worries and problems," Emil wrote. "What do I know of your domestic troubles, of your health, of your thoughts? What do you know of my difficulties?" It was hard to believe a time would come when they would be together again. How much longer would they have to wait? The waiting seemed endless.

28. INTO THE FALL (1942)

*"Your letters are all I have to live from at
the present and my memory and my hope."*
—EMIL TO DETA, JULY 22, 1942

ver the summer of 1942, battles raged in the Pacific,
North Africa, and in the Soviet Union, with heavy losses
on all sides. Far from the fighting, Hanover was peaceful.
On a warm Sunday in October, Emil took a long walk and
thought of Deta and his parents. "You will learn to like fall
almost as much as spring," he wrote her that evening, "once
you live in New England. The leaves of the trees are brown,
some are entirely red. It is a lovely time." The walk was a
reprieve from obligations, but Emil was not a peace. Where
were his parents and Hede and Carl now? If only he had
found the money for Hede's ship passage.

Emil himself vacillated between hope and despair.
Perhaps the visa review committee would consider Deta's
application favorably when he became an American citizen.
In late September, he had received the final application papers
for citizenship.

Deta worried that Emil worked too hard and didn't sleep enough; she feared he might have a breakdown. Wanting to show Deta that he was functioning well, Emil described photographing the rehearsal of a new play at Dartmouth. Imagine, he instructed, "Darkness. I'm sitting high on top of a stepladder. A Leica hanging around my neck, a Speed Graphic [camera] on my knees. The curtain goes up. . . . I follow the scene. If I have the feeling that something of importance is going on, I switch and off go two or three flashbulbs, one on the camera and two on a stand six to eight meters away and connected by wire with the camera. This goes on for between two and three hours, until I am satisfied with the results. The pictures will be used in the paper and in the show windows for official displays." After the rehearsal, he developed his films at the Camera Shop and later sent Deta a copy of the college newspaper with his uncredited photograph. Although the job paid little, Emil found this connection with the theater a worthwhile distraction.

In October, First Lady Eleanor Roosevelt visited American servicemen in England. Perhaps the First Lady could help Deta. There was also recent news that travel on a Greek Ship might be possible. Emil cabled Deta: "Referring letter student friend try DaCasa help see Winant Mrs Roosevelt and get passage Greek ship cable answer result love."

Instead of Deta's reply, Emil received a letter from Commander Andrew W. Cruse, Cable and Radio Censor New York, asking him to explain his cable. Emil's mention of Mrs. Roosevelt had raised a red flag with the Office of Censorship. Regretting having inconvenienced the censor and his office, Emil sent a revised message.

Deta did try, unsuccessfully, to reach Mrs. Roosevelt through the American consulate in London. Writing on the First Lady's behalf, the American vice-consul explained that

Mrs. Roosevelt was unable to reply personally. Once Deta's case was approved, the vice-consul added, they would contact her.

Finally, on November 4, the Department of State official Notice of Hearing for Deta's visa application arrived in Emil's mailbox. The hearing, scheduled for November 16, would begin promptly at 9:00 a.m. in Washington, DC. Emil would be under oath, and his testimony would become part of the official case record. Information on the applicant's understanding of and loyalty to the American system of government, on "the applicant's health, personality, education and training, experience and resources," and evidence that the applicant would become "a useful and desirable member of our community" would be helpful. Since Emil's trip to Washington was for an official government matter, permission from District Attorney Murchie's office was unnecessary.

Emil boarded a train in White River Junction and arrived in Washington the day before the hearing. Seeing the White House, the Capitol, and Pennsylvania Avenue was awe-inspiring, something he had never dreamed of in Guntersblum. He spent some time at the Smithsonian National Gallery, where he bought a souvenir postcard for Deta, and then went to his hotel room. A good night's sleep was the best preparation for the hearing, but whether he slept well that night is doubtful. So much depended on making a favorable impression on the men who held power over his future.

Early the next morning, an express mail envelope was slipped under Emil's door. It contained photostatic copies, made by the Camera Shop staff, of documents Emil would present to the committee. The staff had stayed late Saturday evening after Emil left to make the copies, which had to be hand photographed and printed.

Grateful the documents arrived on time, Emil walked to the State Department Building at 1712 G Street, where the hearing would take place. Addressing representatives of the State Department, Immigration and Naturalization services, FBI, and military and naval intelligence was intimidating, but Emil came prepared. He presented five statements from people who had known Deta in Germany and who confirmed her loyalty, abilities, her opposition to fascism, and her support of democratic ideals. Emil also presented twelve statements about his own character, a two-page letter from Mr. Carter, and one from a local judge.

Emil's references applauded his integrity, loyalty, his knowledge of photography, and his contribution to the community, attributes that earned him unqualified support for his efforts to bring Deta to the United States. As one supporter wrote, "I can say without hesitation that in allowing her a passport you will do no harm to our country and will add to the Hanover population a woman we shall be glad to have among us." Another writer stated that given Emil's character, he was "confident that his fiancée must be a woman of comparable value."

To Emil's surprise, there was also a testimonial from the Camera Shop staff. Emil was more than an employer, the employees wrote; he was a teacher and a friend, interested in their problems, never too busy to give advice to anyone who asked. He was generous with his time, spending hours with a customer, often at the expense of profit. The letter ended: "There are thousands of mortal wounds being struck that we can do nothing to relieve, but that does not lessen the importance of an individual wound if we can find it in our power to help it. The strength of us in America to fight is built on our charity to our individual fellow man."

At the hearing, one committee member asked Emil why he hadn't married Miss Bickel when he was in London. "Sir," Emil answered, "I was not brought up to marry a girl when I was poor and with no prospects."

Otherwise believing he had done well, Emil cabled Deta: "Think made good impression today's hearing final decision towards Christmas." If the answer were positive, she would receive a cable from the State Department.

In December, the Camera Shop produced the usual Christmas cards, portraits, and enlargements. The demand for Emil's work had grown so much that he hired two more short-term employees. May this be the last Christmas they were apart, Emil cabled Deta, a wish she echoed: "Happy Xmas and my heartiest wishes for New Year that our only wish will be come true all my love Elisabeth Bickel." The visa review committee in Washington, however, was silent.

❖ HANOVER, NEW HAMPSHIRE

*T*he letter from the Camera Shop employees, which I found in my father's papers, showed the impact he had on others. To the employees he was a good man, a hard worker, and a generous, caring human being. This was his light. People saw him as kind, understanding, and a gentleman, and, although he could be critical, for the most part, he saw the good in others.

In 1966, an unhappy and confused student broke into the Camera Shop at night. This was not a criminal act, my father told me, but an indication the young man was having difficulties. My father refused to press charges. Concerned the student might be depressed, my father urged the police to make sure the young man wouldn't harm himself. The story of my father's decency and his compassion for the student has stayed with me. I wish I had appreciated more the qualities that made him stand out, rather than focusing on our differences.

29. WASHINGTON ANSWERS (1943)

"Do not worry, I won't rest, even if they
say no in Washington. . . . Anytime in my life,
if I felt treated badly, I fought it harder."
—EMIL TO DETA, JANUARY 3, 1943

January 30, 1943, marked the tenth anniversary of Hitler's rise to power, a date Emil preferred to ignore. The RAF recognized the occasion with its first daytime bombing of Berlin, forcing Göering and Goebbels to postpone their anniversary speeches for over an hour. Emil celebrated a different milestone, namely that the United States Department of Justice acknowledged that he was not a German citizen. Of course, as a stateless person, he did not have a citizen's rights and protections, but this was not a time to be German.

It had been two and a half months since Emil testified in Washington, and the visa review committee still hadn't decided on Deta's application. Was this a good sign? Perhaps on March 20, he and Deta would celebrate her thirty-fourth birthday together. Hoping for good news, Emil checked his Hanover post office box several times a day.

Finally, Washington answered. After careful consideration by the visa review committee and the Board of Appeals, the result, dated February 25, 1943, was "that a favorable recommendation for the issuance of a visa is not warranted at this time." No reason was given for the denial, and the case could not be reconsidered before six months. Emil could request reapplication papers a few weeks prior to July 25, the six-month date, and not before.

Why was Deta's visa denied? The most probable explanation was that a German citizen with family in Germany was considered a liability to American national defense. Emil's statement about Deta's family's whereabouts—"Unknown, last heard of in the Rhineland, any or all of these may be dead"—was inconsequential. That Emil's parents might also be dead was irrelevant. In war, lines were drawn, and those in power enforced rules to protect their side. There was no room for empathy for two ordinary people who wanted to be together.

Had the members of the visa review committee met Deta, all 110 pounds of her, they might have concurred that denying her a visa was senseless. Espionage or sabotage were not in Deta's vocabulary; her one "political act" was to love a German Jew. To the committee, however, Deta was a case number, one of many, not a flesh-and-blood human being. Despite testimony from people who knew her, despite two American sponsors vouching for her sight unseen, Deta was deemed a threat. That a woman might think for herself and leave family and country for the man she loved defied the imagination of the committee members, probably all men.

Or did the committee have reason to mistrust Emil? In the State Department files, a notation under Emil's name from October 8, 1941, read: "Corresponding with German prisoner of war in Canada. Refer any application to Fraud Section of the Passport Division." The mistakenly labelled "prisoner of war" was Carl Hartogsohn's brother Hartog Hartogsohn, arrested in Frankfurt on November 10, 1938, and released with other Buchenwald detainees after the British consul offered entry permits for England. In the spring of 1940, classified as an enemy alien by the British, Hartog was sent from London to a detention camp in Canada. From Canada, he wrote Emil to ask about Carl and Hede. Neither Emil nor Hartog, victims of German fascism, posed a threat. The impact of this entry in Emil's file is unknown.

The State Department denial was a blow, but Emil was persistent. He would reapply in six months and, if necessary, travel again to Washington, DC. He tried to remain positive, but he felt increasingly lonely. Sundays, when the store was closed and people were with their families, were especially difficult. To American friends in California, he asked, "Please continue writing me those wonderful letters which make me think of a happy home and that something like a home still exists in this world." Sometimes, he found relief from loneliness: "Last night I had a nice time," he wrote Deta. "A lady of a neighbor town left me her dog, a French 'Pudel.' He is a well-educated boy. I invited him to supper." The poodle and a letter from Deta got him through the weekend.

The State Department's refusal to admit "a woman of such extraordinary qualities and bravery," as Emil wrote the American Committee for Christian Refugees, made no sense to him. Yes, regulations must be enforced, but "must all human actions be abolished?" Emil asked. How could he not take the State Department denial personally when it was his personal and private life that was on the line?

The caseworker from the American Committee for Christian Refugees commiserated with Emil's frustration. The rejection, she reassured him, was not personal but reflected the State Department's cautious approach to immigration applications. She knew of only one case approved by the visa review committee, that of a woman in England whose husband and children were in the United States. Yet the woman was still in England, unable to get passage to the States. Had Emil submitted proof from the Home Office of Deta's unconditional release from internment? This proof was a prerequisite for an American visa.

No, Emil had not. If this statement was needed, Emil would obtain it. On April 29, he wrote the London Home Office for documentation of Deta's unconditional release and enclosed international reply coupons for an airmail response. Another round of tilting at bureaucratic windmills began.

The Home Office replied in May that to release this information, an official request from the American State Department was required. Three months later, in August, the State Department made the request to the Home Office, and in late September the Home Office forwarded the statement of unconditional release to the U.S. consul general in London. Now the document had to cross the Atlantic to the State Department in Washington. Such was bureaucracy in wartime.

In mid-July, Emil started another visa application. With less time to write to Deta, he compensated by sending food parcels and a subscription to *Reader's Digest* magazine. Running the store required "the flexibility of a commanding officer," Emil explained, to overcome the many difficulties that arose during the day: "The tools refuse to work. A camera won't work. A developer stains. An assistant is sick suddenly. A client badly needs a portrait, a copy of a document, an enlargement. Somebody's camera does not work. But I love it, Detalein, I like the struggle." Clearly, Emil liked being his own master. What he didn't like was feeling powerless before the visa review committee.

Letters from customers and from soldiers on the front praising Emil's pictures of their loved ones were a small but satisfying reward for the long hours in the darkroom. A student friend commented that Emil worked at a frenetic pace to resolve "all the little problems . . . that slowed down the production of the Camera Shop" and to achieve his goal of making the store "the best one in all of New Hampshire. And the orders for photographs and for finishing work come in from places which are miles away."

Deta too struggled with loneliness. In August, she vacationed in Cambridge, at the home of a friend's relatives. Sitting on the grass by the river, Deta wrote to Emil: "The food, which is rather a problem in these days, is good and enough. . . . I quite often sit here watching the boats passing by. And then always dream of you and how happy I could be if you were sitting beside me. I am lonely, always alone where I am. No that's not true, but I sometimes get that feeling, and today I got it." She hoped her birthday letter would arrive on time and wished she could celebrate with him. "But my thoughts will be with you, all day long—Emil, you surely will feel it."

Letters and presents from Deta and Susan did arrive for Emil's thirty-seventh birthday.

Although he couldn't take the afternoon off as Deta had wished—the store was short-staffed—he was hopeful. The State Department's insistence on verification of Deta's unconditional release from detention was, he thought, a good sign.

In November, a ray of sunshine for Deta came in the form of Cousin Lotte's new husband,

"We both send you our love and the best wishes for today, 23 August 1943."

Hans Lowenstein.[84] An American army soldier stationed in England, Hans met Deta in London. Having visited Emil in Hanover, Hans could tell Deta how Emil lived and worked. But not having known Deta in Germany, he couldn't say whether she was the same woman Emil remembered. Nonetheless, he reported, "[S]he certainly is a swell girl." That Hans had recently seen Emil brought him closer to Deta, at least in spirit.

The war, with all its misery, dragged on. In July, the RAF bombed Hamburg and by early August had practically leveled the city. In October, the industrial areas of Kassel were bombed, and in November, the RAF bombed Berlin.

It would be, Emil wrote Deta, another Christmas apart. A pile of films waited to be processed, and the Camera Shop was "stormed" by customers wanting their pictures. In the last ten days, Emil estimated that he had pressed the camera shutter eight hundred times and photographed twelve babies, whose parents asked every day if their pictures were ready.

It snowed in Hanover, and Emil took time to photograph the snow paradise he had come to love. He also saw two movies, "of the better type." The first was *Casablanca*, whose final scene, when the French Commander "gives orders for the usual roundup of two hundred people," he especially liked. One can forgive Emil for misquoting the famous line "Round up the usual suspects" since his English lagged behind the level required for movies. "Marvelous is the singing scene," he continued, "in the restaurant. Conrad Veidt!" The German actor Conrad Veidt, a Lutheran with a Jewish wife, played the Nazi Major Friedrich Strasser. Veidt, an anti-Nazi, left Germany and a successful film career when

---

84. John Hans Lowenstein, a German Jewish refugee, was a Ritchie Boy, one of 15,200 servicemen trained for U.S. Army Intelligence at Camp Ritchie, Maryland. Because they spoke German, the Ritchie Boys participated in counterintelligence and interrogating prisoners. Hans's name appears in the list of Ritchie Boys in Bruce Henderson's *Sons and Soldiers*, Harper Collins, 2017, p. 401.

Hitler came to power. His name undoubtedly had meaning to Emil and Deta.

The second film Emil mentioned was *Five Graves to Cairo*, directed by the Austrian Jewish director Billy Wilder. The movie began with a scene of a dead driver in a tank in the desert. "The lonely tank in the desert, the dead driver, and the rolling of the vehicle in the first ten minutes is unforgettable to me. A fine record and a beautiful scene. One actor—a tank—the desert." The film received Academy Award nominations for Best Film Editing, Best Cinematography, and Best Art Direction.

"Merry Christmas to you, Detalein," Emil ended his letter. "A kiss and the wish you may be with me soon. All my love E."

Christmas letter from Deta to Emil, 1943.

On the world stage, the *New York Times* December 25, 1943, headlines stated, "Eisenhower Named Commander for Invasion; 3,000 Planes Smash French Coast; Berlin Hit; Roosevelt Promises Nation a Durable Peace." On Christmas Eve, President Roosevelt informed the nation that 3.8 million Americans were in the armed forces overseas, more than double the number of soldiers from the previous year. By July 1, 1944, that number would increase to over 5 million men and women.

There was still, the president continued, "much to face in the way of further suffering and sacrifice, and personal tragedy. . . . But, on Christmas Eve this year, I can say to you that at least we may look forward into the future with real, substantial confidence that, however great the cost, 'peace on earth, good will toward men' can be and will be realized and insured." This the president said with certainty, "though the cost may be high and the time may be long." Emil, too, looked ahead, praying that 1944 would bring Hitler's defeat, news of his parents, and reunion with Deta.

30. A YEAR OF UNFINISHED
BUSINESS (1944)

*"There are several possibilities to
get reunited with you:*

1.) To go to England and to marry you.
*2.) To get you over to Canada or another English
possession where I can meet and marry you.*
*3.) To leave temporarily the U.S.A. and to go to
South America, where I would expect you.*
*4.) To leave the U.S.A. and to go to one of the
South American countries for good."*
—EMIL TO DETA, APRIL 30, 1944

On Thursday, May 11, 1944, Emil and Cousin Lotte sat
side by side in Bryant Park behind the New York Public
Library, each writing a note to Deta for Lotte to mail. In half
an hour, Emil would board the train at nearby Grand Central
Station for White River Junction, Vermont. Although the sky
was overcast, the day was warm with a forecast of seventy-
seven degrees. Lotte had removed her sweater, and Emil's

folded raincoat lay over his suitcase. A vegetarian lunch from Lotte and the May 11 *New York Times* were in Emil's briefcase for his journey. On the train, Emil would read on the front page that the Allies were bombing German defenses in Western Europe "with methodical ferocity."

A month earlier, on April 8, despite Emil's second Washington appearance before the visa review committee on March 24, the State Department had again refused to grant Deta a visa. With the second denial, Hanover without Deta felt unbearable, so Emil went to New York to investigate alternatives for their reunion. There he traversed the city, approaching one refugee organization after another about Deta's chances of coming. He even interviewed, unsuccessfully, with the assistant picture editor of *LIFE*, thinking that a staff position with the magazine would get him to England; the sticking point was that Emil still wasn't an American citizen. Emil dreaded returning to his lonely existence.

When the year began, Emil had had high hopes. Deta's new visa application and, after eight months, verification of her unconditional release from internment were at the State Department. Although in the dark about where and when, Americans knew that Allied forces were preparing to invade Europe. Invasion meant defeating the Third Reich and, for Emil, the possibility the Rübs and the Hartogsohns might still be alive. In January, things seemed to be moving in a positive direction.

On March 10, 1944, Emil had passed the exam for American citizenship. If all went well, by August 1944 Emil would be a full-fledged American, perhaps even married to Deta. The possibility of citizenship made him feel "like one who was stranded and adopted suddenly and given a home." It would take another ninety days to receive his final papers, but he could soon call himself an American. Deta's visa would have been a better gift, but passing the exam would have to suffice. Deta cabled her happiness at this "wonderful birthday present."

But now, in May, after another denial that kept Deta from him, Emil was deeply discouraged. He had struggled for so long, first under Hitler, then as a refugee with no real job and no money. Besides the challenges of the Camera Shop, constant worry for his family sat in the pit of his stomach. Deta was his reason for living; she would bring light to his darkness. "You are," Emil told Deta, "the only person I feel close to, [whom] the Nazis could not take away from me."

He was also angry. He resented completing application forms when the State Department apparently had no intention of approving his request. A well-known artist or writer stood a chance of being admitted, but a regular person like Deta didn't seem to matter. In Emil's view, the State Department was rigid and inhumane; they couldn't see past Deta's label as a German enemy alien. Never mind that her expired German passport made her stateless or that her fiancé was a German Jewish refugee—they refused to acknowledge that not all Germans were the same.

Frustrated, Emil considered giving up the Camera Shop to be with Deta; he wanted Deta more than the business. At the same time, he didn't want to go through another uprooting. Alarmed that Emil might act precipitously, in April Deta cabled: "Please do not undertake steps." Emil calmed down, promising he would relinquish the business only if doing so brought him to her.

Although Emil didn't know it, there would soon be reason for optimism. In the early hours of June 6, 1944, the D-Day invasion on the Normandy beaches began. At 9:30 a.m., the first official communiqué was broadcast over the BBC: "Under the command of General Eisenhower, Allied naval forces, supported by strong air forces, began landing Allied armies this morning on the northern coast of France."

In Hanover, on June 6, all conversation was about the invasion.[85] Churches were open and services held throughout the day. Main Street was lined with flags; stores had their radios on and their doors open so passersby could hear the latest developments. One store, Michael's Radio Shop, installed a loudspeaker outside to broadcast the news. In the Camera Shop, upstairs and in the downstairs darkroom, the radio brought the events in Normandy to Emil. By the end of the day, 150 thousand Allied troops, thousands of vehicles, and tons of matériel had landed on the Normandy beaches. The human cost that day would be ten thousand Allied lives.

On August 26, 1944, General de Gaulle arrived in Paris, and the U.S. Third Army under General Patton advanced eastward toward Germany. The closer the Allies got to the Rhine, the more hopeful Emil became. Surely Germany would lose the war before the end of the year.

On November 19 Emil informed Deta that Kaiserslautern, thirty-six miles west of Worms and fifty miles from Guntersblum, might soon be occupied by American troops. But on November 23, 1944, the Allies were only in Metz, France, seventy-five miles from Kaiserslautern. On December 16 an unanticipated German offensive attacked Allied Forces in the Ardennes Forest in Belgium, a disappointing setback to the Allied advance into Germany. Known as the Battle of the Bulge, it was the bloodiest battle the Americans fought in the war, with heavy casualties and loss of nineteen thousand U.S. soldiers. The war was far from over.

Swamped with work, Emil had no time for a Christmas letter. Instead, he wrote a few lines on the back of a photograph he took on December 13 of the poet Robert Frost. One of Emil's photographs of the poet would be included in a 1945 calendar of Dartmouth Portraits. Frost, intrigued by Emil's small camera, asked if he could try it; he then photographed Emil, who sent the resulting photo to Deta.

---

85. *Hanover Gazette*, June 8, 1944.

Robert Frost; Photo by Emil Rueb.

Emil Rueb; Photo by Robert Frost.

On New Year's Eve at 10:30 p.m., before joining the Silvermans for an evening of music at their home, Emil wrote to Deta. "It's already January 1, 1945, in England, and I know your thoughts are with me," he began. "I take the opportunity to thank you for all your love and assure you that I love you with all my heart as much as ever before. . . . Take all my love tonight and all the wishes a man can express towards his lovely wife-to-be. Ever yours E."

The year 1944 was ending with unfinished business— Deta's third visa application, submitted December 1; Emil's pending citizenship; and the war in Europe and the Pacific, which seemed interminable.

❋ HANOVER, NEW HAMPSHIRE

The photograph Robert Frost took in December 1944 tells me more about my father.

The worn sports jacket my father wears appears in other photographs from his early Hanover days. Was this his only jacket?

He looks unshaven, which was unusual. The father I later knew shaved every day. Perhaps he couldn't afford a new razor or didn't take the time to buy one. What stands out is how thin he is. This is partly from his vegetarian diet. Back then, whenever he ate in a restaurant, he would order a vegetable plate because it was cheaper. Although he is smiling, I see fragility and sadness behind his smile.

When I look at the photograph, I want to put my arms around the young man standing by the window, to tell him how courageous I think he is, that I recognize how hard he worked, and that I believe he did the best he could.

31. ENDINGS AND BEGINNINGS

(JANUARY–JUNE 1945)

"The war must be waged . . . with
the greatest and most persistent intensity.
Everything we are and have is at stake.
Everything we are and have will be given."
—PRESIDENT ROOSEVELT, STATE OF THE
UNION ADDRESS, JANUARY 6, 1945

On January 10, 1945, a ceremony took place in Lebanon, New Hampshire. American soldiers advancing into Germany might have said the event in Grafton County Superior Court was one of the reasons they fought. Compared to the fighting in Europe, the ceremony—in Emil's words a "simple but solemn affair"—was inconsequential. For the participants, however, it had enormous significance. On that day, Emil, along with fifteen others (mostly former Canadians), became an American citizen.

"Citizen of the U.S.A.," Emil announced to Deta two days later. "It's hard to describe how much it means to me. A free man again! A man who has rights. Nobody to fear.

It's wonderful. . . . Once we are married it will take only 1/3 of the time it took me to obtain your citizenship." And how did Emil feel? "I am quite proud to be a member of the most powerful country on earth." Deta cabled her congratulations. Surely Emil's American citizenship would persuade the gentlemen in Washington to issue her a visa.

On February 1, Emil informed New Hampshire district attorney Alexander Murchie, to whom for the last three years he had applied for permission to travel and to photograph, that as an American, he was no longer under Murchie's jurisdiction. Ever gracious, Emil thanked Murchie and "the ladies and gentlemen of your office for the fair treatment you gave me during the period of the war."

If Emil's citizenship ended his statelessness, uncertainty about Deta's visa still prevailed. Although the State Department hadn't confirmed the date for his third appeal hearing in Washington, Emil was confident that this time Deta's visa would be approved. Furthermore, despite Roosevelt's State of the Union caution that "the Germans weren't beaten until the last Nazi surrendered," Emil expected Germany to collapse in a month or two. He could then cross the Atlantic himself to bring Deta back.[86]

By the end of March 1945, the Allies had taken Köln, from where Emil flew to England in 1938, and Mainz, where in 1937 Emil passed his note to Deta. On March 21, a spring day as warm as in summer, Allied troops entered Guntersblum and met with no resistance. On March 25 the Fifth Infantry Division crossed the Rhine at Oppenheim, where Emil had gone to school as a young boy. By March 29 Frankfurt, from where the Rübs and the Hartogsohns were deported, was under Allied control.

---

86. Crossing the Atlantic was not as easy as Emil thought. He would have needed a British visa and fare money of $150 to $200. Travel agency Thomas Cook & Son wrote Emil (October 18, 1945) ". . . there is no choice of accommodation at the present time and passengers are usually booked from four to eight in a cabin."

Emil anxiously followed the Allies' progress in his *Heimat* and awaited the call from the visa review committee. Finally, the State Department notified Emil to present himself in Washington on May 7. For his third appearance before the committee, he would bring reinforcements. Dr. Marie Frommer, a German Jewish architect and city planner who fled the Nazis for London in 1936, would accompany him. Dr. Frommer knew Deta because she often visited the Marx family. Now living in New York City, Dr. Frommer would also testify on Deta's behalf.[87]

Writing Deta about his upcoming Washington trip, Emil noted, "Just now the radio reports of the meeting of the Russian and American armies," on April 25, 1945, at the Elbe River. He did not mention President Roosevelt's death on April 12, for there was news of more personal relevance: "My paper yesterday reported that about four thousand Jews may have survived the bloodshed in Germany. No hope for Hede or my parents being alive." Emil was referring to Buchenwald, the German concentration camp liberated on April 12 by the Americans, and Bergen-Belsen, liberated on April 15 by the British. Of the approximately twenty-one thousand surviving inmates of Buchenwald, four thousand of them were Jews. Photographs of the camp—piles of dead bodies, emaciated living skeletons—appeared in the May 4 edition of *LIFE* magazine. Had Emil's family suffered the same fate as those in the photographs? What dark reality would Emil have to confront when the war ended?

Deta too was anxious for news about her family. Through the Red Cross, she had last heard from her parents in September 1944. "Mother sick many months, otherwise all healthy," her father had written. "As soon as there will

---

87. Dr. Marie Frommer (1890–1976), German Jewish architect, one of the first women to study at the Royal Technical University in Berlin and to receive a doctorate from the Technical University Dresden; emigrated to New York in 1940 and worked as an architect for the State of New York. en.wikipedia.org/wiki/Marie_Frommer.

be a possibility," Emil told Deta in late April, "I shall make inquiry about your parents and other relatives. . . . Let us hope that we have the chance to help the surviving of our relatives with money and food soon."

On May 7, 1945, Germany surrendered to the Allies. The same afternoon, accompanied by Dr. Frommer, Emil testified before the visa review committee in Washington. After the hearing, he and Dr. Frommer boarded a late train to New York. On May 8, V-E Day, Emil returned to Hanover, missing the boisterous celebration in Times Square and taking in the end of the European war quietly and alone.

If anyone had asked Emil how he felt on V-E Day, he probably would have answered in his accented English, "I have so many feelings, I can't begin to describe them. Deta is safe from Nazi bombs. Now everyone knows she isn't a threat to the United States, and hopefully she will be here soon. I thank God the Nazis are defeated. I fear that my poor parents haven't survived, but perhaps my sister managed to stay alive after all. I wonder about Guntersblum, my friends, Deta's parents, her brothers and sisters. And I am grateful that Deta and I left Germany when we did. Now we can look to the future."

Too impatient to wait for Washington's decision, on May 18 Emil contacted Senator Styles Bridges of New Hampshire: "As a citizen of the United States and a resident of this beautiful country, which became a haven to me and which you represent, I ask you for your help to build a family." Could the senator either "convince the Department of State that there is no necessity for refusing a visa to my fiancée" or, "if for unknown reasons a visa cannot be granted," help him obtain a passport so he could travel to England and marry her?

The good news finally came. On June 5, 1945, the acting visa division chief informed Emil that the American Embassy of London received authorization to issue an immigration visa to Deta. Senator Bridges replied on June 8, confirming that on June 6 the State Department sent advisory approval for Deta's visa to London. Deta's June 8 cable was more to the point: "Emil at last our only wish has come true am overcome with happiness shall cable again after having found out about passage all my love Elizabeth Bick [sic]."

Now Deta had to wait for her appointment with the American consulate in London and find transportation across the Atlantic. The American Friends Committee cautioned Emil not to expect Deta to arrive soon. But nothing could take away from Emil or Deta the joyous anticipation that they would be reunited by Christmas, perhaps even earlier, and the long wait for each other would be over.

❊ HANOVER, NEW HAMPSHIRE

orn in the United States, I always took for granted the American citizenship that was my birthright. From my father's writings about becoming an American citizen, however, I begin to comprehend what it meant to him. The United States would never replace the *Heimat* he lost, but here he found acceptance and belonging. He knew American democracy was imperfect, that racism and antisemitism still reared their ugly heads, but he was loyal to the country that gave him opportunities and a home. Perhaps this was why he became so reactive when I criticized his adopted home. "Ignorant girl," he must have thought, "you have no idea what it is like to be without a country." And he was right.

32. NEWS FROM GUNTERSBLUM

(JULY 1945)

*E*arly morning in mid-July, Emil walked from his rooming house to the store. It had rained the night before, and in the sunshine Hanover looked and smelled fresh. The war over, the town was returning to normal. Emil longed for the normalcy that Deta would bring. What wasn't normal was that he still had heard nothing about his parents.

As he walked up the street, he thought about the concentration camp photographs he had seen in *LIFE* magazine. More than likely Hede, Carl, and his parents were dead, their bodies lying in a similar pile of lifeless bodies. Yet Emil still hoped. Perhaps, instead of going on a "trip," as the "Erika" postcard reported, the Rübs had gone into hiding. And didn't that postcard, surely written by Hede, suggest she was not deported with her parents? Maybe she was conscripted to a labor camp in Poland. She might be alive. Hope would live until dispelled by facts.

Before crossing Main Street, Emil stopped at the post office. Opening the Camera Shop box with his key, he retrieved several pieces of mail. There were the usual bills, letters from customers and suppliers, nothing from Deta. But one envelope made him gasp. Postmarked "Guntersblum *den* 7.6.45"—June 7, 1945—it had been mailed through military channels by a sergeant in the 223rd CIC detachment. His heart beating, Emil unlocked the Camera Shop and dropped the mail on his desk. Then he went downstairs to read the letter.

When the war had ended, Emil had asked anyone he knew with connections to the American military in Germany to contact Dr. and Mrs. Huhn in Guntersblum, in whose home he first met Deta. Dr. Huhn's wife was Jewish. Emil hoped that she and daughter Erika, whom Deta had cared for when she was born, were still alive. He also was sure that if anyone had information about his parents, it would be the Huhns. Emil sat down and opened the envelope. Inside was a letter from Bertel Huhn.

Emil quickly found the one sentence he'd been dreading: "As much as it pains me, I must tell you the truth, for I believe with complete certainty that your parents died in December 1943 in Minsk."[88]

The knot in Emil's stomach tightened. He had tried to prepare himself for the worst, but seeing the information in black and white was a shock. Tears filled his eyes, a few rolling down his cheek. There was little doubt: what Bertel had written must be true.

Bertel and little Erika had survived, thanks to Dr. Huhn's reputation and connections, and that he was "Aryan." A year before the war ended, Bertel wrote, the Nazis had started arresting and deporting Jews married to "Aryans." Since Dr. Huhn was well-loved in Guntersblum, Bertel's Jewish background was initially overlooked. But Jews were still in

---

88. There is confusion about the Rübs' death date. Helene (Lenchen) Schniering was in Minsk from October 1942 to circa September 1943. In 1961, she testified that the Rübs family died on December 26, 1942. Bertel Huhn's letter says they died in 1943. This must have been a typo. Given the terrible conditions, my grandparents couldn't possibly have survived longer than 1942.

danger. Two months before the Americans arrived, a friend of Dr. Huhn's recommended that Bertel and twelve-year-old Erika go into hiding. The friend, Nazi resistor Jakob Steffan, had Gestapo contacts in Mainz that he used to warn persons who were going to be arrested. Leaving home late at night, Bertel and Erika hid with friends in Mommenheim, eighteen kilometers north of Guntersblum.

"These two months of my life," Bertel stated, "I wish on my enemies—this agony day and night, will the Gestapo find you or not, what are they doing to Ernst [her husband]. This torment for Erika cannot be described in words.

"It was the most wonderful hour of my life," Bertel continued, "when the Americans arrived in Mommenheim . . . to finally be free without any fear and above all for my child. I was the first civilian brought home through the front." She was also, the American major told her, the first living Jew he had encountered in Germany.

"In the year 1941, the Nazis began evacuating all Jews to the East, among them, dear Emil, your parents, sister, and brother-in-law. I had visited them a few weeks before in Frankfurt when I was at the Eugen Wolfs' [Bertel's relatives]. Your parents, sister, and brother-in-law with all other Frankfurt families went to Minsk in Russia. [The German Wehrmacht had invaded the Soviet Union in 1941 and controlled Minsk.] From the Wolfs I received a letter through roundabout ways, and a girl from here was [in Minsk] as an assistant in the Air Force—that's how I found something out. . . . Whether Hede and your brother-in-law returned to Poland with others I was not able to find out. I heard nothing more since January 1944 because the Luftwaffenhelferin was transferred. In case you want to know about the cause of their deaths, I will write in the next letter."

Emil folded the letter and put it back in the envelope. Soon the staff would arrive, the store would open, and customers would come with questions and orders. Today was like any other day in Hanover. Emil would continue just as he had been doing since receiving his parents' final letter from November 1941—he would keep going. The Camera Shop needed his full attention; there was no time or space for emotions. Tonight, he would call Lotte, and she would comfort him as best she could over the phone. He would also write to Deta. Wiping his eyes with a handkerchief, Emil put the letter back in the envelope and went upstairs. It was going to be a long day. He didn't want to know more about how his family died. Details would not bring them back, would not help them or him.

But there are details, some surfacing later, some unclear, which must be included here. The young woman from Guntersblum in Minsk whom Bertel Huhn had mentioned in her letter was Helene "Lenchen" Schniering. Lenchen, whose father was a social democrat and former Reichsbanner member, was not in Minsk by choice. As a single, able-bodied young woman, she was required to join a work detail and had been sent to Minsk in October 1942.

In Minsk one morning, Lenchen heard someone calling her name. It was Frau Wolf from Guntersblum, whose daughter, Marianne, Deta had looked after in 1932. Frau Wolf was in a work brigade on the way to a forced labor assignment. Later that day, a German Jewish woman who cleaned in the building where Lenchen worked found Lenchen and brought greetings from Frau Wolf.

Somehow Lenchen managed to see Frau Wolf, who told her that David and Bertha were also in Minsk. They lived in a small room with six other people and were unable to work, probably because they were ill and weak from hunger. Lenchen saw Frau Wolf once more and learned from her that Bertha and David had died. How they died is unknown. They may have been shot or herded into the mobile truck units that served as gas chambers. Had the Rübs lived till December of 1942, David would have been sixty-four and Bertha sixty-one.

And Hede and her husband, Carl? Lenchen had not seen them in Minsk. If the Hartogsohns weren't sent to Minsk, where had they been taken? Or had they died on the train ride to Minsk? Their names, along with David and Bertha Rüb and the Eugene Wolf family, were on the list of persons deported November 12, 1941, from Frankfurt to Minsk; the Nazis kept meticulous records, which the American military found at Frankfurt Police headquarters after the war. David and Bertha are listed as "declared dead," but Hede and Carl are "*Verschollen*,"—missing, presumed dead. There is no mention of Hede's unborn child. In 1942 Hede would have been thirty-two, Carl thirty-eight.

It would take several days, Bertel's letter continued, to describe her experiences during the war. Later the Huhns would tell Emil how at the end, Dr. Huhn rode his motorbike to the entrances of Guntersblum to advise the eleventh hour Volkssturmer, old men and young boys recruited to save the Reich, to throw down their guns and shovels. "Go home and greet the soldiers with a glass of wine," Dr. Huhn is supposed to have said, and they gratefully complied. Thanks to Dr. Huhn and other resisters, Guntersblum capitulated peacefully to the Americans.

"Therefore, dear Emil," Bertel closed, "as soon as you can, come for a visit to Germany but never again to stay, for always the horrors overwhelm you, when you see these cities and also the small towns, because nothing is whole here. . . . There is unemployment and hunger. . . . What you hear on the radio about concentration camps and other barbarities are true."

As he unlocked the Camera Shop front door, Emil mentally answered Bertel's letter: *I will never return to live in Guntersblum or anywhere else in Germany.*

❀ HANOVER, NEW HAMPSHIRE

"One never stops searching for
relatives that have vanished, even if
one burrows only in one's soul."
—JOSEPH BERGER[89]

*I*n 1953 the German government established the
process for victims of Nazi persecution to apply for
Wiedergutmachung—restitution. Literally "to make good
again," the word means atonement, remediation, compen-
sation. My father spent time, money, and emotional energy
seeking reparations for the loss of his family, their business,
and their property. But money would not compensate
him for these losses. It did not ease his guilt or buy the
tremendous effort required to continue living, knowing
that his parents were murdered and he couldn't save them.
The application for *Wiedergutmachung* was complicated and
lengthy. My father's case wasn't completed until the early
1960s, and although I was unaware of what was involved, it
cast a shadow over our family.

89. Joseph Berger, *Displaced Persons: Growing Up American after the Holocaust,*
New York, Scribner, 2001, p. 327.

In 1995 when I visited Guntersblum, Lenchen Schniering told me the same story Bertel Huhn wrote my father. I picture my grandparents, ill, starving, exhausted, and Hede and Carl, their bodies in some unknown place. These lost family members live unresolved with me.

The Minsk ghetto is gone, but I wanted to see the place where David and Bertha Rüb died. It is the closest I can come to visiting their graves. Traveling to Belarus, however, was not advisable, because of political unrest there.

My grandparents watch me from portraits my father took, now on the wall of my study.

In November and December, when it is dark and cold, I think of Bertha and David, of Hede and Carl. I hope they were together when they died.

33. ALL FOR EACH OTHER (1945)

"Detalein, I am so excited expecting
the cabel [sic] which will announce
your coming. We shall have some lovely
weeks before we settle down to work."
—EMIL TO DETA, SEPT. 9, 1945

With the war in Europe over, Deta didn't think about bombs when she boarded a London-bound train in Gerrards Cross. On July 13, 1945, London was a different city from the one Deta first saw in 1938. Now there were ruined buildings, and the passersby looked shabby and tired. But Deta hardly noticed; she focused on her 2:15 p.m. appointment at the consular section of the American embassy. After seven long years, internment, and dark days of worry, her visa application had finally been approved.

With time to spare, Deta stopped at a Lyons Corner Shop for a cup of chocolate and a bun. She had hardly slept the night before and had eaten little. But she was too nervous to finish her refreshment. Pushing the bun away, she checked her handbag for the documents and six passport photos she was told to bring. And then it was time. With the same determination that had brought her to England, she stood up and went outside. As she walked, it wasn't London she saw but Emil's dark brown eyes, his warm smile. Would they really be together again?

At 2:00 p.m., she reached 1 Grosvenor Square, the location of the American embassy and consulate. There she presented her appointment summons and was shown to the reception room. As she waited, she imagined Emil beside her, telling her to be calm. "Miss Elisabeth Bickel," a consulate employee called her name. Her heart beating fast, Deta stood up to follow the official.

As if in a dream, she sat through a short interview, answering questions about why she wanted to go to the United States and what her intentions were once there. Then she was escorted to another room for the medical examination. Next, she had to verify her signature on the numerous forms she had signed. A little after three o'clock, Deta walked out of the consulate into the warm afternoon. As soon as she obtained a ticket to the United States, her visa would be issued.

That evening in Gerrards Cross, Deta wrote Emil about her day. "The only difficulty is to get a passage but I am very hopeful in spite of these difficulties. I try to come by plane never mind what high price I have to pay for it." Deta had money and if necessary, would ask the Marxes for a loan. "Emil, Darling," she continued, "I promise you that I shan't rest now and will do everything in my power to come to you as soon as possible. It is so hard now to wait—but Emil please do not get impatient—I shall come to you soon—I promise! I need you as badly as you need your Detalein." She would have to apply for an exit permit and a British Certificate of Identity since she didn't have a passport, but compared to obtaining an American visa, these were straightforward formalities.

On Thursday, August 23, 1945, Emil's thirty-ninth birthday, he wrote to Deta, "I'm sitting on the roadside, somewhere near Hanover watching the clouds and the trees and feeling the wind, things which are almost strange to me." It was good to be outdoors. "It's a lovely day and I took off," he continued, "leaving a note in the store that I would plan to be back sometime." He expected Deta would join him soon which made him happy. "You are the great thing in my life to look forward to. . . . After I failed to make you happy seven years ago, I shall do everything in my power to make good for that. Let us hope that I can take you in my arms very soon."

Emil crossed the bridge over the Connecticut River to Vermont and found a spot to sit overlooking the water. As he watched a lone figure paddling a canoe, he thought about where he had come from and where he was now. Had it really been six years since he landed in Hanover, seven years since he arrived in New York from Germany? Much had happened in that interval. The war in Europe and the Pacific was over; Deta had a provisional visa, to be finalized once she had proof of transport; and he knew about his family. Deta's news and Bertel's letter about his parents, Hede, and Carl had arrived only a few weeks apart. This made his thirty-ninth birthday a day of celebration and of mourning.

He identified with the lone figure paddling on the river, for he too was making his way through uncharted waters. Regarding Deta's coming, Mr. Carter had written on June 1, "You will probably have to get used to the idea slowly, after many years' sustained fight against almost invincible odds." Emil would also need time to accept the loss of his family and to grieve.

Had his parents, Hede, and Carl died while he was still in Guntersblum, Emil would have known what to do. But now his knowledge of Jewish burial rites—washing the body, remaining with the body until the burial, saying Kaddish at the gravesite—was useless. There were no bodies to bury and no salve for his pain. Religious ritual would not help him mourn his family or come to terms with how they died.

He told Deta only that his family had been killed. Grief was dangerous; it could unleash emotions too overwhelming to manage. Where Emil opened his heart was toward little Susan, concerned she would suffer when her "Detale" left: "I am so sad for Susan and so helpless. Every day I am thinking of her, and I only can hope that she will have friends enough to get over the great loss." Perhaps Emil projected his own loss and guilt, not only for taking Deta away from Susan but for having failed his family.

In the cool morning, Emil wondered if Deta would find him changed? Would she still want him? He stretched out in the grass and watched the puffy clouds in the sky. Holding grief, guilt, and joy simultaneously was exhausting. His thoughts turned to the High Holy Days in early September. There was a time when he celebrated Rosh Hashanah in the little Guntersblum synagogue, his mother and Oma Dina upstairs in the women's gallery. Emil might have been one of the men called to the podium to read from the Torah. After services, the congregation would exchange New Year's wishes, and friends would come to his parents' house for a glass of wine and some cake.

But those days were gone. There had been no Rosh Hashanah greetings from his parents after 1941, and their good wishes would not come again. Rosh Hashanah 1945 would only remind him of what was lost.

Now Emil faced another challenge. With thousands of American soldiers returning home, the ships from Europe were full; only American civilians with priority could get passage. How would he bring Deta over the Atlantic? Focusing on Deta's travel and their future together would keep him occupied. Grieving would come later. Closing his eyes, he dozed a little before getting up and walking back to town.

On October 3 Deta cabled: "Passage perhaps possible in two months. . . . We cannot do anything to improve position as I have not priority." Ship berths were given primarily to American and Canadian soldiers returning home from Europe, North Africa, and the Mediterranean. Some ships carried as few as three hundred passengers, while the larger ships squeezed in fifteen thousand. There were not enough ships to meet the demand.

Hoping Deta would arrive by Christmas, Emil was running out of patience, his anger and anxiety manifesting themselves in stomach complaints. He considered selling his part of the Camera Shop back to Mr. Carter and traveling to England to marry Deta. Fortunately, by early December 1945 the travel landscape was improving. Emil cabled Deta to contact American Airlines because they did not operate on a priority system; Deta could obtain passage based on when she had registered. Two other U.S. airlines served the London–New York route with comparable fares—around $275 (over $4,000 today).

There was also some good news. Bertel Huhn forwarded a letter from one of Deta's sisters. Deta's parents were alive, confirmed by two photographs enclosed in the letter.

(Left) Deta's mother and sister Karola. (Right) Deta's father and Karola.
Deta's sister wears the habit of a Lutheran deaconess, a Protestant nun.

On December 15 Emil wrote to Deta, "I take this opportunity to assure you of my great devotion and admiration. The people who know me believe—I am sure—that you are a saint. How lovely to know that you are made out of blood and flesh and willing to have me enjoy it as well as your fine heart."

Two days later, Emil acknowledged that the Christmas gift he most wanted wouldn't happen: "It seems to be that we shall be longing for each other as so many times before. . . . Take care of yourself and Susan and don't be sad. I shall be with you on X-Mas Eve. Where else could I be? Ever yours E."

Gradually the transportation knot loosened, thanks to a Dartmouth student, son of a Cook's Travel official, whose father intervened with Pan American Airways. On December 29, 1945, Deta cabled: "Today interview pan airway. . . . Am overjoyed Thanks great love which I return This is happy new year for us." Emil's constant conviction had been correct: the involvement of an influential person had made a difference. "I am full of hope," he wrote Deta on December 30, "that we shall succeed to have you here pretty soon."

❉ *Hanover, New Hampshire*

My Peruvian husband and I lived in Lima until 1972 when we returned to the United States for graduate school. After receiving our degrees, my husband applied for a resident visa so he could live and work in the United States. My husband had a job offer, and we innocently thought the resident visa would easily follow. To our dismay, this was not the case. In fact, we were told it could take up to three years for the visa to come through. What were we going to do? We did not want to return to Peru.

My father, well-acquainted with visa applications, stepped in. A retired former American ambassador to Peru lived in Hanover and was a customer and a friend of my father. My father asked him if he might intervene on my husband's behalf.

It took one letter to the American Consul in Toronto, Canada, from the former ambassador. Within a week my husband was summoned to the American Consulate in Toronto to receive his resident visa. My father knew all along that this was how the world worked.

34. FINALE–PART ONE (1946)

"Expect Pan American Call You Soon
Please Prepare Susan and Family Carefully
All Love to Susan And Good Trip To You."
—CABLE FROM EMIL TO DETA, JANUARY 7, 1946

*O*n Monday, January 21, 1946, the phone in the Camera
Shop basement rang loudly as Emil helped an employee
dry and sort black-and-white prints made earlier that morning.
Normally an upstairs employee would answer the phone, but
this call was different. Emil took a deep breath and lifted the
receiver. "Camera Shop," he said. "Hello."

For the prior two weeks Emil had been on alert for Deta's
cable announcing her arrival date in New York. He had not
heard from Deta since January 8, when she had brought to the
American consulate a coupon for her prepaid airplane ticket
and money for the visa fee. She was to return to the consulate
the next day for her visa, and with visa in hand, she expected
Pan American Airways to give her a reservation within ten days.

But on January 8 at 7:10 a.m., seven thousand Western
Union workers went on strike, resulting in the shutdown of
almost all transoceanic cable and radio messages. How would
Emil learn when Deta was coming? The closer Deta got to a

plane reservation, it seemed, the more obstacles there were to overcome.

Emil wrote Pan American Airways on January 9, 1946: Could they telephone him at his expense with Miss Bickel's London departure date? Unfortunately, no. Pan Am did not receive advance lists of incoming passengers. On January 17, at Emil's request, Lotte and Hans in New York instructed Deta: "Cable immediately to us date of departure." Still no reply from Deta. Was she ill? Was Susan sick? Beside himself with worry, Emil was certain something was wrong.

The only option, an expensive one, was to telephone. Making a transatlantic call in 1946 was complicated and time-consuming. First, one contacted the local operator, who transferred the caller to a traffic operator. The second operator got in line with the transatlantic operator for a circuit. With the limited number of circuits, it could take twenty-four hours for a call to go through.

On Monday morning Emil arrived early at the Camera Shop to place the call. He had tried the day before and waited three hours without success. This morning, to improve his chances, the Camera Shop's line was blocked, so only the operator could get through. As the hours passed, Emil tried not to think about the connectors and wires carrying his call across the Atlantic, more slowly, it seemed, than the years of waiting. When the phone rang shortly before noon, he knew the call had gone through.

"Camera Shop," he spoke into the receiver. "Emil Rueb speaking." In London it was five o'clock in the afternoon.

"Mr. Rueb," said a woman's voice. "This is the operator. Your call to London is ready. Please stay on the line, and I will connect you. One moment, please."

Emil's heart raced. Till now, Deta was her handwriting on blue paper and the smiling two-dimensional woman in a photograph. She spoke only in Emil's dreams. In a moment she would be at the other end of the line, a living, breathing person. What would Deta sound like? It had been seven years since he last heard her voice. Would they speak English or German? Would it be awkward after so long?

While Emil waited, a London traffic operator called MAIda Vale 1454, the Marxes' number. When someone answered at 6 Aberdare Gardens, the American and London operators connected the Camera Shop with London.

"Go ahead, sir," said the American operator after a few moments. "London on the line."

"Hello, hello," Emil said. His mouth was dry. He wished the Camera Shop employee would disappear so he could have some privacy. However, the employee, impressed that his boss was speaking with someone in England, stayed put.

"Hello, hello," a woman's voice said.

Despite the poor connection, Emil immediately recognized Deta's voice.

"Deta," he said in English, "how are you? Are you all right? I have been so worried. You haven't written or cabled. Did you get Hans's cable?"

"*Ach*, Emil," Deta answered. "Is it really you?"

"Yes, yes, it's me. Did you get the cable Hans sent?"

"Yes," Deta replied. "I got the cable yesterday." Deta's voice faded in and out. "Emil, can you hear me? The consulate says the German and Austrian quotas *sind voll*," Deta drifted into German.

"I beg your pardon?" Emil had trouble understanding Deta through the static on the line.

"Emil, the quotas are full," Deta repeated. "Now I wait again until February 4. Emil, I have been sick about this and couldn't write."

When Deta had returned to the consulate on January 9, she was informed that the German and Austrian quotas had been filled and that she would have to wait to receive her visa. Having been so close to leaving, this news made Deta ill, which was the reason she hadn't written. She too was low on emotional reserves and less able to withstand another roadblock to a reunion with Emil.

"I look into this." Emil tried to remain calm. "I let you know. I say goodbye now. Try to stay calm. We will be together soon. Be strong. Goodbye."

The employee returned to work, and Emil went upstairs to his desk. Would Deta not get her visa, even after it had been approved? Emil was adamant that she needed to travel before her visa expired on September 1, 1946.

The phone call was the first time Emil had heard Deta speak English, but he couldn't bask in how her voice sounded; he had to act. Picking up the phone, he gave the operator the number for Senator Bridge's office. "Please," he asked the senator's secretary, "could the senator call the State Department to find out about the quotas?"

"By God," he swore to Deta when he wrote her the next day, "if they do not issue this visa to you by February 4, I shall start selling out my part of the Shop by February 5." He would also apply for an American passport to travel to England in case Deta's arrival was further delayed.

Senator Bridges replied that Deta's information was accurate: the German quota was full. A new quota was in process, however, and there was no reason that Deta should not receive her visa soon. Emil was reassured but still anxious. That he might soon hold Deta in his arms was hard to imagine.

On February 5 the American vice-consul stamped and signed Deta's long-awaited visa on her British Certificate of Identity. But the wait wasn't over. At the Pan American office, Deta learned that the next available departure date was April 23. No sooner did Deta advance, another setback appeared.

Emil, of course, immediately contacted the Pan American traffic manager in New York about how they could disregard their previous commitment to give Deta a seat within a week of her getting a visa. There were multiple reasons for the delay, the manager explained: the British government had restricted more planes from landing, which meant fewer flights to the United States; with the tremendous winds of the last several weeks, airplanes were taking on more fuel and fewer passengers; and finally, a United Nations conference finishing in London limited seat availability on the forty-four passenger DC-4. Once again Emil and Deta were under a cloud of uncertainty. How much longer would it take for Deta to get a plane reservation? Hovering in limbo between 6 Aberdare Gardens and Hanover, Deta hardly slept or ate.

On Tuesday, February 19 Deta presented herself at the London Pan Am offices and learned she could get a reservation for "week's end." After not hearing from Pan Am by Monday, February 25, Deta again contacted the airline. The agent promised to confirm her departure the following morning. But when she called the next day, the agent still had no information; Deta should telephone again that afternoon.

The day wore on, and Deta became more anxious. Her small suitcase was packed, her room cleaned, her remaining belongings in the same trunk she had sent in 1937 to England from Germany. Promptly at two o'clock, Deta phoned Pan American again. This time there was news. Deta was to be at Hurn Airport in Bournemouth, 107 miles south of London, that evening at six o'clock. With such short notice, the Marxes would have to send her trunk by ship. Deta cabled Emil that she hoped to land in New York by March 1.

As she finished packing, she recalled that Emil had suggested they spend a few days together in case Deta had second thoughts about marriage. Second thoughts? Impossible. For this man she had withheld the truth from her parents, left Germany, and endured internment. Deta dressed in the tailored suit she had ordered from a London seamstress and looked at herself in the mirror one last time. Then she picked up her suitcase and closed the door to her room.

Taking leave of Dr. and Mrs. Marx was difficult. They had survived the war together and watched Susan grow from a baby to a little girl. Deta had become part of the family, and she would miss them, especially Susan. But the next month, Deta would be thirty-eight years old; it was time to start her own family. With the same determination with which she had boarded the train in Mainz in 1937, Deta left 6 Aberdare Gardens. A taxi took her to London's Waterloo station for the train to Bournemouth. It was her turn to depart, and she was not going to cry—Emil was waiting.

On Thursday, February 27 at 4:30 in the morning, Pan American Flight 101 took off from Hurn for the seventeen-hour journey to New York. Thirty-one passengers were on board; six of them, Deta included, were listed as "stateless" on the flight manifest. With one exception, the destination of the passengers was New York City. The exception, Elisabeth Bickel, was bound for Hanover, New Hampshire. After refueling in Shannon, Ireland, and taking on twelve additional passengers, the pilot headed the plane across the Atlantic.

That Deta was on an airplane over the ocean was unbelievable. The long wait was almost over.

35. 1946—PART TWO

"May I have your attention, please?" the flight hostess said over the intercom, waking Deta from a deep sleep. "We will be landing shortly at LaGuardia Airport in New York. Please make sure your seatbelts are fastened and your seats upright for landing." It was now Friday, February 28.

Out the window that early morning, Deta could see the lights of New York. "Dear God, please don't let me get airsick," she prayed silently as the plane descended. She had not appreciated the descents in Shannon and in Gander for refueling. The plane banked on a turn and the earth slanted sideways. "Dear God, please let us land safely," she added, gripping the armrests of her seat.

Emil would be at Haven Avenue since Deta couldn't give him an exact arrival time. But there would be a note from him at the Pan American desk with instructions, of that she was certain. "Deta arrives, March 1" was noted and underlined in Emil's pocket calendar, a Christmas gift from little Susan. In between two red hearts, Susan had written at the front: "For a lucky New year."

The plane continued its descent and landed safely at the Marine Terminal, LaGuardia Airport. Soon the stairs were pushed up against the plane, and the cabin door opened.

Deta put on her coat and disembarked with the other passengers. It was a relief to be back on the ground and in the fresh air. As she took her first step onto American soil, she pinched herself. Was she really here? Was she awake, or was she dreaming? She followed the passengers into the terminal.

The first American Deta encountered was a gum-chewing immigration officer. "What is the purpose of your trip to the United States?" the official asked her.

Thrown off guard by the man's New York accent, Deta said, "I beg your pardon?"

The official repeated his question.

"I come here to get married. My husband," she added quickly, "is an American citizen." Tired from her journey, she realized she had mixed up "husband" and "fiancé." Hopefully this was not a problem.

The official looked over her immigration document and checked her visa. Deta was not the first stateless person he had encountered. "Welcome to the United States," the official said after a few moments. He stamped Deta's Certificate of Identity "Admitted Permanent at New York, N.Y." Perhaps later that day, when he got home, he would tell his wife about the woman in the camel hair coat who came here to get married. It would make a nice story.

After retrieving her suitcase and going through customs, Deta left the passenger-only area. Everything looked strange, and she hesitated. It was one in the morning, and other than the passengers from her flight, the Marine Terminal was empty. Deta reminded herself that she had survived new situations before. She would manage here too.

She found the Pan American Airways passenger service counter and asked whether there was a message for her. "No," the agent said. "There is no note for Elisabeth Bickel here."

"Please," Deta responded, "could you look again?" She knew in every part of her being that Emil had left a note.

"I am sorry, madam, I don't see any note for you," the woman behind the counter said.

"Please," Deta insisted, "be so kind as to look once more."

Slightly impatient, the airline representative ruffled through some envelopes. This time she found an envelope with Deta's name on it and handed it to her. Inside was a note: "Deta, Welcome to the United States. Telephone WAdsworth 8-4208. As soon as you call, I will come get you. Yours, E."

The Pan American representative allowed Deta to use the desk phone and dialed the number for her. It rang once, and Hans answered. "Emil is here. We are on our way."

When the call came, Emil and Hans were talking quietly in the living room; they didn't want to disturb Lotte, who was sleeping. The two men grabbed their overcoats and left the apartment. The early morning air was brisk, but Emil didn't feel the cold. They walked one block and hailed a passing cab.

"LaGuardia, Marine Terminal," Hans told the driver. "How soon can we get there?"

"'Bout half an hour," the driver answered. "Not much traffic this time of night."

Hans tried to make conversation with Emil during the ride. Meeting an incoming passenger at the airport instead of at a West Side Highway pier was a new experience. "What do you think her trip was like? How was the food on the plane? Deta must be exhausted from the long flight."

Emil barely answered. He had dreamed of this moment for so long, and now it was here. He would see and touch the woman who would heal his loneliness and make him whole. She would help him move from grief and guilt into enjoying life again.

Knowing that Emil was on his way, Deta could be patient. In England, some people had asked her, "Why hold out in the middle of a war for someone so far away?" "What man would wait so many years for a woman? Emil might meet someone else." But Deta never wavered. She trusted that the bond between her and Emil, stretched over time and space, was intact. It had, in fact, become stronger. In her handbag was the note Emil slipped into her hand at the Mainz train station: "All for you."

After a while, Deta noticed two men walking toward her. She recognized Hans, whom she had seen several times when he was stationed in England. Next to Hans, slightly taller, smiling broadly, was Emil.

Deta got up from the bench where she had been sitting. The long wait was over. In a few seconds, she and Emil would embrace. So much love and yearning had gone into this moment. Together at last. All for each other.

Together!

EPILOGUE–FROM EMIL
AND DETA'S DAUGHTER

*"If this marriage is as successful as it was difficult
in attaining and endures as long as the interval
seemed, it will be happy throughout eternity."*
—Toast made at a dinner following Emil
and Deta's wedding, March 8, 1946.

I wish I could describe Deta and Emil's first embrace, what they said to each other, and how they felt, but I can't. My mother never told me. And their first night at Haven Avenue? Did they sleep together in the bedroom overlooking the George Washington Bridge? Deta would have liked the lights on the bridge. Or were they in separate bedrooms? Perhaps they didn't sleep at all but talked until morning. How would a man and a woman be together after such a long separation?

What I know is that my parents spent a long weekend in New York with Hans and Lotte. On Monday they saw *Hamlet* with renowned British actor Maurice Evans, the tickets an early wedding gift from one of Emil's friends. On

Wednesday Emil and Deta departed for Hanover from Grand Central Station. After taking this journey alone so often, Emil must have marveled that Deta sat beside him. At the White River Junction station, Emil's friends the Silvermans met them and took them out for supper.

Two days later, March 8, 1946, Emil and Deta were married by a justice of the peace, with Dr. Syvertsen as one of the witnesses. Afterward the newlyweds were invited to dinner at the Hotel Coolidge in White River. "Uncle Emil and I married today," Deta cabled Susan, "Am touched by welcome in Hanover please be happy with us Love you and family Detale Uncle Emil." In her datebook, Deta wrote, "My only wish [has] come true. I am more than happy." In his calendar, my father wrote "married."

Their reunion did not go unnoticed by local newspapers. The March 14, 1946, *Hanover Gazette* editorial, "Emil and Elizabeth Escapees from Hitler's Wrath Find Haven Here," recounted their story and concluded, "The climax of this story has the character of an Easter festival literally and figuratively speaking. Two people can tell you what it means to be in the land of the living." An article in the March 15 *Daily Dartmouth* began, "A quiet wedding ceremony on Friday, 8 March, marked the happy ending to a story of enforced separation lasting seven and one-half years for Hanover's newest couple, Mr. and Mrs. Emil Rueb." The article ended: "Answering the proverbial question as to how she liked the United States, Mrs. Rueb wisely refrained, claiming that she was still too overwhelmed to consolidate her first impressions."

The March cold and her new living situation were a shock for Deta. Hanover was not London, and Emil's boarding house room was a far cry from the Marxes' well-appointed household. Deta cooked vegetarian food over a small burner in the Camera Shop basement, a challenge she accepted. Two years later, shortly before I was born, my parents moved

So many good people have given us a lift during the years of our separation that we had to choose this somewhat impersonal way to announce our reunion and marriage. Please take our thanks for your interest in our cause. Credit: Emil Rueb.

nearby to a small furnished apartment. In the early 1950s, they purchased land and built a simple, modern house where we moved in 1955. "Guntersblum II," my father noted on a photo of the house.

My parents' reunion was as close to "happily ever after" as circumstances allowed. They were together until Emil's death, thirty-four years later. Love and loyalty were the foundation of their marriage, but it was a foundation with cracks. My father was not the person Deta had known in Germany. He was quick to get angry or impatient; he was easily depressed and had somatic complaints. Despite support from a psychoanalyst, he couldn't forgive himself for having failed his family. The years of waiting for Deta, the repeated ups and downs between hope and disappointment, also had taken their toll.

If Deta were disappointed, if the castles in the air she had built while in England never materialized, she did not let on. She dedicated herself entirely to her husband and never regretted the choices she made, for they were based on her unending love for him.

Working six days a week, my parents built the Camera Shop into a successful and respected Main Street institution. Without Deta bolstering Emil, the store might have failed. When I was an infant, she waited on customers while carrying me against her shoulder. When they could not pay their bills and Emil wanted to throw in the towel, Deta insisted they wouldn't give up. It was not easy. Still, together Emil and Deta found joy in their home, in their friends, and in our family. They did their best to give me a normal childhood.

My father never forgot the people who helped him rebuild his life, especially Philip Carter. "You were kind enough to say," Mr. Carter wrote after visiting us in the mid-1950s, "that I was one of several who had helped you. While I would like to believe that such was the case, my own analysis is that your and Elisabeth's achievement has been possible in spite of and not because of my involvements with you when you first came to Hanover."

Emil felt indebted to the community that had taken him in, and he gave back generously. And always Deta was there, the helpmate without whom he could not have achieved what he did or become the person he wanted to be.

In 1952, the three of us travelled to Germany, my parents' first trip back. Meeting Emil for the first time, my Lutheran grandparents welcomed him warmly. My father found Guntersblum to be basically the same, but the people he saw there, none of them Jews, "had no real conception of the enormous grief the actions of their chosen masters had brought upon the entire world."[90] The Germans he met preferred to forget rather than repent, to focus on rebuilding instead of on the past. Only Deta's mother took responsibility: "We are all guilty," she told her newest son-in-law. "We did not stand up for our Christian beliefs and did not protest the mistreating of other human beings."

My father went alone to Seilerstrasse 9 in Frankfurt. After knocking on several doors, he found an elderly woman who remembered his family. She told him about the family's last days before being deported, that Hede was pregnant and worked the night shift cleaning streetcars, that Hede was angry at him for not getting them out of Germany. For a few moments, Emil couldn't breathe. "It will be hard . . . to continue to live knowing of my guilt. It is heartbreaking to think that nothing will bring them back," he wrote his analyst. Of the Rübs and the Hartog-sohns, what remains are the few things my maternal grandfather retrieved after the war, and their absence, their silence.

We left Germany by train. On the way, there was a bad accident, delaying the train for several hours. I remember nothing of this; it was night, and I was asleep. Unfortunately,

---

90. From the booklet my father wrote about our trip, which he gave to friends as gifts.

someone was killed. "Your father broke down," my mother told me years later, "and cried bitterly. He couldn't stop crying." The accident triggered the grief Emil could no longer repress, a replay of September 1938 when he saw his parents for the last time on the Mainz train platform. This loss permeated all subsequent losses.

Yet Emil never disconnected himself from Germany, later in life traveling there every fall. Guntersblum was and would always be Emil's *Heimat*, the place where he was born and raised. This was one thing the Nazis could not take from him. Sometimes Emil got angry at this *Heimat*. In 1969, finding that the Guntersblum Jewish cemetery had been vandalized, Emil declared he would not return until the gravestones lying on the ground were restored. The tombstones of his grandfather and great-grandparents had survived the Third Reich, he commented, but not Germany's second republic.

My father died before Guntersblum began acknowledging its past. He never saw artist Gunter Demnig's *Stolpersteine*— "stumbling stones," brass-covered cobblestones engraved with a person's name, birth year, and where they died, and placed before the last known voluntary residence of individual victims. There are four such markers in the sidewalk at 4 Wormser Strasse. A street in a housing development honors David Rüb; a plaque on the former Jewish school names the Guntersblum Jews who were killed in the Holocaust; and there is a book on the Guntersblum Jewish community and one on the Guntersblum Jewish Cemetery. My father also didn't know that his German citizenship was restored to me, to my son, and to my grandchildren.

When Emil died in 1980, words could not contain the enormity of Deta's loss. But my mother was a survivor. She lived another twenty-one years and ran the Camera Shop until her retirement in 1986.

The Camera Shop closed in 2007. In death, Emil and Deta lie side by side in the Hanover cemetery. Deeply committed to each other, my parents lived through and survived extraordinary times. Their story is one of steadfastness, loyalty, and perseverance—and above all, love.

❈ HANOVER, NEW HAMPSHIRE

On March 30, 1945, shortly before the war ended, my father wrote to my mother, "The world wasn't good to us. Let's try to be better to the world." Doing and being better to the world was how my father lived. Justice, not retribution, mattered to him—and decency. More than anything, he wanted to be a good man, a responsible citizen, and a good Jew. He worked hard to rebuild his "shattered life"—his words—and to give me the security and opportunities he hadn't had.

The letters I found so long ago took me into my father's past. For the shy young man with little self-confidence, the journey from Guntersblum to Hanover was long and arduous, yet my father found his way, adapted, and eventually thrived. Learning about his story has given me a deeper appreciation of his struggles and his accomplishments.

The events that brought my parents to Hanover were traumatic, and that trauma affected our family. Even as a high-functioning adult, my father's depression always lurked in the background. Yet my father kept going. To honor the dead, he named me after his mother and grandmother. Becoming a husband and a father was how he joined the living. In his kindness and generosity to others, especially to the newcomer and the stranger, he found healing for himself.

The echoes of what happened in Germany reverberate today—their impact is not over. New information is uncovered, personal accounts continue to be written. These stories must be told, to prevent denial of the past and to ensure that no group considered "other" is mistreated, persecuted, or discriminated against. In sharing my family story, I too have found healing because I no longer carry it alone.

If I could speak to my father today, I would say, "You had every right to think it was a miserable world; you knew misery firsthand. Now I know more about your struggles, your loneliness and frustrations, and the emotional rollercoaster you rode waiting for your Deta. The guilt you carried was a heavy price for failing to save your family. It is not for me to absolve your guilt, but I offer you empathy, support, respect, and love. You built a life, as you said, 'out of the ashes.' Today I celebrate you by recounting your story."

NOTES

The following sources are displayed in footnotes throughout the book and organized by topic here.

Guntersblum

- Frey, Frank and Langenbach, Albrecht. *Guntersblum: So war's einmal,* Volumes I and II. Geiger-Verlag, Horb am Neckar, 1993.
- Kellerhoff, Sven Felix. *Ein Ganz Normales Pogrom: November 1938 in einem deutschen Dorf.* Kleet-Cotta, Stuttgart, Germany, 2018.
- Michaelis, Dieter. *Die Jüdische Gemeinde Guntersblum: Von den Anfängen bis Zur Vernichtung durch den National-sozialismus.* Wissenschaftlicher Verlag, Berlin, 2014.
- Michaelis, Dieter, and Hager-Latz, Jutta, and the Agency for the Conservation of Cultural Monument, Rhineland-Palatinate. *The Jewish Cemetery of Guntersblum.* 2002.
- *Guntersblumer Blaette: Stolpersteine in Guntersblum.* Verein zur Erhaltung Guntersblumer Kulturgutes e.V., Auflage 3, Ausgabe 02/2020.
- Newspaper articles from the research of Guntersblum resident Volker Sonneck.
- Arbeitskreis Stolpersteine of Guntersblum provided information and documents.
- Interviews: Marianna Flinner; Frau Simon; Elisabeth Rueb, Hans Jacob Schmitt.

- Emil Rueb: oral and written narratives and restitution documents.
- Research by Karin and Konrad Holl on the history of Guntersblum.

Frankfurt and Frankfurt-Hoechst during the Third Reich

- Beck, Waltraud; Fenzl, Josef; Krohn. Helga. *Juden in Hoechst: Die Vergessenen Nachbarn.* Jewish Museum Frankfurt, Drückerei Henrich GmbH, 1990.
- *Dokumente zur Geschichte der Frankfurter Juden 1933–1945.* Verlag Waldemar Kramer, Frankfurt am Main, 1963, p. 435.
- Geiler, Inge, *Wie ein Schatten sind unsere Tage: Die Geschichte der Familie Grünbaum.* Schöffling & Co., Frankfurt am Main, 2012.
- Kingreen, Monica. *Nach der Kristallnacht: Jüdisches Leben und antijüdische Politik in Frankfurt am Main 1938—1945.* Campus Verlag, GmbH, Frankfurt/Main, 1999.
- Krohn, Helga et al, *Ostend: Blick in ein jüdisches Viertel.* Jüdisches Museum Frankfurt am Main, Societäts Verlag, Frankfurt am Main, 2000.
- *"Und Keiner hat für uns Kaddisch Gesagt . . ." Deportationen aus Frankfurt am Main 1941 bis 1945.* Jewish Museum Frankfurt, Stroemfeld Verlag, Frankfurt am Main, 2004.
- Wolfgang Wippermann. *Das Leben in Frankfurt zur NS-Zeit: Die nationalsozialistische Judenverfolgung.* W. Kramer & Co., Frankfurt am Main, 1986.

Internment of Enemy Aliens in Britain

- Chappell, Connery. *Island of Barbed Wire: The Remarkable Story of World War Two Internment on the Isle of Man.* Robert Hale Limited, London, 2005.

- Gillman, Peter and Leni. *'Collar the Lot!': How Britain Interned and Expelled its Wartime Refugees.* Quartet Books Limited, London, 1980.
- Seller, Maxine Schwarz. *We Built up Our Lives: Education and Community among Jewish Refugees Interned by Britain in World War II.* Praeger Publishers Inc., Westport, Connecticut, 2001.
- The Manx National Heritage, Douglas, Isle of Man.

Emigration from Germany to the United States
- Dobbs, Michael. *America, Auschwitz, and a Village Caught In Between.* United States Holocaust Museum, Alfred A. Knopf, New York, 2019.
- Palmier, Jean-Michel, *Weimar in Exile: The Antifascist Emigration in Europe and America.* Translated by David Fernbach. Verso, London, 2006.
- Zuckmayer, Carl. *A Part of Myself.* Translated by Richard and Clara Winston. Carroll & Graf Publisher Inc., New York, 1966.

The Third Reich
- Haffner, Sebastian. *Defying Hitler: A Memoir.* Translated by Oliver Pretzel. Farrar, Straus and Giroux, New York, 2000.
- Yahil, Leni. *The Holocaust: The Fate of European Jewry, 1932–1945.* Translated by Ina Friedman and Haya Galai. Oxford University Press, New York, 1990.

The Minsk Ghetto
- Smolar, Hersh. *The Minsk Ghetto: Soviet-Jewish Partisans Against the Nazis.* Translated by Max Rosenfeld. Holocaust Library, New York 1989.

ACKNOWLEDGMENTS

This book would not exist without the support and assistance of many people.

From Guntersblum: I am indebted to Dieter Michaelis and his late wife, Hanneliese; Fred Trumpler, Melitta Bender, and the dedicated members of the Stolpersteine Gruppe; the late Hans Jakob Schmitt and his wife, Erika; Karin and Konrad Holl; the late Frank Frey; Volker Sonneck; and the late Liesel and Walter Vatter. All provided information, documents, and answers to my questions. I treasure the friendship and hospitality that my family and I experienced in Guntersblum.

I am also deeply grateful to:

- Helga Krohn (formerly of the Frankfurt Jewish Museum), the late Franz Fenzel, Waltraud Beck, and the Höchst Stolpersteine Group;
- The late Dr. Fritz Neubauer; my friend Dr. Fritz Kilthau; Dr. Franz Baumann, who corrected an early draft; and my friend Bernhild Voegel, who taught me about historical research;
- Members of the Wednesday Morning Writers Group, who encouraged, suggested, and always asked, "What happened next?"

- Margaret Williamson, who advised me about London and connected me with her cousin;
- Janet Broady, researcher par excellence, who found wonderful details about airports, planes, trains, and buses in 1930s and 1940s England;
- The Goethe Institute in Boston for the small grant to transcribe my grandparents' letters;
- Amy Reytar, National Archives & Records Administration, for information that Emil corresponded with a German prisoner of war in Canada.
- The late Margaret Robinson, who transcribed my grandparents' letters;
- Anna Thornhill, her sister Teresa, and the late Allen Thornhill for information about Stewart Thornhill and for their kindness;
- The staff of the Manx Historical Society, Douglas, Isle of Man and of the Howe Library of Hanover, New Hampshire;
- Ulrike Rainer and Monika Otter for advice on German translations;
- Bill Murphy, my colleague and former high school social studies teacher;
- Rabbi Mark Melamut for answering questions about Judaism;
- Alice Carter (Philip Carter's daughter) for finding me and for telling me about her parents;
- Vadim Altskan of the United States Holocaust Museum, who reviewed my chapter on Minsk;
- Gunnar Berg of YIVO Institute for Jewish Research, who sent me my grandparents' and Hede's identity cards;
- The friends who kept me going: David T., who reviewed an early draft; Kathy G., Susan P., and Geraldine, who said, "Just start writing"; and always Esther, who listened, encouraged, and understood my need to write this book;

- Susan White, my first professional editor, for her honest feedback;
- Editor Laura Matthews with thinkStory.biz, who taught me about emotional beats and helped prepare this project for submission;
- Gretchen Cherrington for sharing her publishing experience and for recommending SheWrites Press;
- Project Manager Shannon Green of SheWrites Press for her patient assistance and SheWrites Press for bringing my family story to life;
- My family—Kim, Oscar, and my late husband—for their love and caring;
- My partner, Octavian, who shopped, cooked, stopped me from giving up, and who made me laugh;
- My parents, to whom I owe so much.

ABOUT THE AUTHOR

*D*ena Rueb Romero grew up in Hanover, New Hampshire, the daughter of a Lutheran mother and a Jewish father, both refugees from Nazi Germany. Her Jewish grandparents were killed in the Holocaust. Although she was raised as a Jew, her parents celebrated both Jewish and Christian holidays. The family traveled regularly to Germany to visit Dena's Lutheran grandparents, aunts, and uncles. Dena graduated from Brandeis University and received an MA in English from the University of Virginia and an MSW from Boston College Graduate School of Social Work. Previous publications include: *Gretel's Albums*, a collaborative bilingual Internet project with researcher Bernhild Vögel (www.birdstage.net/kleeblatt/); and an essay about German citizenship in *A Place They Called Home: Reclaiming Citizenship, Stories of a New Jewish Return to Germany*, Donna Swarthout, Editor, Berlinica Publishing LLC, 2019. *All for You: A World War II Family Memoir of Love, Separation, and Loss* is her first full-length book. Dena still lives in Hanover, where she sings in a women's chorus and volunteers at a daycare center as well as with an organization supporting refugees and asylum seekers.

Author photo © Octavian Godeanu

SELECTED TITLES FROM SHE WRITES PRESS

She Writes Press is an independent publishing company founded to serve women writers everywhere. Visit us at www.shewritespress.com.

Quest for Eternal Sunshine: A Holocaust Survivor's Journey from Darkness to Light by Mendek Rubin and Myra Goodman. $16.95, 978-1-63152-878-1. Following the death of Mendek Rubin, a brilliant inventor who overcame the trauma of the Holocaust to live a truly joyous life, his daughter Myra found an unfinished manuscript about his healing journey; this inspirational book is that manuscript, with the missing parts of Mendek's story—along with his wisdom and secrets to finding happiness—woven in by Myra.

Irma's Passport: One Woman, Two World Wars, and a Legacy of Courage by Catherine Ehrlich. $16.95, 978-1-64742-305-6. After two European cataclysms disrupt the life of Irma—the wife of the leader of Vienna's Jewish community—she escapes to London and New York, where she restores her life by saving child refugees. This true story, told in Irma's words and narrated by her granddaughter, reveals an inspiring woman who used languages as her passport to a safer, more hopeful world.

Jumping Over Shadows: A Memoir by Annette Gendler. $16.95, 978-1-63152-170-6. Like her great-aunt Resi, Annette Gendler, a German, fell in love with a Jewish man—but unlike her aunt, whose marriage was destroyed by "the Nazi times," Gendler found a way to make her impossible love survive.

Newcomers in an Ancient Land: Adventures, Love, and Seeking Myself in 1960s Israel by Paula Wagner. $16.95, 978-1-63152-529-2. After leaving home at eighteen in search of her Jewish roots in Israel and France, Paula learns far more than two new languages. To navigate her new life, she must also separate from her twin sister and forge her own identity.

Shedding Our Stars: The Story of Hans Calmeyer and How He Saved Thousands of Families Like Mine by Laureen Nussbaum with Karen Kirtley. $16.95, 978-1-63152-636-7. From his post at the headquarters of the German occupation during World War II, Hans Calmeyer surreptitiously saved thousands of Jewish lives in the Netherlands. Here, Laureen Nussbaum describes how Calmeyer declared her mother non-Jewish and deleted her and her family from the deportation lists—and traces the arc of both her life and Calmeyer's in the aftermath of the war.

Api's Berlin Diaries: My Quest to Understand My Grandfather's Nazi Past by Gabrielle Robinson. $16.95, 978-1-64742-003-1. After her mother's death, Gabrielle Robinson found diaries her grandfather had kept while serving as doctor in Berlin 1945—only to discover that her beloved "Api" had been a Nazi.